TRANSPORTATION OPERATIONS MANAGEMENT

TRANSPORTATION OPERATIONS MANAGEMENT

DARREN J. PROKOP
Professor of Logistics, College of Business and Public Policy, University of Alaska Anchorage, Anchorage, AK, United States

ELSEVIER

Elsevier
Radarweg 29, PO Box 211, 1000 AE Amsterdam, Netherlands
The Boulevard, Langford Lane, Kidlington, Oxford OX5 1GB, United Kingdom
50 Hampshire Street, 5th Floor, Cambridge, MA 02139, United States

Library of Congress Cataloging-in-Publication Data
A catalog record for this book is available from the Library of Congress

British Library Cataloguing-in-Publication Data
A catalogue record for this book is available from the British Library

ISBN: 978-0-12-815415-1

For information on all Elsevier publications
visit our website at https://www.elsevier.com/books-and-journals

Publisher: Joseph P. Hayton
Acquisitions Editor: Kathryn Eryilmaz
Editorial Project Manager: Fernanda A. Oliveira
Production Project Manager: Sreejith Viswanathan
Cover Designer: Victoria Pearson Esser

Typeset by STRAIVE, India

Dedication

This book is dedicated to my wife, Stephanie, whose love and support were instrumental in helping me get this book to the finish line.

Contents

Author's biography

Darren J. Prokop is Professor of Logistics in the College of Business and Public Policy at the University of Alaska Anchorage. He is an active consultant to government and business and has published seminal research in the microfoundations of logistics, cabotage regulations, air cargo logistics, and supply chain security modeling. His other books include *The Business of Transportation*, *Concepts of Transportation Economics*, and *Global Supply Chain Security and Management*.

Preface

Transportation operations management is a critical element of logistical processes that support every link along a supply chain. Without careful planning and management of transportation operations, commercial markets—from raw material extraction through to retail delivery and final consumption—would not function properly. In short, all trade, from local to international, would slow down or even shut down. Even governments, in times of emergency, rely on having sound transportation operations in place in order to maintain or restore the socioeconomic fabric on which all commercial markets depend.

It is interesting to consider the curious position that transportation holds in the business world and in business schools. To many it is an invisible industry—a black box in between pickups and deliveries. As long as the shipment arrives intact and on time, why think much about what goes on inside? Of course, if the shipment does not arrive or is damaged along the way, the consequences could be dire. At that point, consternation replaces complacency. Certainly, when it comes to doing business, no one thinks that ignorance is bliss. Yet, since transportation operations are so specialized, it is not exactly a straightforward activity for nonspecialists to think about.

Perhaps one reason for this black box attitude is that, despite its seeming invisibility, transportation operations can be highly complex. This leads nonspecialists to want to leave it to experts. However, transportation operations are vulnerable to risk and uncertainty from many sources. In other words, a shipment from point A to point B may travel on multiple types of conveyances, over land, air, and water. Several for-hire carriers may be responsible for the shipment along the way. Various ports of call may be visited as the shipment is transferred from carrier to carrier. In other words, a lot of things can impact the integrity of the shipment or the delivery schedule.

This book outlines transportation operations not as a unilateral exercise handled by for-hire carriers but as a collaborative activity that facilitates trade between buyers and sellers of raw materials, subassemblies, and finished goods. For-hire transportation is a contractual activity; therefore, it is open to critical analysis just like any other business activity between two or more parties. Of course, transportation operations can lead to unique problems in costing and pricing. Since transportation, like any other production process, is built into the price a final customer pays, it is important to consider for-hire carriers as supply chain partners rather than as necessary, but merely transactional, agents between buyers and sellers of tangible items.

This book is an attempt to delve into the nuts and bolts of transportation operations management in order to make the invisible visible for those business managers and students who wish to shine a light into this metaphorical black box. This opens up a wide array of challenges and opportunities for all business managers. For students, it applies similar tools of analysis to the transportation industry which is, by design and by regulation, nonhomogenous across the five basic modes of transport—motor carrier, water vessel, air, rail, and pipeline.

No business or government organization can manage its activities without reliable transportation operations using suitable infrastructure. The only exception is a fanciful organization where all input supply and consumer demand were located in the same small area. This certainly does not apply to modern economic activity in the age of high-tech manufacturing, information technology, globalization, and the desire for travel.

To introduce the transportation problem, Chapter 1 outlines some key foundational concepts. Supply chain management is defined including how transportation impacts it. Issues are explored that involve transport network design, pricing at value versus cost, and contractual obligations. The relationship between the consignor of the shipment and the for-hire carrier will be a major theme throughout the book. Since transportation is not a homogenous activity, distinctions in operations will be made from among the five basic carrier modes. The complexities of transportation planning that will be touched upon deserve the attention of the buyers and sellers of the items to be shipped. They may have to resort to outsourcing this function to an intermediary that would arrange for transportation on their behalf. Issues will arise when it comes to negotiating freight rates, terms of payment, and the contents of the contract of carriage known as the bill of lading. Transportation represents, therefore, yet another important dimension in the negotiating and contracting processes found in modern supply chain management.

The role of transportation in the economy—specifically, its role as a facilitator of production and trade—is the subject of Chapter 2. Balancing transportation operations given that there are multiple competing sources of economies of scale and diseconomies of scale is highlighted. The role of government is outlined in terms of market intervention. This creates a distinction between private efficiency and social efficiency. To highlight this complicated relationship, some unique examples of transportation regulations are discussed. These may be seen as operational constraints that affect how transportation networks are designed and the routes taken along them. Basically, all for-hire carriers must devote time and money toward regulatory compliance.

Transportation operations are examined in Chapter 3 within the contexts of determining supply chain efficiency and resiliency. Of course, these two contexts need not be interdependent. Transportation facilitates value-adding activities such as procurement, production, inventory management, and distribution. Each of these activities requires adjustments to be made to transportation provision. Shipper and for-hire carrier relationships are also examined within the context of bills of lading. Of course, information gathering and sharing among these various players help mitigate supply chain disruptions. The five basic modes of transport and their different support infrastructure are under increased pressure to provide customer fulfillment. This necessarily requires improvements in supply chain resiliency and cooperation along the supply chain.

Chapter 4 considers the interface between long-distance transportation operations and physical geography. There are logistical implications of doing business on a round, nonhomogenous earth with a population that is unevenly distributed. Seasonal patterns and routing via orthodromes are discussed. Managing network choke points and traffic congestion is a necessary consequence of geography and limited infrastructure. This is examined from a game-theoretic perspective. Transportation technology may improve over time, but seasonality and the earth's topography will remain constraints to stability in transportation markets. The complexity of traffic planning is examined in terms of a growing tension between self-interest and authoritative control. Adding to the challenge is that each mode of transport has different mixes of private control and government regulation. As such, each mode is not likely to adopt new technologies in the same way and at the same speed.

In Chapter 5, fleet management techniques are examined and their modal differences highlighted. In particular, the choice between a shipper developing a private fleet and using for-hire carriers is considered. Regarding conveyances themselves, there is also the choice between owning and leasing. No matter which choices are made there will still be the fundamental problem of balancing front-haul and back-haul shipments. This is examined in the context of market competition and the nature of the logistical constraints of time, physical space, and location.

Chapter 6 examines the degree to which generating and sharing data is transforming transportation operations. In particular, the processes of digitization, artificial intelligence, machine learning, and blockchain technology are evaluated. The analysis is taken in the context of data as an input to production and as a price-excludible public good or club good. There are incentives and disincentives to sharing data among the various players within transportation markets. Issues surrounding security, electronic documentation, contracting, and customer service are outlined. The use and diffusion of these various technologies across the different modes of transport are not likely to be uniform, and this creates particular challenges in international transportation.

Problems in measuring the cost of transportation are explored in Chapter 7. These include distinguishing between joint costs and common costs, which opens a debate on the nature of what transportation as a service is supposed to achieve. Also, the full set of costs involved in arranging for and providing transportation are considered in the context of the total cost of ownership from the perspectives of consignors, for-hire carriers, and consignees. The costs of demurrage and detention are used to illustrate the problem of timing and coordination in international transportation. Several examples of the cost of regulatory compliance are outlined to contrast how efficiency and fairness are handled. All modes of transportation are regulated and to varying degrees. This means the full cost of transportation can be quite different across modes.

Chapter 8 covers problems in measuring revenue flows in transportation. Increasing revenue need not mean increasing profit. For-hire carriers, therefore, have a strategic decision to make when they consider how to price their products and services. Revenue is compared to cost in order to determine the level of profit over a range of supply. The components of revenue management systems are examined in passenger and cargo contexts. The practice of price discrimination is examined from a revenue perspective. A degree of revenue certainty in transportation is best characterized by the limited antitrust immunity granted by the US government to international containership lines handling US exports and imports. Standard and reverse auctions are explored as a method to promote competition through finding a suitable price rather than having the for-hire carrier set it independently. In this regard, a critical piece of the process between the for-hire carrier and the consignors wishing to enter bids is a detailed request for proposal that forms the basis of the eventual contract with the winning consignor.

Distinguishing between risk and uncertainty is the subject of Chapter 9. Both are unavoidable, yet their effects are manageable to some degree. The role of transportation is explored in terms of the support it provides to normal market activities and to emergency management. Risk and uncertainty, when they impact transportation, can permeate through multiple supply chains leading to significant consequences. Risk assessment procedures are introduced with the purpose of developing a risk management plan. Supply chain partnerships offer opportunities to share in risk mitigation provided, of course, that trust and information sharing are well developed. Service contracts are an attempt to codify these relationships. The concepts of force majeure and general average highlight special conditions that can have significant impacts on transportation despite having well-thought-out plans in place.

Finally, Chapter 10 looks to the future of transportation operations. It pulls together some common themes from the book and shows that many of the challenges facing transportation operations today will remain in the future. Of course, degrees may vary in the years ahead. The physical environment, infrastructure, support technology, the demands of consignors, and final customers at the end of the supply chain will always be a source of coordination problems leading to risk and uncertainty. The chapter looks ahead and explores automation and energy usage: two concepts that bring together many of the forces and constituencies that characterize for-hire transportation.

CHAPTER 1

Introduction to the transportation problem

The role of transportation in operations management

What is operations management?

Operations management involves the application of purposefully designed processes or systems in order to better understand or improve specific business activities. The activity that tends to be the most prominent in operations management is the production process (i.e., turning inputs into outputs). This is because successful production serving today's marketplace takes place when there is a production plan or system in place. Imagine trying to produce something as complex as an automobile—or even something much simpler like the piece of glass used in its rear view mirror—without a step-by-step process in place. Using the piece of glass as an example the following questions need to be addressed for the production process to be purposeful as opposed to haphazard:

(1) What are the specifications (i.e., size and thickness) of the glass for it to fit into the mirror's frame?

(2) Is the glass made in-house or bought from a vendor (i.e., an upstream supply chain partner)? If it was the latter what criteria was used to choose a particular vendor?

(3) How many finished pieces of glass are to be on hand for installation per workday? Where will the glass be stored and what materials are required in storing and moving it to the assembly line?

(4) How many pieces of glass should be held in inventory (to guard against shortages, and to reap any savings from buying in bulk)? Apart from the issue of storage and materials noted in question 3, should any inventory not likely to be used over many workdays be stored at the production facility or at some other locale (given that there may be multiple production facilities across the region or country which draws down this inventory)?

The answers to all of these questions will be based on the necessities of the production process (i.e., where the inputs are drawn from, where they can

Transportation Operations Management
https://doi.org/10.1016/B978-0-12-815415-1.00009-4

be used, and where the finished items are sold), and the marketplace (i.e., what the inputs cost and what the customers are willing to pay for the finished items).

The answer to question 2 most likely will be that the glass is purchased from a vendor specializing in the production of tempered glass for car mirrors. In fact, most production processes are not self-sufficient. Resource needs are outsourced so that firms can concentrate on their core competencies. The car manufacturer specializes in the design, functionality, and fit and finish of cars. Outside vendors dealing with specialty items (not only glass, but also tires, paint, brakes, and countless more) use their expertise to try to meet the manufacturer's specifications. Therefore, relationships among many separate parties are necessary for the production process to be efficient. These business connections form what is known as a supply chain.

What is supply chain management?

Supply chain management involves linking organizations together in order to fulfill some strategic purpose. The linkages could be based on merger and acquisition (M&A) or on independent entities setting up contractual arrangements. M&A supply chains imply that operations are characterized more so by command-and-control rather than the market signals of price and cost. This arrangement may make sense if a vendor is supplying a critical resource in the production process and it is desirable to have tight control over its supply. The contractual arrangement, on the other hand, gives supply chain partners more flexibility in that each has to fulfill expectations for the other as enshrined in the legal contract. Precontract negotiations can sort out what these expectations are. Also, if one party is not proving to be a valuable partner the contract could be allowed to lapse and other partnerships could form. This arrangement is particularly useful when the market for vendors or for customers is competitive and made up of many players.

Consider the structure of a supply chain as shown in Fig. 1.1.[a] This is a standard representation that incorporates several support and constraint processes as well as logistics (to be discussed in section "What is logistics?"). The transportation function is not readily apparent but it is implicit here. There are five primary processes proceeding from raw material vendors to the final customer; that is, from production leading to consumption. Each stage adds value to the successive customers who form the interdependent partnerships along the supply chain. Again, this could involve just one vertically integrated firm

[a] This is based on the value chain as first proposed by Porter (1985).

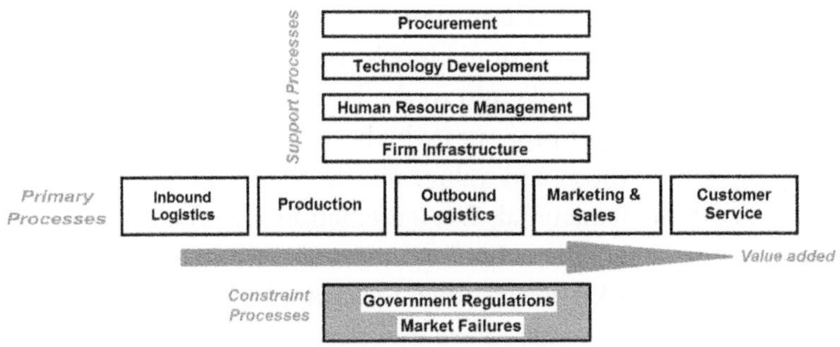

Fig. 1.1 The supply chain with support and constraint processes.

(formed through M&A) selling to an end customer at the retail level or multiple firms all under contract to supply their respective products and services.

Inbound logistics involves purchasing and transporting all necessary inputs from the point of origin to the point of storage and production. The production process uses the collected inputs in combinations necessary to produce subassemblies and/or finished products for immediate sale or storage. If production takes place at multiple facilities, transportation will be necessary in order to fulfill the production plan. Outbound logistics involves the purchasing and transportation of the finished products.

Of course, these three primary processes involve buying and selling. The customer buys from an upstream vendor. Like all transactions, information is exchanged before any buy-sell agreement is made. This is where the other two primary processes come in. Marketing facilitates sales when sellers signal the attributes of their supplies relative to the demand signals sent by their customers. Price, cost, quality, availability, etc., are the signals sent back and forth. Customer service goes beyond marketing and ties all of the other primary processes together so that the customer feels fulfilled. This means the promises contained in the marketing function are to be turned into reality by combining them with the logistics of delivery to the customer at the appropriate time and place. For example, marketing involves promoting a product to a potential customer base. Customer service involves making sure the distribution network (i.e., the outbound logistics) is able to fulfill the marketing message. Think of it this way, marketing tells the potential customer all about something that is not yet in the latter's possession. An expectation is now planted in the potential customer's mind. If the finished product, when bought and in the customer's possession, meets those expectations, customer service is successful.[b] Another important item in customer service is the posttransaction. Here issues related to warranties, repairs, exchanges, and product recalls add to the level of customer fulfillment.

There are four support processes which, in their own way, apply to the primary processes as those add value. Again, transportation is implicit in these. Procurement of material, implementation and maintenance of the hardware used in machine technology, connectivity of human resources over a physical network, and the maintenance of the firm's infrastructure (i.e., buildings, roads, etc.) all require transportation to the extent that items and people must be transported from where they are to where they are needed. In a sense, transportation supports the other support processes shown in Fig. 1.1.

In tandem with the support processes are two sources of constraints to the value-adding process. These are government regulations and market failures. Operations management would not be too hard if there were no constraints to force choices to be made among available alternatives. The constraints shown in Fig. 1.1 are not those resulting from the laws of physics (e.g., machinery will depreciate with use) or the marketplace (e.g., if an item becomes scarce relative to demand it will become more expensive); rather these involve how operations are ill-affected in their smoothness or simplicity by government and/or by markets not working properly.

Transportation is a highly regulated industry. Why? Three reasons are: it contributes to congestion on public roadways, waterways, and airspace; it produces significant environmental pollution; and it requires the building of extensive infrastructure (often at taxpayer expense). All of these by-products can negatively affect the health and safety of the general public. To the extent that they interfere with the leisurely enjoyment or business activities of the general public they are contributors to what economists call market failures. Often governments respond by using regulations to mitigate these causes of market failures. Examples include standards for vehicle maintenance, limitations of hours-of-service on

[b] Successful customer service should not be confused with perfection or 100% fulfillment. With multiple customers, each with their own valuations and aversions to cost and risk, it is impossible to satisfy all customers. To try would be too costly. For example, to guard against all possibilities of a stock-out requires an excessive safety stock. The trade-off is between the actual cost of safety stock vs. the probable cost of some customers demanding more than usual. Each unit of safety stock is, therefore, subject to diminishing returns. The art is to strike the right balance in terms of cost control.

the road, routing airplanes away from suburban areas at night, etc. These man-made constraints may bring about solutions to operational problems that appear counterintuitive at first. One such example might require a shipment using two trucks (and two drivers) instead of one if the jurisdiction does not allow double-trailer trucks. Of course, regulations may be purely political and have no relationship at all to market failures. An example here would be a US-based ocean vessel company buying higher-priced vessels from US shipyards because foreign-built vessels are prohibited under federal law.[c]

Transportation has a unique place in the supply chain. In fact, all supply chains require transportation in order to fulfill their operations and achieve their goals.[d] For proof simply consider the type of supply chain where no transportation is required at all. No matter what physical item or intangible service the supply chain is to produce and sell, if there is no transportation required then all supply (i.e., raw materials, utilities, workers, etc.) and all end customers must be within close proximity. If this were true, a car buyer and dealer, for example, would have to be near an iron ore mine (which is the source of the car's steel). Of course, they would also have to be nearby sources of rubber, aluminum, glass, etc. Since all of these sources are, themselves, not in the same place something and/or someone is going to have to be moved from its origin to where it is needed in the production process. This is where transportation comes in. It allows supply chains to be spread out over long distances and across many different countries and continents. Without transportation there would be no international, interstate, or intrastate trade.

Transportation is an activity requiring special equipment, trained operators of the conveyances used, and each are subject to a variety of government regulations at federal, state, and local levels. Using the choice between M&A and contracting, supply chain partners need to think about which of the two would provide more efficient transportation. A producer of tangible items could provide its own transportation services by establishing a private fleet of conveyances, or it could acquire a transportation carrier through M&A. As noted above, this may make sense if transportation is a critical

[c] This is known as an anticabotage regulation which has been the basis of US law since the Merchant Marine Act (1920) also known as the Jones Act. For a more detailed explanation see Prokop (2014a).

[d] For an introductory overview of the transportation market see Prokop (2014b).

process and the marketplace for such services is not very competitive. On the other hand, rather than being burdened with maintaining a fleet of conveyances, the producer could contract out its transportation needs to a for-hire carrier. In this case, not only does the producer have the flexibility afforded by contractual arrangements but costs (in the form of freight rates) may be lower than the costs incurred in-house. If this is so then a for-hire carrier would be another partner to be added to the list of supply chain partners. Of course, the more the types of transportation necessary to move something from origin to destination the more for-hire carrier partners will be needed.

What is logistics?

Logistics is the art and science of managing the constraints of time, physical space, and location. While supply chain management is about the structure and linkages of organizations, logistics is about the flow of items within that structure in order to fulfill the mutual goals of the supply chain partners. Transportation is a logistics activity that is synonymous with flow. All of the primary processes shown in Fig. 1.1 require it when an item goes from origin to destination; moving from where it is to where it is needed.

In terms of flow, logistics can be seen as fulfilling "seven rights" to downstream customers along the supply chain. This involves:

(1) making sure the right product
(2) is packaged in the right quantity
(3) delivered in the right condition
(4) to the right customer
(5) at the right time
(6) in the right location
(7) and doing all of this for the right price

Getting all of these right requires careful planning, knowledge of what the supply chain partners want and what they are capable of, and being flexible when something should change that is beyond one's control. Logistics planning means understanding points of origin and destination, what could happen in-between, and which mode or modes of transportation are best equipped to fulfill the seven "rights." Whatever the product is, points 1–2 require consideration of the size and configuration of the conveyance transporting the shipments. Point 3 relates to storage technology. Points 4–6 relate to the infrastructure of the transportation network and route chosen. Point 7 means that the other six points where handled efficiently with no unnecessary waste.[e]

It was noted in section "What is supply chain management?" that production costs may be lower if transportation is contracted out. Why is this the case? Basically, transportation is the most outsourced logistical activity. Supply chain partners typically do not want to maintain a private conveyance let alone an entire fleet of them. At the same time, transportation is often seen by nonspecialists as a "black box" where items are shipped from origin to destination with supply chain partners only concerning themselves about what is happening during this process when something goes wrong along the way (e.g., the delivery is projected to be late). In other words, transportation is a special activity requiring specialized technology, trained operators, and subject to specific regulations at all levels of government. It is little wonder, then, that many companies involved in manufacturing would rather hire this service than perform it in-house.

The black box of transportation

When something or someone must be transported from origin to destination what sort of planning is involved? First there is a presupposition that this move will add value (be it financial, personal, or social). Another is that the actual cost of the move is less than the value to be added. In other words, there should be net value added. Who determines whether or not there is a net value? Basically, it is the person making the arrangements for transportation. As a simple example, consider traveling along a jammed freeway or through a crowded airport. Why would someone put up with the inconvenience? Presumably, it is because the value added at the destination more than compensates for the time and energy used up while waiting in a queue. Also, travelers and shipments may not have much flexibility with their

[e] A useful way to think about efficiency is in terms of production and allocation of resources. Productive efficiency means that the activity was handled in the least-costly way. In other words, no other mode of transport or route could have moved the product from origin to destination at a lower cost. Allocative efficiency means that the activity was handled to meet all the expectations of the customer. For example, if speed is paramount then air delivery is more efficient than, say, motor carrier when the distance is in thousands of miles. Notice that allocative efficiency is the precursor to productive efficiency. The right time and right condition of a shipment may require a seemingly more expensive form of transportation; but it is efficient to use it so long as the customer is willing to pay extra for a speedy delivery.

schedules so the infrastructure can get very congested during morning/evening rush hours and holiday seasons.

When planning transportation from origin to destination the "black box" effect comes up when planners consider it as simply two points to connect. But it is not that simple. There can be a multitude of intermediate points along the way. This is due to the real-world constraints that arise when working within a transportation network. Consider these questions.

(1) How many modes of transport are needed?

(2) What is the nature of the transportation network to be used?

(3) Is there a back-haul available?

If more than one mode of transport is needed the shipper may have to deal with each modal carrier individually. Another possibility is that the shipper hires an intermediary known as a third-party logistics provider (often abbreviated, 3PL) to handle these complications on its behalf. Either way, any and all carriers and 3PLs imply more supply chain partners. The need for different modes may be due to geography. For example, shipments from China to the United States, because of the Pacific Ocean, require either air or ocean vessel transport. It may be due to available infrastructure. For example, a rail shipment would have to move to its final destination by truck if a railroad spur does not reach that point. In either case, transfers of shipments from one mode to another add to shipment time, may require lay-over storage, and are more vulnerable to damage and theft.

Even if the same mode of transport is used, the transportation network may require layovers and transfers between conveyances in the same fleet or among different carriers using the same mode. Many examples arise in international transportation. If a motor carrier does not have a license for travel into another country it may choose to transfer the shipment at or near the border to another carrier domiciled in that country. This operation is known as interlining. Another reason may be that the destination is so far into the other country that the carrier worries about empty back-hauls (discussed below). International airlines may be restricted by governments in the number of, and frequency of visits to, airports in other countries. This means that passengers and/or cargo would have to switch airlines to reach final destinations elsewhere in the country.[f]

[f] These restrictions are set out in bilateral air service agreements that are negotiated between two sovereign nations in order to determine how each may conduct business in the other's airspace. For a more detailed overview see Prokop (2014c).

Consider the back-haul problem. For every front-haul move there is a back-haul move (with or without a shipment in toe) to the point of origin (i.e., the domicile of the conveyance and/or its operator). If a back-haul load is not available, the front-haul shipper will have to absorb some or perhaps all of the costs of an empty back-haul or repositioning move to find a haul elsewhere. These extra costs may limit the amount of shipments tendered or eliminate them completely. Of course, the back-haul problem is an important reason why most shippers prefer to use a for-hire carrier. If a car manufacturer transports finished vehicles to car dealerships, what shipments could it take back to the car factory? There are no real options here. This, again, is a reason why transportation is so often outsourced.

Efficiencies in shipment consolidation, networks, and tracking

In section "The black box of transportation" interlining was discussed as a source of extra cost. However, interlining can also be a source of efficiency and cost savings. The primary reason for this is capacity utilization. A conveyance that is not being utilized fully is foregoing revenue.[g] Fig. 1.2 demonstrates how interlining works. Two round-trip routes are shown: A–B and C–D and these are traveled by two conveyances performing front-hauls and back-hauls on each. However, since the two routes have a cross-point there is an opportunity to transfer loads and, in effect, offer four more "round-trip" routes: A–C, A–D, C–B, and B–D. If a warehouse is built at the interline point there is no need for the two conveyances to

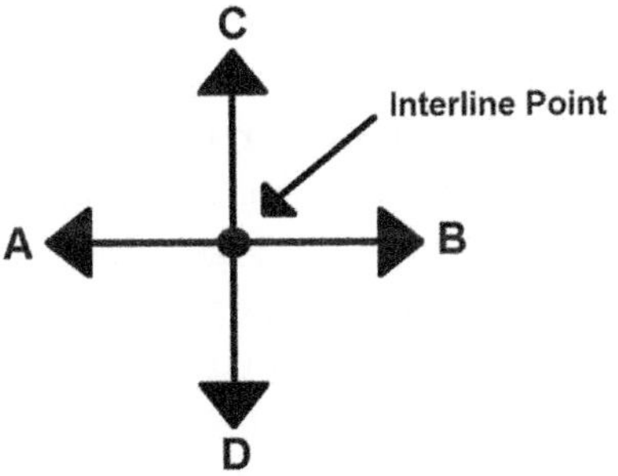

Fig. 1.2 The interline point

[g] Fully utilized does not necessarily mean the conveyance is filled to 100% capacity. Sometimes fill rates well below 100% are optimal. It also depends on what is being transported. Not all shipments are brick-like and stackable so that no gaps exist between packages or pallets. Optimality in shipping will be discussed in subsequent chapters.

physically meet there. Using two conveyances on two routes to, in effect, travel six routes enhances efficiency since they are filled with shipments going where they are not necessarily traveling to. Also, avoiding the need to expand the fleet when adding routes reduces costs and increases the opportunity for back-haul shipments on a given conveyance. For example, the A-B front-haul has the option to be topped-up at the interline point with C–B and D–B shipments. On the back-haul it may have B–A loads over the entire run, loads to be dropped off at the interline point (i.e., B–C and B–D), or it may top-up its back-haul with loads available at the interline point (i.e., C–A and D–A).

A phenomenon related to interlining is the hub-and-spoke network. In this case, a fleet is made up of different sized conveyances. Smaller quantities of loads and/or passengers are moved when the demand at the point of origin is low. These are the spoke-to-hub routes. More popular routes are serviced by larger conveyances. These are the hub-to-hub routes. This network design is very popular with both passenger and cargo airlines. Routes between large cities are fairly easy to plan for because of the high demand. It is simply a matter of using conveyances large enough to handle the flow. But if the city is small, and there is a demand for transport to a variety of cities (both large and small), there is a danger that there will not be enough demand at a given time to fill an airplane (even if it is a small one). In this case, the airplane should travel to one hub city and the passengers will connect to other airplanes to reach their various final destinations. In this way, the spoke-to-hub route will transport passengers who are, in effect, traveling to multiple destinations across the region, country, and the world. This allows spoke cities to create efficient routes that would be impossible without hubs. The smaller airlines have more opportunities to increase capacity utilization of the front-haul and the back-haul. While passenger airlines' hubs tend to be in larger cities air cargo carriers need not have their hubs there because the cargo is moved to smaller airplanes and/or trucks to reach destinations within the state or region.[h] Fig. 1.3 demonstrates how the hub-and-spoke model works. The thick lines show hub routes while the thin lines are the spoke routes. With cities A and E being

[h] The superhubs for FedEx and UPS are Memphis, TN and Louisville, KY, respectively. There is an advantage to having a locale with a large workforce nearby but less of the airspace congestion to be found around passenger airline hubs. Anchorage, AK is a gateway city and regional hub for both FedEx and UPS. This is due to the cost savings in gas-and-go operations which will be discussed in subsequent chapters.

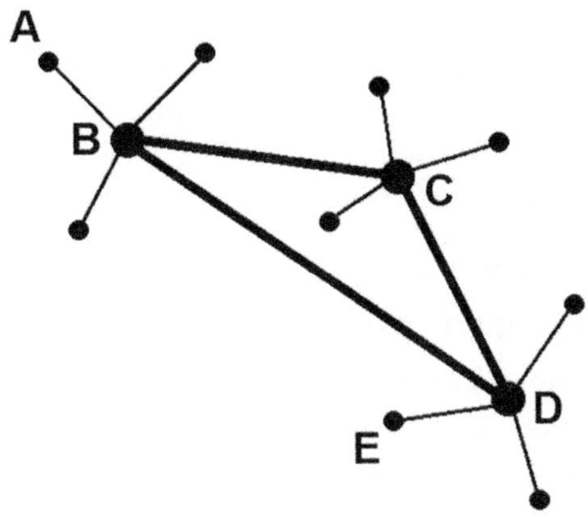

Fig. 1.3 The hub-and-spoke network.

small and far apart it would be hard to validate a direct flight in terms of demand; yet some people need to fly an A-E route. By consolidating passengers at point A on a flight to hub B passengers can make connections to take them to any other hub or spoke in the network. The A–E route proceeds as A–B–C–D–E or A–B–D–E. The passenger may choose the longer route if there were a price saving to compensate for the extra travel time and other inconveniences.[i]

Interlining and network design highlight the idea that shipments do not necessarily move along the shortest distance between origin and destination; and the route may be "broken" into different legs. The longer a shipment is *en route* the greater the risk of damage and theft.[j] On the other hand, tracking shipments means that congestion points along the network can be avoided or, if they are unavoidable, downstream supply chain partners can be informed and plan accordingly. The technology used in tracking shipments and conveyances include global positioning systems (GPS) and radio frequency identification (RFID). The challenge today, as discussed in Chapter 6, is to handle the avalanche of data gathered daily on the movement of conveyances and their shipments. Still, it must be kept in mind that interline points and hubs create efficiency through funneling traffic to them. However, if these central nodes are disrupted it can affect the performance of

[i] Airline prices do not always correlate with the distance traveled. Airlines practice a system of revenue management, which looks more so at what a passenger is willing to pay than what it costs to provide the service. Chapter 8 will discuss this issue in more detail.

[j] A complete discussion of transportation risk management may be found in Prokop (2017).

the entire network. It is, therefore, necessary to build resiliency into those points by having alternative routes available. There is a tension between cost control through building sufficient infrastructure and taking on the extra costs of ensuring more than sufficient infrastructure.[k]

Transportation value vs. cost

Variable cost and fixed cost

Cost management in transportation focuses on two operational sources: variable cost and fixed cost. Variable costs include wages for labor (i.e., conveyance operators, support staff, and managers), fuel, licenses, insurance, etc. These costs rise as the operations increase. Fixed costs include support infrastructure (e.g., leases on terminals, warehouses, rail lines, etc.). These costs remain constant (and positive) whether or not there are any operations. Only after the terms of these costs expire can the carrier either forgo or renegotiate them.

The sum of these two costs is known as total operational costs. A schematic presentation of these costs is provided in Fig. 1.4. For a given quantity of transportation services fixed cost is constant at some monetary value. Variable cost would be zero if there were no operations and rises (in a linear fashion, here, for simplicity) as operations increase. The rate of increase is constant (i.e., linear) though more complex models discussed in subsequent chapters will have nonlinear variable costs. Total cost is simply the vertical sum of the other two costs.

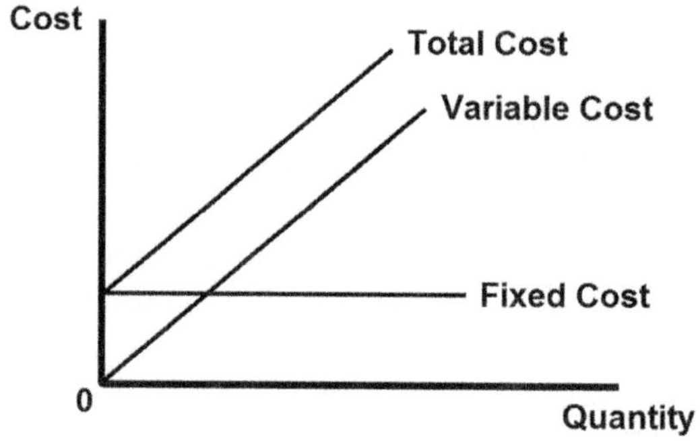

Fig. 1.4 Operational cost structure.

[k] For a discussion of the difference between efficiency and effectiveness see Prokop (2017; p. 186).

What is important to note is that each mode of transportation has different proportions of fixed and variable costs in total operational costs. As a result, carriers within these modes face different cost control challenges. For example, railroads require a lot of infrastructure built up-front (e.g., rail lines, switches, etc.) before operations can even begin. Motor carriers, on the other hand, can make use of public roads, bridges, etc. These differences have implications for the level of competition within the transport mode.

Cost of service and value of service

When a carrier sets a freight rate there are two distinct methods: pricing at cost of service (with a profit margin included) and pricing at value of service (i.e., what the market will bear). Most carriers do not have the luxury of choosing the method. Often market realities force adoption of one of the two methods. Also, each method has its challenges when trying to implement it. Cost of service pricing sounds simple enough since it is just a matter of covering cost. The problem is that some costs are not that easy to breakdown on a shipper-by-shipper basis. These are known as the joint cost and common cost traceability problem. Value of service pricing may mean that some shippers are charged below cost while others are charged more.

The traceability (also called the separability) problem is the main reason why front-haul shipments tend to cost more than back-haul ones (even if it were the same type of shipment hauled over the same distance). This is the case with joint costs. On the other hand, when common costs are present it is very difficult to trace them to their original source. With value of service pricing the carrier needs to be able to separate shippers into different groups based of their willingness to pay. Economists call the process price discrimination. Subsequent chapters will examine these rival methods in more detail and how they are deployed by different modes.

Introduction of the players

The five carrier modes

For-hire carriers are the providers of transportation services to the benefit of their shipper customers. There are five basic modes of transportation:

- air carrier
- motor carrier
- pipeline

- railway
- water vessel

For-hire carriers need not be restricted to only one of the five modes. Many carriers provide multimodal services. For example, FedEx and UPS maintain fleets of airplanes to move packages around the world; but they also have fleets of trucks to pick-up and drop-off packages at the doorsteps of their customers. Carriers may also partner with other carriers when interlining is necessary to move the item from origin to destination.

There is a rough relationship between the mode of transportation and the proportion of fixed cost necessary to operate. Also, the greater the proportion of fixed costs in the total cost of operations the less competitive the modal subsection of the transportation industry is. This is because fixed costs, being up-front and constant, tend to act as a barrier to entry. More competition tends to incentivize cost control and suppress profit margins. In short, more competitive modes tend to be less stable price-wise and cost-wise than less competitive ones. This relationship is shown in Fig. 1.5.[1] Note the inverse relationship between the fixed cost proportion and the degree of competitiveness.

A special type of operation is known as intermodalism. In this case more than one mode of transport is used from origin to destination. The multimodal activity of FedEx and UPS are examples of intermodalism. Of course, different carriers using different modes is another example. A shipment from China to the United States, which is not amenable to air cargo travel, will

	Fixed Cost	Variable Cost	Level of Modal Competition
Motor Carrier	5 20%	1 80%	1 many
Water Vessel	4 40%	2 60%	2 numerous
Air	3 50%	3 50%	3 few
Rail	2 60%	4 40%	4 few/regional
Pipeline	1 80%	5 20%	5 none

1 = highest / most
5 = lowest / least

Fig. 1.5 Operational costs and the level of modal competition.

[1] This figure is adapted from Prentice and Prokop (2016, Fig. 6.8).

have to be an intermodal shipment. A water vessel would arrive at a US port and the shipment would be transferred to motor carrier or rail for shipment inland.

The modern shipping container is a common denominator in many intermodal activities. Indeed, the rationale for containers was the idea that a shipment could be loaded at point of origin and be shipped using multiple modes without unloading and reloading the container's contents when transferred from mode to mode. This reduces risk of damage and theft and lowers the cost of stevedoring.[m]

The shippers/consignors

One thinks of the shipper as simply the demander for the services being supplied by the for-hire carrier. Technically, the consignor is the legal term for the individual who actually arranges for the transportation service. If the consignor is not willing to pay spot rates then the freight rate is open to negotiation with the carrier. After all terms regarding carriage are agreed to, the consignor and carrier sign a contract of carriage known as the bill of lading.

Consider a simple supply chain where a manufacturer needs to buy raw material from a vendor in order to complete the production process. If their places of business are a considerable distance apart, and neither owns a private conveyance to move the material, a for-hire carrier is needed to facilitate transportation. The question is: Who is the consignor? It could be the buyer of the item to be shipped, its seller, or even a third-party hired by one of the other two to act as an agent. When exactly does ownership pass from the seller of the item to be shipped to its buyer? Is it at the point of origin, destination, or some intermediate point along the shipping route? These are very important operational questions and open to negotiation when transportation services are being planned.

Many might say the seller of the raw material ought to be the consignor. After all, the item is at the seller's premises and it makes sense for the seller (as a vendor) to add the icing to its customer service cake by arranging the transportation and making sure the item reaches its buyer with all logistical aspects of time utility and place utility satisfied. But it is not that simple. The shipper could be either the buyer or the seller of the item. In fact, it could be neither. If both parties do not feel comfortable negotiating their

[m] For a complete history of the shipping container, see Donovan and Bonney (2006) and Levinson (2006).

way through the market for transportation services, one of the two may simply elect to deal directly with a third-party logistics provider (3PL) which will make contact with an appropriate for-hire carrier and arrange for transportation on its client's behalf. Things can get even trickier when multiple carriers and multiple modes of transport are necessary to move the item from seller to buyer. So, this seemingly simple buyer-seller transaction of raw material may need multiple players to support it and one of them will need to deal with one or more intermediaries in order to facilitate the transaction.

The consignor is the buyer of transportation services (i.e., the party responsible for directly paying the carrier). The consignor makes the item available for pick-up by the carrier (i.e., it consigns the shipment to the carrier) and is, by law, the party entitled to recover any damages to the item while in transit (i.e., under the for-hire carrier's control). The for-hire carrier is the supplier of transportation services and is required to meet all state and federal regulations applicable to that mode of transport, especially regarding the holding of freight insurance. As noted, the carrier is the other party to sign the bill of lading. By law, for-hire transportation cannot take place without a signed bill of lading between the consignor and the carrier. The carrier also needs to have freight insurance. This is a legal requirement so that the consignor can be made whole should a claim be made regarding loss and/or damage. Finally, the party designated to receive the shipment at the point of delivery, and take final possession, is known as the consignee. Of course, if the buyer of the item wants to be the shipper as well, then the consignor and consignee are the same person. In any case, the buyer of an item being shipped is always the consignee.

The intermediaries

An intermediary, known as a third-party logistics provider (3PL), may be hired by the buyer or seller of an item to be shipped when neither wishes to arrange for transportation. If the 3PL deals directly with the carrier on behalf of its client the shipper (who, again, can be either the buyer or seller of the item) then the distinction between shipper and consignor gets a little blurry. It is important to understand what the responsibilities are when an agency relationship is added to the mix. If the 3PL negotiates the terms of transportation, agrees to directly pay the carrier, and signs the bill of lading then it becomes the consignor acting as an agent for the true shipper. In fact, the place on the bill of lading where the consignor signs is typically listed as "shipper." But since the 3PL is not really the shipper it makes sense for it to protect itself by also including the name and address of the true shipper. In this way its agency function becomes clear on the legal contract and keeps the 3PL out of disputes that might not concern it. For example, if the consignee finds that the item was damaged in transit, it needs to deal directly with the carrier and not the 3PL who hired the carrier. Or, if the item appears defective in its original manufacturing or packaging, the consignee will want to deal directly with the seller, the true shipper. Also, from the carrier's perspective, the consignee could outright refuse delivery of the item. What then? In effect, the buyer refuses to pay the seller and the original transaction dissolves. In that case the seller would obviously like to have the item returned. However, the carrier is only obliged to contact the "shipper" as listed on the bill of lading before being legally entitled to dispose of the item in its charge. The carrier has a lien on the shipment in its custody until it is paid by someone: the buyer, the seller, or the 3PL.

Apart from 3PLs there is another important intermediary in transportation planning. Suppose the for-hire carrier feels it necessary to involve other parties in order to ship the item from origin to final destination. Many motor carriers, for example, use owner-operators (i.e., independent drivers using their own tractor trailers). Note that owner-operators allow large carriers more flexibility in their fleet management and help them avoid unnecessary fixed costs. Such things serve to keep freight rates lower than otherwise. In any case, the carrier contracted by the consignor (which is now not doing any actual carrying here) is still bound by the bill of lading it signed and is responsible for any of its own agent's acts in carrying out the contract. Suppose the carrier does not normally travel to the required destination but promises delivery because it arranges an interline operation to another carrier. Again, this other carrier would be, in effect, a hired agent of the contracted carrier with the latter still responsible for the former's performance. Finally, suppose multiple modes of transport are needed to move the item from origin to destination. Likely, multiple bills of lading will be needed if the various carriers only wish to contract for their own portions of the desired route.

Contractual interaction: The bill of lading

For-hire transportation is an important contractual activity just like others seen among customers and their vendors along a supply chain. A big difference, however, is that the law requires a for-hire carrier to issue the bill of lading. By giving the signed copy to the consignor and taking charge of the shipment, the carrier is holding itself liable to the consignor in case of loss or damage due to its own negligence. The bill of lading also serves as the consignor's receipt for the item the carrier is picking up and delivering. Both the consignor and the carrier should take comfort in a well-drafted and executed bill of lading.

Here is an important question: Could the consignor prepare the bill of lading instead? Yes. The law requires that a contract be issued by the carrier; it does not say who draws it up. For many reasons a shipper, or a 3PL acting as consignor, may want to forego a carrier's "uniform" bill of lading and spell out certain particulars in the contract (e.g., specific freight handling requirements, liabilities, etc.). If it is important to the shipper then it is better to spell it out to the carrier in writing at the contracting stage rather than hoping, for example, its loading dock personnel and the carrier's driver can sort out any ambiguities between themselves. Another important point in US transportation law is the Carmack Amendment to the US Interstate Commerce Act. This law allows the carrier to require that damage claims be made in writing and within 9 months of the date of the loss. Furthermore, the carrier may limit its liability to the lesser of: (1) the reduction in the item's value due to the damage and (2) the cost to repair the damage. As in all contracts there should be a meeting of the minds; in this case between the consignor and the carrier. Uniform bills of lading and the Carmack Amendment are the carrier's default positions. Basically, it is up to the shipper to decide to agree with this or propose alternatives as part of a negotiation.

The variations involved in the shipper-carrier relationship show how important a supply chain partner the carrier is. Here is another question: the bill of lading may be necessary by law but is it the only binding contract between the consignor and the carrier? Well, it should not be. As a contract of carriage the bill of lading is somewhat limited. True, the bill of lading designates who directly pays the carrier. In fact, some diligent consignors even like to reference on the bill the exact amount to be paid. However, it is important to understand that transportation pricing needs to be set forth in a different contract which notes an agreed-to freight rate or freight tariff schedule (if the carrier uses one) and any other terms and timing of payment.

During this entire process, as outlined above, when does the item's title of ownership pass from the buyer to the seller? Perhaps surprisingly, it is not in the bill of lading because that is not the appropriate legal document. Again, the bill of lading is a contract between the buyer and seller of *transportation*, not the buyer and seller of the item being shipped. The consignor may actually own the item in-transit or it may act as an agent for the true owner at the time of transport. The bottom line is the ownership of the item to be shipped passes between buyer and seller when each says so as specified in their separate contract of sale. If such terms are noted in a shipper's bill of lading it is not relevant and nonbinding within that document. To see this, imagine if the buyer and the seller agree that the item's title of ownership passes to the buyer before transportation takes place. Imagine as well that the seller, acting as consignor, is willing to arrange transportation with the carrier. What happens when something goes wrong in fulfilling the bill of lading? The seller for its part cannot legally claim that resolving the problem should now pass to the item's true owner because the buyer cannot be bound by the bill of lading—a document to which it was not even a party. The seller, as the agent for the buyer, needs to exercise reasonable care in its duties. The bottom line is that free on board (FOB) at origin shows that the consignee owns the item in transit while FOB-destination shows that the consignor does (or the seller, specifically, when the consignor is a 3PL in an agency agreement).[n] On top of the FOB-origin or FOB-destination designations other items need to spell out which party is actually paying the carrier. "Freight collect" means the consignee is paying the carrier while "freight prepaid" means the consignor is paying. In this case there are four possible combinations; and like all things in supply chain management one has to choose, or negotiate over, how much responsibility to take on and how much risk to pass along to others.

Issues and problems going forward

Buyers and sellers of items often see transportation as a means to an end. It is not something that is necessary enjoyable to deal with. But, since shippers rely on transportation, here are some things to keep in mind when dealing with carriers. Shippers should try to limit legal liability on both sides and keep disputes from becoming unnecessarily time consuming. For example, make sure all parties are listed on the bill of lading with accurate contact information. Pick-up and delivery times and places should comport with the shipper's expectations and be listed accurately on the bill of lading. But, like all things, offering lead times can help carriers better plan their services. Last-minute requests lead to risks and freight surcharges. As they say,

[n] FOB is part of a collection of international commercial terms (abbreviated, Incoterms), which will be discussed in greater detail in subsequent chapters.

time is money. But it is a two-way street. In other words, if the shipper expects a pick-up at a certain time it makes sense, therefore, to assist the carrier in performing its duty. Shippers should try to avoid dock delays and bottlenecks so that the driver is not left idling. Shippers need to make sure their yards have signage to help the driver find the dock. The yards also need the space necessary to navigate the type of conveyance the carrier assigns to the shipment. A conveyance in motion is earning revenue while one that is parked is only incurring costs. If shippers can think from the point of view of the carrier then keeping things moving helps keep costs down. When it is possible shippers should schedule travel on off-peak hours or weekends. In the case of motor carriers, it is important to know that their drivers face an hours-of-service limit of 11 h on the job. Shippers and carriers who work well together know how to work within this time window and, if they happen to bump up to it, a courteous shipper should make his yard available for the truck to park during the driver's requisite 10-h rest break. These plans and courtesies are expected when a carrier is looked upon as a supply chain partner in the same way a vendor of inputs is to a manufacturer.

The buyer and seller of an item must navigate through the market for transportation in order to keep their supply chain working smoothly. Yet transportation is often considered to be a "black box" by those who do not work directly with for-hire carriers. One reason for this may be the belief that only consignors need to worry about the transportation process (as if the other partners farther upstream or downstream along the supply chain do not have an interest in keeping items moving along). Another reason may be that too much leverage is ceded to the for-hire carrier in the contracting process. The complexities of transportation planning touched on in this chapter may seem far beyond the core competencies of buyers and sellers. But buyers and sellers can hire a 3PL to help level the playing field with the carrier. Also, while carriers have certain legal requirements to fulfill, shippers also have options when it comes to negotiating freight rates, terms of payment, and the contents of the bill of lading. Transportation represents another important dimension in the negotiating and contracting processes found in supply chain management. If buyers and sellers come to think of for-hire carriers as important supply chain partners, and worth investing the time to build strong relationships, a lot of light will shine into a once black box. These ideas should be kept in mind as subsequent chapters unfold.

References

Donovan, A., Bonney, J., 2006. The Box that Changed the World. Commonwealth Business Media, East Windsor, NJ.

Levinson, M., 2006. The Box: How the Shipping Container Made the World Smaller and the World Economy Bigger. Princeton University Press, Princeton, NJ.

Porter, M.E., 1985. Competitive Advantage: Creating and Sustaining Superior Performance. Simon and Schuster, New York, NY.

Prentice, B.E., Prokop, D., 2016. Concepts of Transportation Economics. World Scientific, Hackensack, NJ.

Prokop, D., 2014a. International transportation management. In: Prokop, D. (Ed.), The Business of Transportation. Modes and Markets. Vol. 2. Praeger, Santa Barbara, CA, pp. 70–89.

Prokop, D., 2014b. Transportation in business decision-making. In: Prokop, D. (Ed.), The Business of Transportation. Modes and Markets. Vol. 1. Praeger, Santa Barbara, CA, pp. 1–14.

Prokop, D., 2014c. Government regulation of international air transportation. In: Peoples, J. (Ed.), The Economics of International Airline Transport (Advances in Airline Economics, Volume 4). Emerald Publishing Limited, Bingley, UK, pp. 45–59.

Prokop, D., 2017. Global Supply Chain Security and Management: Appraising Programs. Preventing Crimes, Butterworth Heinemann, Cambridge, MA.

References

[illegible]

CHAPTER 2

The economics of transportation operations

Transportation and the economy

As long as the processes of resource extraction and production do not take place in the same locale, transportation is necessary. It is also necessary if workers and managers do not live where they work and if production and consumption do not take place in the same locale either.

Economic theory is not homogenous. Rather, there are differing theories of how profits are generated, capital is formed, etc. As such, there are different policy prescriptions for how to deal with interest rates, the money supply, unemployment, etc. However, the role of transportation in the economy is fairly clear.

Transportation facilitates trade which means that it not only facilitates multistage production processes but also facilitates their being spread over vast distances and across multiple countries. Traversing across continents and oceans is now commonplace and this has implications not only for production but also for the economy as a whole. With more stages of production taking place in-between resource extraction and final consumption of a finished good, there are more nodes susceptible to different levels of volatility in input prices, employment, inventory, and production. This may result from misallocations of investment capital and credit. This is the challenge facing supply chain coordination. Economic theory tends to treat the distribution of government-induced increases in the money supply as uniform across sectors. The same goes for the effects of price inflation.[a]

At the downstream end of every supply chain is a final customer who will buy the item only if it is affordable and is perceived to add value relative to cost. The latter is always a subjective valuation on the part of the customer. Upstream along the supply chain, various producers and vendors make

[a] In essence there is a tension in economics between two schools of thought known as neoclassical monetary theory and Austrian capital theory. For a full discussion see Skousen (1990).

Transportation Operations Management
https://doi.org/10.1016/B978-0-12-815415-1.00002-1

Table 2.1 Cost of transportation by top sectors in 2018.

Top sectors (descending order)	Transportation cost per dollar of output	Percentage share of for-hire transportation
Wholesale and retail	$0.086	49
Utilities	$0.055	96
Natural resources and mining	$0.043	65
Manufacturing	$0.041	78
Construction	$0.037	47

Source: Modified from Transportation Statistics Annual Report (2020). Washington, DC: US Department of Transportation. Fig. 5.3.

decisions that are determined less so by customer psychology. They buy inputs in order to facilitate production and not consumption. The final customer is, indeed, the wild card at the end of every supply chain.

In 2016, the transportation labor force in the United States totaled 13 million people and facilitated the transport of almost 5 trillion ton-miles of freight and 5.3 trillion passenger-miles.[b] Table 2.1 summarizes the cost of transportation services required for the production of output by sector.

The balance of the percentages shown in the second column represents private, in-house transportation. Thus, while wholesale/retail and construction are on opposite ends for how much transportation costs factor into the cost of output, private transportation accounts for slightly more than half of the cost of transportation they incurred. In other words, these sectors are comfortable maintaining private conveyances. This makes sense for the construction sector since conveyances are on-site working with excavation equipment, cranes, etc. Many wholesale/retail businesses make use of private vehicles for last-mile delivery to households. The high percentage share shown in the utility sector is accounted for by the separation of companies engaged in energy generation versus energy distribution over a dedicated infrastructure.

Economies of scale

The US Navy can project its military power using the largest piece of military equipment ever built. The *USS Gerald R. Ford*, commissioned in 2017, is the first of the new Ford-class aircraft carriers. The Ford-class also offers

[b] Calculated from National Transportation Statistics (2017), Tables 1-40, 1-50, and 3-23.

efficiencies compared to the similar-sized but older Nimitz-class. These include 700 fewer crew members and lower maintenance costs from its two nuclear reactors which, at 600 MW, generate triple the electric power of the Nimitz-class and enough to light up a city of half a million people. Newport News Shipbuilding charges about $13 billion for a Ford-class carrier, which is twice as much as the last Nimitz-class, the *USS George H. W. Bush* commissioned in 2009. These prices, of course, do not cover the cost of aircraft. Currently, the United States maintains a fleet of 11 aircraft carriers and no other navy comes even close.

From a military perspective, aircraft carriers have allowed the US Navy to establish air superiority off the coast of any nation thus alleviating the need to secure access to neighboring countries' airspaces let alone being granted permission from them to establish airbases. However, aircraft carriers are also multibillion-dollar targets that are vulnerable to attack from enemy submarines, aircraft, ballistic missiles, and, perhaps one day, drones. As such, aircraft carriers need to be positioned farther off enemy shores (perhaps as much as 1000 nautical miles) to be able to avoid today's modern and maneuverable missiles. Each nautical mile offshore presents the trade-off of keeping the military asset safe while limiting the range of its fighter and recognizance aircraft. More escort vessels and submarines may allow for closer positioning but that ties up even more assets. Despite the increased efficiencies of Ford-class carriers, navy strategists are no doubt wrestling with the thought that these supercarriers may be suffering from a nonmilitary concept known as diseconomies of scale. In the business world, a company needs to guard against becoming too big to fail. The military needs to guard against weapons that are becoming too expensive to lose.

Chapter 1 outlined the gains to be had through interlining operations and the hub-and-spoke model of network design. To the extent that these options can lower the cost of transportation per unit, they are examples of economies of scale. If expanding the size of an organization sees long-run costs rise at a decreasing rate (i.e., long-run average costs are falling) economies of scale are present. Interlining and hub-and-spoke networks are benefits that can arise from fleet expansion. The standard definition of economies of scale relates to a generic increase in the scale of the operation. For-hire carriers have options for many variations of scale.

Economies of scale, due to lowering a carrier's long-run average cost, can provide a rationale for lowering the freight rates charged to consignors. The term can be simplified to mean that bigger is better (i.e., bigger vehicles, bigger fleets, and bigger shipments). The downside is that economies of scale, as

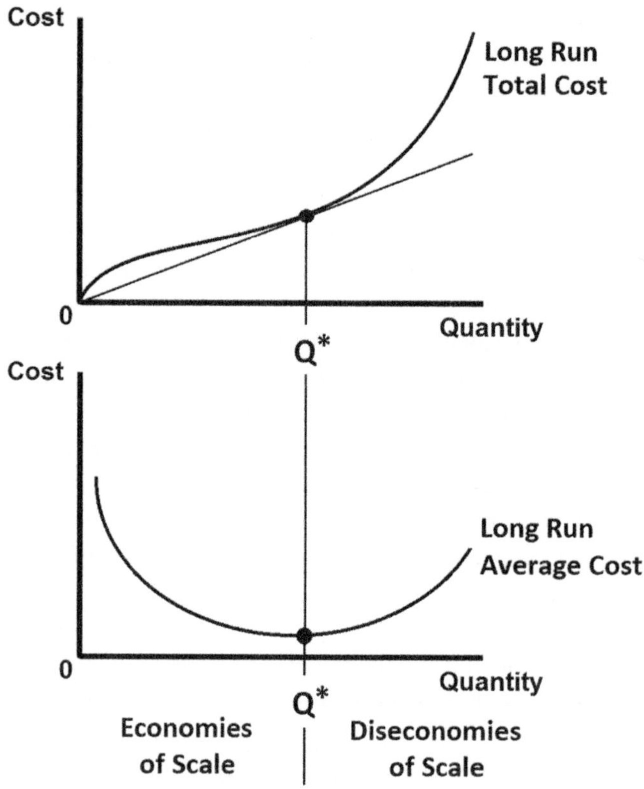

Fig. 2.1 Economies and diseconomies of scale.

a phenomenon, do not go on indefinitely. There is a point when long-run average costs will begin to rise as scale increases. This is known as diseconomies of scale. Both of these concepts are shown in Fig. 2.1. The "quantity" in the figure can be taken to mean ton-miles which increase as the scale of the for-hire carrier's operation expands.

Economies of scale describe what happens to operating cost as the size of the operation itself increases. The term does not directly relate to sales revenue or to profit. Specifically, as a business takes advantage of economies of scale, its total cost rises at a decreasing rate. It is easy to make the mistake of thinking that costs will fall when economies of scale are exploited. Technically, as total cost rises at a decreasing rate, it is only the *average* cost that is decreasing. After all, it is hard to think of a business that increases its scale of operation by, say, 25% and finds that with all the extra labor and capital now employed that its total cost has actually fallen. What is happening is that the scale of operation increases by 25% and total costs increase by some lower percentage. Since the average cost is defined as the ratio of total cost divided by the current level of production, the ratio declines as the scale increases when economies of scale are exploited. Conversely, when facing diseconomies of scale, the total cost rises at an increasing rate meaning that average cost rises.[c]

Economies of scale are assumed to occur over a production process experiencing no technological change. Simply put, the means by which inputs are turned into outputs (i.e., the production function) as shown in Eq. (2.1) does not change as the business increases its scale of production.

$$Q = Q(L, K, N, E) \tag{2.1}$$

where Q is the quantity of output; L is labor; K is capital (i.e., machines and infrastructure); N is natural resources; E is entrepreneurship (including management).

The implication is that qualitative inputs such as managerial skills remain constant and there are no scientific innovations taking place which would impact the production process. Of course, these assumptions do not hold in the real world. However, the reason for the assumption is that economies of scale apply to how a given set of inputs are turned into specific outputs. Changing the quality of inputs or substituting with other (more innovative) inputs means the equation for the production function would have to be redefined to account for these. This changes how total and average costs behave. In this context, economies of scale would have little meaning. The good news for businesses seeking innovations is that technological change has a long history of reducing production costs and bringing improved products to the marketplace. Innovations in science or management can, indeed, make a business more scalable; but one cannot build them explicitly into production plans. The sources of economies of scale are more systematic.

It is important to note that economies of scale are what economists call a long-run concept. This means businesses must plan in advance for a certain scale of operation and, once it is achieved, they have to live with the consequences until, in the long run, the plan can be revised to meet new market

[c] This is what the ray from the origin in Fig. 2.1 is highlighting. The slope of the ray is defined as rise-over-run or (TC − 0)/(Q − 0) or simply, TC/Q which is the average cost. In other words, the falling slopes of the rays from Q = 0 to Q*, and the rising slopes beyond Q* trace out the average cost curve.

realities. This interim period of time is known as the short run where some components of a business' operation are fixed in size (e.g., the capacity of a warehouse, duration of a lease on a vehicle, union wages set through collective bargaining, etc.). Thus, the choice of scale is a strategic exercise because it involves a forecast of what market conditions are expected to be over the short-run interim. Three important questions from a supply chain management perspective are as follows:

(1) Will the chosen scale provide enough products to meet downstream customer demand?

(2) Will upstream vendors be able to provide enough inputs to facilitate the level of production necessary to fulfill point (1)?

(3) Will financial and operational costs be low enough to set a product price that will generate enough sales revenue to stay in business in the long run?

To complicate matters, a business may face competitors which are likewise trying to achieve an appropriate scale of operations. With a fixed level of consumer demand, vendor supply, and financial capital it becomes harder for one business to achieve higher scale if one or more are already larger and with a lot of market share. Each business is striving for so-called internal economies of scale. On the other hand, more competition may be beneficial for all competitors in an industry if it attracts external players which help to grow the entire industry. This is what is meant by the term external economies of scale.

Consider the internal and external sources of both economies and diseconomies of scale. Internal circumstances can lead to either a decrease or an increase in long-run average costs as the business grows larger. As a business increases in scale from a small labor force, it makes sense to divide production into more specialized tasks with specific departments set up to manage these tasks. This division of labor can lead to efficiencies. The modern assembly line is the best example of this. However, if tasks become too narrow they can become mundane and quality control can become a problem. Also, as the business becomes large it may become more bureaucratic, mired in red-tape, and less flexible because of the time spent in pushing papers, having meetings, etc. Guarding against these pitfalls is an important organizational task. In fact, it is a balancing act between lean and lethargy; flexibility and inflexibility. As for external circumstances, as a business becomes larger it may make sense for the local government to improve transport infrastructure in the vicinity in order to get workers, vendor supplies, and customers to and from the place of business. On the other hand, a business can become so large that it creates traffic congestion within a given infrastructure, or it begins to exhaust a free publicly available input (e.g., clean water from a lake) and costs begin to rise. Thus, it is also incumbent on a business to follow the workings of government and plan accordingly in order to strike the right balance when trying to exploit external economies of scale.

There is also an interplay between internal and external economies of scale through the set-up or sunk costs of a business. Any business will incur such costs because the production plan must be conceived, vendor relationships must be established, distribution channels must be created, etc. The larger the business the more these set-up costs are distributed over the pool of output. In this way, long-run average cost declines. As a simple example, consider advertising as an upfront cost to set up a distribution channel. A minute of commercial television time during the Super Bowl is so expensive it only makes sense for the largest businesses to pay for it. They have more output and sales revenue to validate such a purchase.

Standard economics looks at scale in a singular fashion; basically, just the "size" of the operation. Regarding a for-hire carrier, the scale of an operation can take many forms. These include the size of a vehicle or shipping container; the number of vehicles in a fleet; transportation network efficiencies; and a shipment's weight and distance carried. But, recall, such sources of economies of scale will eventually become diseconomies of scale. Therefore, striking the right balance in transportation planning is critical.

Economies of vehicle or container size come about because the volume or carrying capacity of a truck trailer, rail car, airplane, ocean vessel, and pipeline increases faster than the quantity of side material needed to build it. For example, compare a $3' \times 3' \times 3'$ container with a $6' \times 6' \times 6'$ container. The material used on each side would increase by 4 times; that is, each side increases from 9 to $36\,\text{ft}^2$. However, the capacity of the smaller container is $27\,\text{ft}^3$ while the larger one is $216\,\text{ft}^3$, which is an increase of 8 times.

For a pipeline, consider a sheet of metal that is $10' \times 30'$. It is wrapped around to make a section of a pipeline that is $10'$ in circumference (C) and $30'$ in length. Finding the radius (r) is a matter of using the equation $C = 2\pi r$. The radius is, therefore, $1.59'$. Finding the volume (V) that can pass through is a matter of using the equation $V = \pi r^2 h$ where the height (h) is $30'$. Volume is $238.3\,\text{ft}^3$. Of course, if the section were double in length (i.e., $10' \times 60'$) the volume would merely double as well. However, economies of scale comes, instead, from increasing the circumference.

If the metal sheet is $20' \times 30'$, the circumference doubles. The radius is found by solving $20 = 2\pi r$ which is $3.18'$ which is double the radius. The volume is $\pi(3.18)^2(30)$ or $953\,\text{ft}^3$. Thus, doubling the material cost of the outer shell of the pipeline increases its volume by 4 times.

Carrying capacity (which is a source of carrier revenue) increases faster than the material cost involved in expanding that capacity. However, the vehicle or container can become too big to haul shipments along a given road, canal, etc. An airplane could be so big that it takes too long to load and unload passengers. The pipeline could collapse under its own weight when loaded. These are all examples of diseconomies of scale.

Economies of shipment weight and distance come about when considering all the costs which increase as the shipment's characteristics change. For example, doubling the size of a given shipment or hauling a given shipment double the distance should not double *all* of the costs associated with the shipment. Just one pilot and one copilot are necessary for a fully laden cargo jet traveling 5000 miles or 10,000 miles or carrying 50% capacity or 100% capacity. Compare a fully laden 10,000 twenty-foot equivalent unit (TEU) container vessel with one that is double in size. Does doubling the size mean that the crew size doubles? Does it require double the amount of gantry cranes to load and unload the containers at a port? Does it require double the amount of bunker fuel to steam from point A to B? Does it require double the amount of office workers to handle the doubled flow of container shipping documents? The answer to these questions is no. The fact that not all sources of cost rise at the same rate as others means that a double-sized TEU operation will indeed cost more but it need not cost double when economies of scale are present.

An ocean vessel carrier offering a lot of capacity in one large vessel gives consignors with high demand for transport (e.g., Walmart, Home Depot, etc.) a chance for even larger bulk discounts on their freight rates. There are external benefits to be had as well. A vessel that is double in size does not double its burn rate of bunker fuel. This means that the fuel savings per TEU lessen the environmental impact of air pollution per TEU.

These costs will taper off as weight and/or distance increases. In other words, these costs are spread over the extra revenue to be had through hauling more or hauling for longer distances. This is good news. The bad news is this only continues until it is necessary to increase the labor involved in the shipment. This could involve adding more shifts of drivers over long distances or more personnel to load and unload vehicles. Suppose the container becomes so large that its sidings collapse due to the weight of the shipments loaded into it. Suppose the new 20,000 TEU vessel is too big to be handled by the gauges of the gantry cranes available at the required ports of call. Suppose the vessel takes too long to load and unload given the time constraints of the consignors and/or the workday requirements of unionized dock personnel. Suppose the increase in office workers and management oversight lead to bureaucratic red-tape. In other words, the sources of revenue and cost savings afforded from higher carrying capacity begin to disappear under the limitations of container engineering, the indivisibilities of labor, the cost of bureaucracy, and the patience of consignors. Longer load and unload times per TEU and the extra time moored offshore waiting for other large vessels to be serviced lead to extra fuel burn in idle time. This, of course, increases the environmental impact of air pollution.

Diseconomies of scale can also occur when infrastructure's capacity must be expanded but indivisibilities require expansions larger than needed. For example, if a truck trailer is at capacity and there is a desire by the motor carrier to expand operations, it must increase in increments of one trailer even if that is much more capacity than is desired. If a road is congested by traffic it must be expanded in increments of an extra lane. On the other hand, if market demand sufficiently expands over time then the investment in a new trailer, extra lane, etc., does offer economies of scale up and until capacity is maximized yet again.

An intermediate point between economies and diseconomies of scale is constant returns to scale. This is the absence of either economies or diseconomies of scale. Constant returns to scale occur when there is a built-in rigidity or independence to the operation. Fig. 2.2 shows the cost effects.[d]

Long-run total cost expresses neither acceleration nor deceleration as scale increases. Each increment of scale (i.e., an increase in fleet size) offers no gains to the other conveyances. This is why long-run average cost is constant over all quantities of output.

As an example of constant returns to scale, consider US-Asia ocean vessel shipping. Many container vessels travel to and from ports on the US West Coast to ports in Japan, South Korea, and China with no stops along the way. Of course, the vastness of the Pacific Ocean necessitates this nonstop service. These vessels follow similar routes along the "great circle" (or orthodrome) between the US West Coast and Asia (taking them through or near the Aleutian Islands of Alaska). While their routes may cross one another in

[d] Since total cost itself is a ray from the origin and the slope is constant it means that the slope itself is, by definition, average cost.

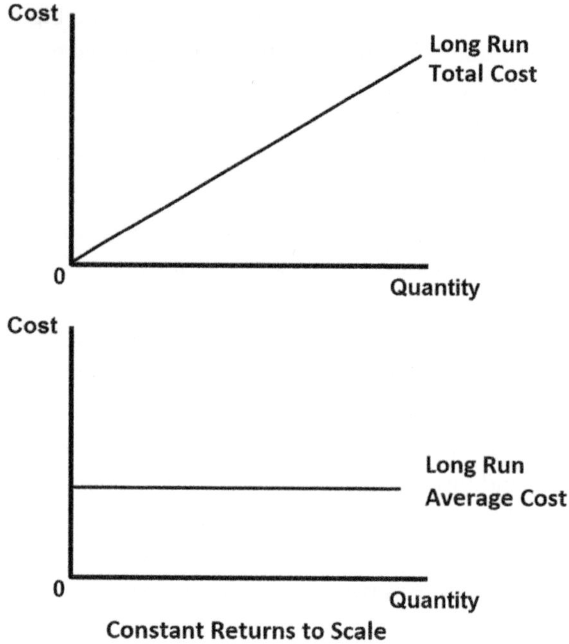

Fig. 2.2 Constant returns to scale.

the Pacific Ocean there is no possibility of interlining in the way trucks, trains, and air carriers can. Each vessel in the ocean carrier's fleet in these waters serves an independent route and enjoys no economies of fleet size. Expanding operations in these waters requires a different vessel, crew, port dockage authority, etc. For these reasons, the carrier does not see its average cost rise or fall as the fleet expands. Long-run average costs are constant and face indivisibilities as the fleet expands one vessel at a time. Of course, interlining in the ocean vessel sector does occur in other routes. The Port of Singapore is an example of an important container transfer point along Europe-Asia trade lanes.

Economies of scope is a term related to economies of scale. While constant returns to scale is about rigidity, economies of scope is about flexibility. In this case, the carrier is trying to achieve efficiencies through a mixture of services instead through a larger scale of a particular service. Economies of scope offers carriers a chance to diversify their operations in order to expand market share or mitigate a decline in a current market. Many examples exist in transportation. A commercial airline can offer charter service if scheduled service is in less demand. A less-than-truckload (LTL) carrier can offer truckload service (TL) if the consignor is willing and able to fill an entire truck and pay a dedicated freight rate. Of course, it is certainly easy enough for a rail carrier to attach boxcars to passenger cars and provide a mixture of haulage services.

Diseconomies of scope emerge, however, when the carrier begins to forget its core competency and diverts too many resources into its secondary operation. In transportation, this is best explained in terms of cargo services versus passenger services. Cargo transport is always a part of the production process while passenger travel (for nonbusiness purposes) is a part of the consumption process. Inputs are cargo. The carriers facilitate the production process by moving inputs to where they need to be. Passengers on vacation are enjoying the "consumption" of their leisure time and carriers facilitate this consumption process. Indeed, cruises, train tours, etc. are themselves an act of consumption. Why is this distinction important? Because production is governed by the state of technology and this is an important factor used in pricing transportation. Consumption is governed by tastes and preferences, user income, etc. and pricing transportation is more nebulous in this case. Furthermore, passengers are "freight that complain" and, therefore, must be treated differently than cargo.

As noted above, economies of scale do not directly relate to a business's sales revenue and profit. Achieving the lowest long-run average cost makes sense when market conditions suggest that low-cost businesses will have staying power. But there is no reason to believe that such a business will maximize profits. Markets that are easy to enter and exit tend to be very competitive and do not offer many options to increase scale at the expense of competitors. However, for some businesses (e.g., the railroads and pipeline companies) economies of scale can act as a barrier to entry for other competitors. Once the railway or pipeline infrastructure is in place there is little incentive for a direct competitor to challenge the incumbent along that route. In this way, monopolistic profits are possible if the market is unregulated or uncontestable.

When considering transportation hubs, it is no coincidence that consignors and carriers tend to locate in areas that are hospitable to them. Chicago (for Class I railroads), Memphis (for FedEx and air cargo), and Singapore (for ocean vessels) are important examples. These are also sources of external economies of scale because business and government are able to serve each other's needs. Businesses benefit from government-provided infrastructure and the government benefits from the taxes and fees it can collect from successful businesses. Urbanization and agglomeration policies that take into account these businesses help to ensure a steady pool of labor, vendors, and customers. Applicable research and development (R&D) through local universities and think tanks may come about as well. Of course, as noted above, R&D benefits deviate from the assumption of constant technology within the definition of economies of scale. Nonetheless, these are all important aspects of successful logistical hubs and knowledge clusters.

While all five modes of transport (i.e., truck, rail, air, water vessel, and pipeline) have been used to illustrate various examples of economies of scale, some modes are more prone to it than others. For a variety of reasons, it is more likely that less competitive markets will benefit from economies of scale. Why? Basically, it is due to barriers to entry in the form of set-up costs. As long as most roads are publicly provided it will always be easier for a motor carrier to buy a truck and offer, say, a 100-mile route than would a railway or a pipeline company. Worse still, if railways and pipeline companies are less competitive, why should they take full advantage of economies of scale and try to lower the costs of their operations? The answer, in part, lies with intermodal competition. If one mode offers some level of alternative service in the eyes of consignors then these "contestable" markets may see greater exploitation of economies of scale than might otherwise be the case. Consignors must maintain a discriminating eye when it comes to the mode of transportation they choose.

Transportation planning is a complex task. It is dependent on the nature of the marketplace, the state of technology, government regulation, and cost control. Economies of scale is an important concept when it comes to cost control. Transportation offers rich variants on the concept of "scale" and these demonstrate that transportation is by no means a homogenous activity along the supply chain.

"Build it and they will come" is no guarantee in any mode of transportation—especially in ones that are competitive and prone to economic downturns. More flexibility is afforded through fleets of smaller and more nimble conveyances. This overcomes the indivisibility problem and the dangers of excess capacity if and when consignors become scarce. A single large vessel is either at sea with any excess capacity resulting from lack of demand or is out of business in dry dock. On the other hand, a fleet of several smaller vessels with aggregated TEUs equal to the large one has more options. These include making adjustments in routing to avoid congested ports, seeking out scarce freight from more ports of call, and moving to dry dock on a piecemeal basis if business declines.

As mega-vessels dock at fewer ports, there will also be more drayage, more trucks on the road, and more trains moving containers to and from places all over the country. All of these activities will concentrate on a few large ports able to handle the world's largest vessels. Economies of scale require careful planning and timing in order to adjust to changes in consumer demand and technology. A good rule of thumb for all businesses is: too big to fail simply means too big.

Market failures in transportation

Taxes and regulations are always politically motivated and they are almost always crafted to meet some perceived lapse in equity or fairness in the judgment of lawmakers. The only exception is when a tax or regulation is used to overcome what economists call a market failure, meaning a failure to achieve social efficiency. Basically, a market fails when the private sector either underprovides what society would prefer more of (e.g., new infrastructure to increase mobility) or overprovides what it wants less of (e.g., air pollution from fuel exhaust).

For-hire carriers and consignors of freight might consider fuel exhaust to be an unfortunate by-product of moving items to destinations where they are more valued. But others who are not a part of that freight market, yet are directly affected by the pollution, might see it as an unwanted cost that they deserve to be compensated for. The market fails to provide this compensation unless the for-hire carriers and/or the consignors were legally required to do so. It is on that basis that government attempts to correct these market failures by taxing or regulating the participants in the market responsible for generating the external effects of pollution.

There are numerous examples of market failures in transportation. A prominent one would be the "public good" aspects of free-access roads. Could we have reasonably expected the current network of highways, roads, bridges, tunnels, and sidewalks to have been built by the profit-seeking private sector? If so, then imagine all of these being subject to a tangle of different toll charges by their various private sector owners. Would any cluster of nearby road owners be able to cover their costs if they were competing against each other for traffic? If not, it might take local monopolies or oligopolies to cover their costs; but then such companies might overcharge their captive markets. The fact that markets fail because of problems like this means that society tends to leave the bulk of this construction to government control. Governments have the legal right to tax and, therefore, to force payment whether or not the taxpayer actually uses the road.

Pure public goods are both nonrival and nonexcludible. This can be thought of as a set of ceiling lights provided in a public library. Illuminating

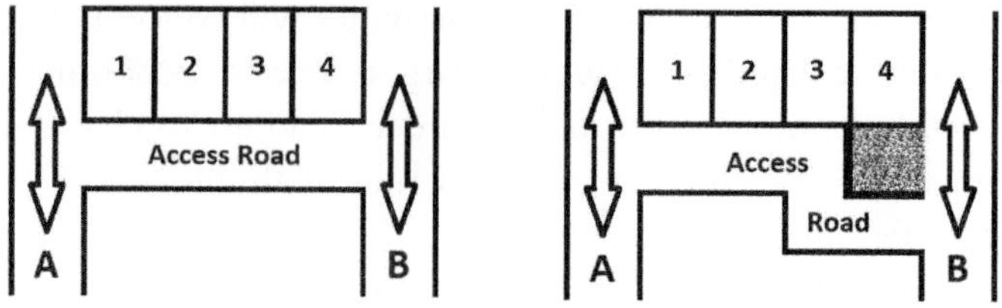

Fig. 2.3 Free riders and access roads.

the room for one reader means it is illuminated for everyone else in the room. No one enjoying the bright atmosphere of the room interferes with anyone else in the room doing likewise. This is what is meant by nonrivalry. At the same time, it makes no sense to try to exclude someone from the room if it is not crowded. In other words, only when the room starts to lose its aspect of nonrivalry does it make sense to enforce a policy that excludes those not willing to pay for access.

It does make sense to enforce a policy of excludability when it is necessary to preserve a market. An example would be an airline choosing not to upgrade enough passengers from coach class to fill every unsold seat in first class. This policy avoids signaling to first-class passengers that their high-priced perquisites may be randomly assigned to those who paid less. Maintaining empty seats, when unsold, keeps the air of exclusivity that validates the premium prices. On the other hand, enforcing excludability may lead to perverse results. Consider this in the context of a homeowner who understands the value of free-riding. Fig. 2.3 shows the layout of a proposed access road.

A private company observes that four homes use a gravel road to access two thoroughfares (A and B) on each side of their block. The company pitches its idea of paving the road and charging each of the four homeowners one-quarter of the total costs. Homeowners 1–3 agree while homeowner 4 feigns his disinterest in the road knowing, of course, that the others have already agreed to it. This puts the company in an awkward position. Building a straight road would be most efficient from a material point of view. Of course, homeowners 1–3 would each be paying one-third of the total cost and homeowner 4 would be free-riding. Homeowner 4 receives the same benefits without any of the cost.

There is no guarantee that one or more of the homeowners will not likewise opt to free-ride. This instability may jeopardize the project. Another solution is to just build the paved road around homeowner 4. While it is true that his direct access to thoroughfare A is blocked, he still has direct access to B.[e] The result is a gangling road that costs more to build and had less people paying for it than if free-riding were curtailed. The incentive to free-ride indicates a market failure. To overcome this, the government would build the road in order to offer the four homeowners equal access to the two thoroughfares. Each homeowner will be assessed his share of the costs via the tax system.

Transportation is a rich area of study and it contains interesting surprises. For example, in some markets, one might think of as prone to failure need not fail. Consider a privately owned lighthouse.[f] Its role is to help ships navigate at night while on their way to a port-of-call some distance away. Surely that is a market prone to fail. How can the lighthouse owner receive compensation from the ships for the valuable service rendered? Other than altruism they have no incentive to pay. If that is the case, we would expect fewer lighthouses to be built and the market for water-based shipping to be less safe as a result. But the lighthouse owner could simply work out a deal with the port-of-call owner to top up the dockage fee by some amount (to be shared between them of course) to compensate for the lighthouse's operation. This insight relieves the government from instituting taxes and regulations to try to improve the market. Assuming there are incentives for the parties to come together and negotiate, the results are more efficient than relying on the government to impose a tax or regulation.

Some markets one might think of as already failed may actually provide a benefit to others. Since government-owned public transit is subsidized to the point where fares cover only a fraction of the operating costs, it might be said that public transit is a failed market. Could a privately run transit company survive outside of highly populated, densely packed urban areas? Probably not. On the other hand, the government's propped-up transit market does relieve traffic congestion that would otherwise occur if riders were forced to switch to private automobiles and carpools. This government-controlled monopoly of buses and exclusive bus stops allow commercial

[e] It would be difficult to exclude homeowner 4 from indirect access to thoroughfare A unless the other three homeowners agree to install gates on each end of the access road. In any case, the example is contrived to the extent that it is even possible for a private company to deny direct access to thoroughfare A using a roadblock of some sort. Typically, the gravel access road would be publicly owned. Of course, the situation is even more tenuous if it was homeowner 2 or 3 who decided to be a free-rider. Leaving a patch of gravel road in front of their homes is possible but there is no way to block them off from a paved access road.

[f] See Coase (1974).

transportation to be more efficient because it reduces the amount of automobiles on urban roads. In effect, taxpayers (most of whom do not use public transit) are cross-subsidizing the fares to give riders (and especially the poor) better options for mobility and access to jobs. Of course, the amount of public transit subsidy is a political question because the money has to be taken from someone.

When it comes to publicly provided highways, roads, etc., all users (i.e., drivers and passengers) are in it together. Certainly, all for-hire trucks and the consignors of freight are in it too. They share an infrastructure that needs further investment and repair. This is most noticeable for highway bridges. Of the 612,000 bridges across the United States, about 10% are structurally deficient and 14% are functionally obsolete.[g] These proportions will increase over time if nothing is done.

In the midst of recent proposals for public-private partnerships to build new infrastructure and finance it through tolls (with some targeted on for-hire trucks), the American Trucking Associations (ATA) is on record proposing a long-neglected option. It proposes raising the federal tax rate on fuel. All vehicles would pay it at the pump and, furthermore, the administrative system to collect it is already in place. Tolls, on the other hand, tend to have higher administrative costs because they do not piggyback on the prices at the pump and they do not have the administrative economies of scale that a nation-wide, fixed-rate fuel tax does.

Introduced at 1 cent per gallon in 1932, yet unchanged since 1993, the federal fuel tax is now 18.4 cents per gallon for gasoline and 24.4 cents per gallon for diesel fuel. Technically, one could add another tenth of a penny to both since it is piggy-backed by another federal tax, established in 1986, paid into the Leaking Underground Storage Tank (LUST) trust fund. Of course, all 50 states assess their own taxes on gasoline and diesel fuel.

The federal fuel tax contributes about 90% of the revenue that goes into the federal Highway Trust Fund (HTF) which was established in 1956. Since then, 100% of all federal fuel tax revenue goes into the HTF, and appropriations are earmarked for the maintenance and construction of interstate highways as well as providing some assistance for urban roads in order to improve public transit. However, as part of an omnibus budget bill in 1990, the tax was increased by five cents per gallon with 2.5 cents going into the HTF and the other half earmarked for reductions in the federal budget deficit. Thus, the fuel tax, while mostly a user fee, became a source of general

[g] State Transportation Statistics (2015. Table 1.7).

revenue to cover government spending in a variety of areas outside of transportation. This was short-lived, however, because the Taxpayer Relief Act of 1997 removed the earmark to general funds and restored the fuel tax revenues to the HTF exclusively.

At the federal level, since 1993 at least, the two fuel taxes have been a very good deal for drivers given that they did not even increase to keep up with price inflation. If they had been indexed to the Consumer Price Index, for example, their respective amounts today would be about 32 and 43 cents per gallon. Early in 2018, the US Chamber of Commerce weighed in with a proposal to raise the fuel tax by 25 cents per gallon (i.e., 5 cents per year over 5 years). Of course, the political mistrust on both sides of the aisle prevented a major infrastruture bill from getting through Congress until late 2021.

The fuel tax is regressive since it is a fixed rate for all users with no check on one's W2 form at the pump. Of course, there are two ways to increase tax progressivity: raise the funds from the already labyrinthine income tax; or provide a fuel tax credit for poorer users. The effective income tax rate on richer individuals can be manipulated and lowered through a clever application of the tax code which defeats some, or perhaps most, of any gains from supposed progressivity. Tax credits, on the other hand, can be targeted to benefit just the poor. In any case, now is the time for a brisk and imaginative debate over the rival taxation principles of user-pay versus ability-to-pay. Bear in mind that doing nothing about the current state of US infrastructure is regressive too. The cost of vehicle wear and tear on subpar roads and the burning of fuel while stuck in congested roads is proportionally harder for the poor to bear.

While all for-hire trucks would directly pay any fuel tax increase, would they bear it equally? Not likely. The tax increase would be on a per-gallon basis so trucks with newer engines that burn less fuel per mile would, therefore, have a lower tax burden per mile. Established trucking companies with dedicated shippers and experience in using the spot market to fill capacity and backhauls could earn more revenue per mile and lower their net tax burden per mile. If the for-hire carrier has some degree of market power it could build a fuel surcharge into its freight rate and pass some or all of the fuel tax onto the consignor. Finally, those with the ability to invest in hybrid or fully electric trucks would be partially or fully exempt from the fuel tax and, in effect, free ride on the infrastructure benefits paid for by other users.

Those likely to absorb the tax would be smaller owner-operators trying to play the spot market or those in the role of agent (i.e., independent contractor) to the larger trucking companies when the latter need to top-up their fleet capabilities. In this light, the ATA's advocacy for a higher fuel tax is not akin to Warren Buffett lamenting that his tax burden is less than his secretary's (though that is simply due to the way the tax code treats Buffett's capital gains vs his secretary's wage-based income). The tax code is a tangle of politics subject to the shifting power of industry and consumer lobbyists. The ATA represents numerous large for-hire trucking companies, and it is not lobbying for a higher fuel tax just to increase the tax burden on its most prominent members. Large companies with market power are adept at shifting tax burdens onto others.

But what about the external effects of road usage? Basically, the fuel tax was designed to finance roads but not their external effects. The LUST tax, as administered by the Environmental Protection Agency (EPA), certainly covers the negative external effects of fuels leaking into the ground. However, there is no federal earmark for any external effects arising from road usage. Air pollution, CO_2 emissions, and accident-related healthcare costs attributed to wasteful and unsafe driving represent another facet to add to the political debate.

Regulation of transportation

Every transportation regulation has a political rationale behind it. All regulations reflect a regulatory agency's interpretation of legislation passed into law by elected politicians. Laws change when the legislation that backs them is revoked or amended. These are political decisions. All regulations, too, are open to revision and they are always open to criticism from any special interest group that does not agree with them. Regulatory agencies work below the Congress and state legislatures and can decide on their own when it is time to update their interpretations. Of course, there will be periods for public comment on any proposed regulatory updates. Ideally, regulations, like laws, are enacted to correct for a market failure. Whether or not they do, consignors, carriers, and other intermediaries must build regulations into their operations and planning in order to be in compliance. This section examines selected regulations affecting each of the five modes of transportation. Each in its own way has significant impacts on transportation operations and planning.[h]

[h] A review and economic appraisal of the regulatory changes across various industries is found in Kahn (1998).

Motor carriers

Hours of service (HOS) regulations are intended to incentivize motor carriers (by the threat of fines) to make sure their drivers have a minimum amount of rest time over specific time periods. Such regulations can be validated when considering that out of the five basic modes of transportation, it is the motor carrier sector that has the closest and most frequent interaction with industry outsiders. They mostly use government-provided roadways, bridges, and tunnels and they share them with the general public who commute in cars, light trucks, and buses. Thus, a fatigued truck driver trying to meet a tight delivery schedule would not only hurt himself but many other nearby commuters and pedestrians should an accident occur. Of course, truck drivers are susceptible to two types of fatigue: physical (i.e., muscle-related) and mental (i.e., boredom and sleepiness).

Given the basic rationale for HOS regulations, there have been several sets of rules since the initial one went into effect in 1938. The Federal Motor Carrier Safety Administration (FMCSA) laid down the present set of rules in 2020 and are summarized in Table 2.2. Of course, nothing is ever final when it comes to transportation policy; therefore, these may be subject to change.

Table 2.2 Federal hours of service regulations.

Property-carrying drivers	Passenger-carrying drivers
11-h driving limit May drive a maximum of 11 h after 10 consecutive hours off duty **14-h limit** May not drive beyond the 14th consecutive hour after coming on duty, following 10 consecutive hours off duty. Off-duty time does not extend the 14-h period **30-min driving break** Drivers must take a 30-min break when they have driven for a period of 8 cumulative hours without at least a 30-min interruption. The break may be satisfied by any nondriving period of 30 consecutive minutes (i.e., on-duty not driving, off-duty, sleeper berth, or any combination of these taken consecutively)	**10-h driving limit** May drive a maximum of 10 h after 8 consecutive hours off duty **15-h limit** May not drive after having been on duty for 15 h, following 8 consecutive hours off duty. Off-duty time is not included in the 15-h period

Continued

Table 2.2 Federal hours of service regulations—cont'd

Property-carrying drivers	Passenger-carrying drivers
60/70-h limit May not drive after 60/70 h on duty in 7/8 consecutive days. A driver may restart a 7/8 consecutive day period after taking 34 or more consecutive hours off duty	**60/70-h limit** May not drive after 60/70 h on duty in 7/8 consecutive days
Sleeper berth provision Drivers may split their required 10-h off-duty period, as long as one off-duty period (whether in or out of the sleeper berth) is at least 2 h long and the other involves at least 7 consecutive hours spent in the sleeper berth. All sleeper berth pairings MUST add up to at least 10 h. When used together, neither time period counts against the maximum 14-h driving window	**Sleeper berth provision** Drivers using a sleeper berth must take at least 8 h in the sleeper berth, and may split the sleeper berth time into two periods provided neither is less than 2 h. All sleeper berth pairings MUST add up to at least 10 h
Adverse driving conditions Drivers are allowed to extend the 11-h maximum driving limit and 14-h driving window by up to 2 h when adverse driving conditions are encountered	**Adverse driving conditions** Drivers are allowed to extend the 10-h maximum driving time and 15-h on-duty limit by up to 2 h when adverse driving conditions are encountered
Short-haul exception A driver is exempt from the requirements of 49 CFR §395.8 and §395.11 if: the driver operates within a 150 air-mile radius of the normal work reporting location, and the driver does not exceed a maximum duty period of 14 h. Drivers using the short-haul exception in §395.1(e) (1) must report and return to the normal work reporting location within 14 consecutive hours, and stay within a 150 air-mile radius of the work reporting location	**Short-haul exception** A driver is exempt from the requirements of §395.8 and §395.11 if: the driver operates within a 150 air-mile radius of the normal work reporting location, and the driver does not exceed a maximum duty period of 14 h. Drivers using the short-haul exception in §395.1(e) (1) must report and return to the normal work reporting location within 14 consecutive hours, and stay within a 150 air-mile radius of the work reporting location

Source: Based on Federal Motor Carrier Safety Administration. Summary of Hours of Service Regulations. Washington, DC: U.S. Department of Transportation. https://www.fmcsa.dot.gov/regulations/hours-service/summary-hours-service-regulations.

There is a distinction in the HOS regulations between a driver being on duty and actually driving a vehicle. Naturally, a truck driver's work encompasses more than just driving. Loading and unloading cargo, dealing with dock personnel, etc. are part of the job. Taking property-carrying drivers as an example, the on-duty shift (whether driving or not) consists of no more than 14 h after which there must be at least 10 consecutive hours spent off duty. If driving occurs during the on-duty period it cannot be more than 11 h. Once 11 h of driving has occurred within a 14-h shift there must be at least 10 consecutive hours spent off duty. If the intent is to drive for long hours there must be non-driving breaks of at least 30 min after every 8 h of driving. Finally, if the intent is to be on duty over 7 (or 8) consecutive days, the cumulative hours spent on driving cannot exceed 60 (or 70). As soon as those hours are reached over those days, an off-duty period of at least 34 consecutive hours is mandated.

Exceptions are made for adverse driving conditions and for short hauls. On-duty time and driving time within on-duty time may be extended up to 2 h when adverse conditions occur and are noted. Examples include adverse weather (i.e., snow, ice, and fog) and adverse traffic that was unanticipated and could not reasonably have been expected by the driver.

Of course, one may wonder how drivers can keep track of all of these requirements let alone the government enforcing them. It turns out that technology called electronic logging devices (ELDs) automate the process and create a permanent record that is used to enforce HOS. Geographic positioning systems (GPS) can also be used to correlate driver positions relative to adverse weather, road work, and traffic congestion. Drivers eligible for the short-haul exception (i.e., those operating within a 150-mile radius over their on-duty period) are not required to use ELDs. They can simply record their start times and end times on duty, and the total number of hours worked per day.

Ideally, what is to be gained by periodically revisiting such regulations is to give regulators a chance to hear from industry stakeholders. In other words, are truck-related accidents down since the last iteration of HOS regulations? Are there any adverse effects on delivery times and transport costs as a result of the mandated rest time? Are there any emerging forms of technology (e.g., driver assistance cameras and semiautonomous vehicles) that mitigate the need to dictate HOS in its current form? All stakeholders should provide experiential and, whenever possible, data-informed opinions on such an important set of regulations. Like so many regulations they filter into people's behavior, the cost of doing business and consumer prices, in ways that are not always easy to see.

Water vessels

Motor carrier HOS regulations are a federal mandate. Modes of transport that engage in international transport may be subject to international regulations meaning those set and enforced by multinational organizations. The United Nations' International Maritime Organization (IMO) implemented a low-sulfur fuel mandate in 2020. Referred to as IMO 2020, it updates Annex VI of the MARPOL (or Marine Pollution Treaty of 1973). Annex VI covers a variety of airborne pollutants from vessels. Local jurisdictions, however, have the option to enforce even tighter standards. Thus, IMO 2020, as a minimum standard, applies to international waters (i.e., those beyond 200 nautical miles of a country's shoreline).

The IMO oversees 174 signatory nations. The global fleet of merchant vessels is around 53,000 units with almost 18,000 being general cargo and 12,000 being bulk cargo. Containerized vessels, typically carrying the most valuable cargo per ton, are barely 5000 in number. Therefore, different types of water-based operations are affected by the new regulation. Some of these carriers are better able to take on the extra cost of compliance.

Under IMO 2020 the maximum sulfur content of bunker fuel used on ocean vessels fell from 3.5% by weight, set in 2012, to 0.5% (i.e., an 86% reduction in sulfur content). This applies to all fuel used onboard meaning in main engines, auxiliary engines, and boilers. Of course, the IMO designated certain Emission Control Areas (ECAs) where the standard is even stricter at 0.1%. The ECAs cover: the Baltic Sea, the North Sea, and designated coastal areas of Canada, the Caribbean (specifically Puerto Rico and the US Virgin Islands), and the United States.

Ocean carriers have three choices: convert to low-sulfur fuels; retain the heavier, and less expensive, bunker fuel but take on the cost of installing scrubbers (i.e., exhaust cleaning systems); or apply to the flag state for a waiver on behalf of the IMO. Of course, the ocean carrier would have to demonstrate that acceptable alternative fuels were not available for purchase. Flag states, for their part, are required under Regulation 18 of Annex VI to "take all reasonable steps to promote the availability of fuel oils which comply with this Annex and inform the [IMO] of the availability of compliant fuel oils in its ports and terminals."[i] The IMO also noted that exceptions are possible for emergencies involving risk to life and damaged vessels. It is also

[i] The regulations set out in IMO 2020 may be found in IMO 2020-Cutting Sulphur Oxide Emissions (2019).

up to each flag state to determine appropriate fines for noncompliance. Thus, while the rules are uniform the sanctions are not.

Basic economics suggests that if demand for low-sulfur fuel rises faster than the available supply (via refinery output and inventory draw-down) prices will rise in the near term. Beyond basic economics are the logistical constraints of time, physical space, and location. This means that some ports may have enough compliant fuel to service their customers while others may not. If this is the case, one cannot expect supply chains and ocean transportation networks to adjust quickly enough to prevent such a price increase. Until adequate fuel supplies are available where needed, the adjustments likely to take place would involve what one would expect in any large neighborhood where there is only one gasoline station. Drivers would either: hoard their fuel early on (creating traffic congestion in the area); or drive more slowly and plan trips carefully all the while hoping that a fresh supply will be on hand before the gas tank runs dry. In like manner, ocean vessels would curtail their speeds in-between ports of call and hope to ride out any shortages.

To date, there has been no price spike in diesel fuel—a low-sulfur option. This is good news given that IMO 2020 indirectly affects other modes of transport that use diesel fuel (i.e., trucks and railways). Very low sulfur fuel oil (VLSFO) also meets IMO 2020 standards and is available at the major ports (e.g., Rotterdam and Singapore). Many carriers will likely invest in scrubbers. Installation cost per vessel starts at about $2 million and can rise to several million more. This is the classic cost-benefit problem of taking on up-front costs versus estimating the present discounted cost of a more volatile commodity over time. Time to recoup up-front cost is dependent, of course, on the installation cost and annual maintenance costs of the scrubbers as well as the daily volume of fuel consumption.

Despite the eventual savings that come from scrubbers relative to VLSFO, there is still a monetary risk from external sources. This is the classic *social* cost-benefit problem where a firm must consider larger environmental impacts beyond its own market. The IMO could eventually ban heavy bunker fuel and thereby invalidate the purpose of scrubbers. The scrubbers themselves could be banned due to the effluent that they generate which must be disposed of after arrival at a port. As scrubbers become more prevalent under IMO 2020 will trading off sulfur particulate matter for effluent waste dumps, and the associated risk of ground contamination while awaiting treatment with caustic soda, be ignored by some future update to IMO regulations?

In any case, ocean carriers will be taking on more costs as they adjust to IMO 2020. They will certainly try to pass those costs along to their customers as a bunker adjustment factor (BAF) or surcharge. Who bears most of the regulatory burden is a problem that economists study at length. Again, carriers buying the same fuel type face roughly the same cost per ton but they may carry bulk or containerized cargo of many different values per ton. For consignors of bulk cargo versus those of containerized consumer goods, if each faced the same BAF in straight dollars, the latter would find it easier to absorb since the value of their shipments is higher on a per ton basis. On the other hand, any excess capacity in a shipping lane puts the consignor in a better position to hold off surcharges. Some consignors may feel pressure to accept the carrier's BAF formula while others may be able to negotiate its structure.

Liquefied natural gas (LNG), which has no sulfur emissions, is another option but the conversion from heavy bunker fuel is even more expensive. Since LNG density is lower than bunker fuel the LNG tanks need to be quite a bit larger. Of course, TOTE Maritime Alaska has been an early adopter of this technology. It was the first carrier in the United States to retrofit a vessel for LNG power. Its two diesel-powered Orca-class roll-on, roll-off (RO-RO) vessels (built in 2003) were retrofitted with two LNG cryogenic tanks placed on the weather deck behind the ship's bridge. Each tank has a $1100\,m^3$ capacity. While less than 5% of the global fleet runs on LNG there is no doubt that IMO 2020 will boost its prospects when carriers consider new vessel orders over the coming decades.

The years of planning for IMO 2020 have paid off. Some flag states may be quick to fine carriers arriving at the port with noncompliant bunker fuel and some may not. Some carriers may choose not to comply with IMO 2020 until caught. Such is the nature of a diverse global industry made up of developed and less-developed nations. In any case, such discretion adds slack when needed in the fuel markets. Green policies for blue skies will surely occupy business and government relations for decades to come.

Railroads

Railroads and pipelines, unlike other modes of transportation, have to finance and build practically all of their support infrastructure. This is why they are very capital intensive and bear a large proportion of fixed costs as opposed to variable costs. They take on a lot of upfront costs before even one boxcar or one drop of crude oil, as the case may be, can be transported in order to begin earning operating revenue.

Railroads, like all other modes of transportation, must deal with various types of government regulation. Unfortunately, some of these regulations were developed in response to tragic events. Positive train control (PTC), a regulation under the supervision of the Federal Railroad Administration (FRA), is one of these. The FRA's implementation of the Rail Safety Improvement Act (2008) included the first set of PTC regulations. The law was enacted in response to the collision of a Metrolink passenger train with a Union Pacific (UP) freight train in Los Angeles in 2008. The engineer of the Metrolink train ignored or failed to notice a stoplight and proceeded onto the track of the UP train. The death toll was 25 (including the Metrolink engineer) and there were 135 injuries making this one of the deadliest train collisions in US history.

Simply put, PTC intends to overlay entire rail networks with an electronic system that can override a train engineer who is either speeding or about to enter an unauthorized area. The engineer would first receive a warning and, if no action is taken, the train would be automatically stopped. The goal is to improve safety by avoiding accidents. But PTC is also an unfunded federal mandate meaning that each railroad must finance the acquisition or construction of the necessary equipment on its own. When the law was enacted in 2008 the required technology did not exist, so the industry had to take on the necessary research and development. Intercity and commuter railroads originally faced a deadline of end-of-year 2015 but it was moved to end-of-year 2018 and finally to end-of-year 2020 as the industry worked with the FRA on implementation plans. Basically, PTC technology is another layer of fixed cost for the rail industry to take on.

The value of PTC is evident over rail networks with characteristics such as high density, high speeds, and mixtures of freight and passenger traffic. The unfunded mandate, being a federal one, also applies to the 470-mile state-owned Alaska Railroad (ARR) since it is a recipient of federal funds. In its capacity as a commuter service provider, ARR shares federal funds with the Municipality of Anchorage to cover public transit. But of the three characteristics noted above only the third applies to ARR. Of course, ARR's passenger and freight services are handled by separate locomotives; and density on the network is low enough such that these trains do not often pass each other except at the depots in Seward, Anchorage, and Fairbanks. Nonetheless, ARR proceeded with PTC implementation.

Since ARR is like no other railroad in the United States, PTC implementation has been a particular challenge. Being the only near-Arctic railroad in the United States it is natural to expect that construction costs would be higher and more time consuming than elsewhere. While the average cost per mile to lay track is about $10 million, ARR's range of costs is $2–60 million per mile. This wide variation is due to things familiar to other railroads such as changes in gradient, the need for bridges/tunnels, and securing rights-of-way. But the largest contributing factors to construction costs are uniquely Alaskan. These involve construction in very remote areas with no road access and under harsh weather conditions involving heavy snow and permafrost.

In order to fulfill the PTC mandate, the technology must be active at all points along the rail network. This is a unique problem for ARR since there are stretches along the network, particularly between Anchorage and Fairbanks, where there is no commercial power source available. ARR faced the extra cost and technological burden of providing power along 200 miles worth of "dark spots" on its wayside in order to generate the steady stream of data and communications that are integral to PTC. Batteries at these remote stations are charged using a variety of options such as solar, fuel cell, and propane generators.

While several railroads in the contiguous United States use cellular technology to meet PTC's 200 MHz requirements, ARR must use private radios over the long stretches with no cellular connectivity. This also means that ARR has to deal with the annual maintenance of their power stations on top of the standard PTC equipment that other railroads are dealing with. The extra costs involve several millions of dollars per year.

Though owned by the state, ARR is expected to be self-sustaining. Thus, any financing for PTC has to come out of its three main sources of revenue which derive from freight haulage, passengers, and returns on leased real estate. The total implementation cost is expected to be about $180 million. Annual operating costs are expected to be $8–10 million. This is a substantial outlay for a railroad that earns annual gross revenue of around $140 million.

Compared to railroads in the contiguous United States, access to power and operations maintenance will add to costs. But lower usage density and the strict demarcation between freight and passenger services should serve to keep costs down. Time will tell how this will balance out along the nation's northernmost railroad.

Air carriers

Air carriers are required to secure landing slots at airports in order to establish their commercial routes. They have to pay the airports for these slots and they have to secure an arrival time at airport B that accounts for the departure time from airport A. Regarding international operations, be it passenger airplanes or air cargo freighters, routing is constrained by what the governments in the origin and destination countries have agreed to. In other words, even if a foreign carrier would pay the required fee for an available landing slot at an airport in the destination country, it may not be legal to do so. Bilateral air service agreements have set out what the allowable routing options are. This contrasts with foreign-based motor carriers and ocean vessels which simply use the domestic road network and ports, respectively, by paying all appropriate user fees.[j] Of course, foreign-based railroads and pipeline companies do require domestic government approval to build their infrastructure but, in contrast to air carriers, they do not have to negotiate landing fees with destination airports. They have to secure right-of-way across different jurisdictions. Railroads and pipelines use fixed routes while airlines try to take advantage of their flexibility in designing efficient networks.

International commercial air transport is the only mode that starts with two governments codifying how their respective airspaces are to be utilized. From there the airlines must work within those confines. This process began with the Convention on International Civil Aviation of 1944 (also known as the "Chicago Convention") and the subsequent point of view that a country's airspace is a strategic asset.

The Chicago Convention's mandate explains why the US government got involved when UPS decided to give up its landing slots used for weekly flights between Hong Kong and Singapore. While these slots are valuable, an airline cannot let them remain unused. They must be used for revenue service or else be relinquished. As such this keeps the air passenger and air cargo markets moving along. Of course, it also challenges some airlines to "loss minimize"[k] in order to keep their landing slots active. This was why so many passenger airlines resorted to carrying cargo-only in their bellies and even strapped onto the passenger seats when COVID-19 fears, combined with

[j] Technically, foreign-flagged ocean vessels can only visit one US port. They can only engage in import or export activity. Picking up and dropping off a given unit of cargo between two domestic ports constitutes a cabotage move which is legal only for US-flagged vessels. For an overview, see Prokop (2014).

[k] Loss minimization is a technique used when a company calculates that all available options create losses. It chooses the option with the lowest magnitude of losses. For example, if a carrier faces a fixed cost of $10,000 that would be its loss if it parked all conveyances and earned no revenue as a result. However, if it stayed in business and earned revenue that more than covered the variable cost of operating, that extra revenue could pay off some of the fixed costs. In this way, losses would be less than $10,000.

government-mandated travel restrictions, severely impacted the passenger market in early 2020.

In June 2020 the US Department of Transportation (USDOT) approved the transfer of UPS' routes to Kalitta Air and FedEx, both of which are US domiciled all-cargo carriers. After considering the carriers' filings, USDOT allocated three of the four Hong Kong-Singapore routes available to Kalitta and the remaining one to FedEx. A fifth weekly slot was already owned by Polar Air Cargo (a subsidiary of US-based Atlas Air).

The bilateral air service agreement between the United States and Hong Kong allows for up to 64 weekly all-cargo flights. In theory, this means a US domiciled air carrier could fly into Hong Kong as part of a flight originating in the United States or one terminating there. There is also the option to include a third country as part of the route because this bilateral agreement allows for so-called fifth freedom routing. If the route did not include a US origin or destination on the part of the US carrier, the resulting all-Asia route would be seventh freedom, which is an even tougher liberalization to negotiate. All of these "freedoms of the skies" grew out of the Chicago Convention. In fact, depending on how one counts, there are eight or nine freedoms in total with the eighth and ninth constituting types of cabotage. Table 2.3 lists the freedoms. It is typical for the rights granted to be reciprocal between the two countries.

Notwithstanding the flight frequencies allowed in the bilateral agreement, their usage presupposes the air carriers can secure and are willing to pay for, the required landing slots. For a fifth freedom route, this requires at least three properly timed slots in order for the route to be viable. This is part of the reason why the Hong Kong-Singapore route discussed above is serviced by only five weekly visits by US air cargo carriers. However, the biggest reason is that USDOT noted that the cap of 64 round trip frequencies per week has been reached. Starting any new route would mean cancelling another.

Another question worth considering is the effect of regulatory oversight on market efficiency. Valuable landing slots confer on the airlines a chance to earn extra profits through limited competition (something economists call economic rent). Problems arise when airlines rent-seek. This means they devote time and money to striving for this monopoly-like power. Only one or a limited number of winners emerge in the process of filing detailed applications with regulators. The other applicants lose. The amount of time and money the "losers" devoted is called rent-seeking waste. What can be

Table 2.3 Freedoms of the skies.

Options in the context of country A granting privileges to country B	
First freedom	An air carrier from country B can fly over country A without landing
Second freedom	An air carrier from country B can land in country A for a technical stop (i.e., an emergency and/or repairs)
Third freedom	An air carrier from country B can land in country A to deliver revenue passengers and/or cargo arriving from country B
Fourth freedom	An air carrier from country B can pick up revenue passengers and/or cargo in country A and deliver them to country B
Fifth freedom	An air carrier from country B can pick up revenue passengers and/or cargo in country A and deliver them to a third country, say country C. The route may also originate in country C and deliver revenue passengers and/or cargo to country A with the route ending in country B
Sixth freedom	Similar to the fifth freedom except that the air carrier's domicile (i.e., country B) is in the middle of the three-country route carrying revenue passengers and/or cargo originating in one of them
Seventh freedom	A three-country route carrying revenue passengers and/or cargo with the carrier's domicile not being a part of the route
Eighth freedom	An air carrier from country B can land in country A to deliver revenue passengers and/or cargo from country B (i.e., third freedom) and, furthermore, it may pick-up and drop-off revenue passengers and/or cargo within country A
Ninth freedom	An air carrier from country B has a route carrying revenue passengers and/or cargo within country A with no passengers and/or cargo coming from or heading to country B

Source: Based on Freedoms of the Air. International Civil Aviation Organization. New York, NY: United Nations. https://www.icao.int/pages/freedomsair.aspx.

done to avoid this? Regulators would have to be willing to let the market pick the winners and losers by auction.

In a contest for the Hong Kong-Singapore all-cargo market, suppose USDOT simply auctioned off the right to a weekly frequency. Of course, USDOT would have to collaborate with the respective airports in order to plan the auction design, set minimum bids, etc. Instead of preparing detailed filings, Kalitta, FedEx, and perhaps other carriers would have submitted financial bids—putting their money where their mouths are so to speak. The "loser" is merely out the time to prepare and submit a bid rather than the time and money involved in submitting a detailed filing. Financial bids are objective while filings, by design, are evaluated subjectively.

The two biggest obstacles to successful auctions for airport landing slots are: (1) not enough bidders to create a truly competitive situation; and (2) the need for an after-market. Basically, in a route from Hong Kong to Singapore the securing of a slot at the former but not at the latter renders the route nonexistent. Since the two airports would be running their own independent auctions, an airport and the regulator would have to grant airlines the freedom to trade slots among themselves. For example, airline X secured a slot at airport A but could not secure one needed at airport B to create an A-B route. If airline Y wanted the slot at airport A to complete a different route it has in mind, and it was willing to give airline X a slot that would create a viable route elsewhere then there is a chance for gains-from-trade.

Basically, if the market is viable for auctions they are superior to regulators merely taking landing slots away due to nonuse and using "beauty contests" to determine which airline deserves the slot. Unless a market failure is demonstrated regulations are not the answer.

Pipelines

Since pipelines are one of the least competitive modes of transport it is natural to expect them to be subject to regulation. Interstate motor carriers, railways, and airlines were deregulated between 1978 and 1980. This means that market conditions determine what freight rates the carriers would set, where they would operate, etc. Interstate water vessels (also known as "Jones Act" carriers[1]) file their freight rates for commercial cargo with the Federal Maritime Commission; but they are, by and large, set based on market conditions.

The Federal Energy Regulatory Commission (FERC) oversees domestic pipeline activity. FERC scrutinizes requests for building new pipelines or expanding existing ones under the concept of "public convenience and necessity." Rates charged to consignors must be "just and reasonable." Basically, FERC interprets this to mean cost-of-service pricing; that is, a rate that covers costs and provides a reasonable return on invested capital. This is thought to prevent a monopoly pipeline from taking advantage of its captive market. Once approved, the rates are fixed in place. Of course, proposals by

[1] The Jones Act is shorthand for the Merchant Marine Act of 1920 which excludes foreign-flagged vessels from engaging in cabotage (i.e., either interstate or intrastate pick-up and delivery of cargo). For an overview see Prokop (2014).

pipeline owners to increase their rates are submitted to FERC and scrutinized.

If FERC deems the pipeline company's market to be sufficiently competitive, it may approve so-called market-based rate increases. The onus is on the pipeline company to demonstrate to FERC that such a rate increase would not significantly add to its market power. Market-based rate applications must include[m]:

(1) A description of the proposed service.
(2) Definition of the relevant product and its geographic markets.
(3) Provision of the applicant's ownership and list of affiliated energy companies, services provided, and their location. If an affiliate operates in the same geographic market, the market shares of the applicant and the affiliate should be combined.
(4) Identification of good alternatives to the proposed service and which parties provide similar services within the same geographic market. Provision of a list of the applicant's competitors and locations.
(5) Include market share and Herfindahl-Hirschman Index (HHI) calculations to measure market concentration. FERC's traditional HHI threshold is 1800.[n]
(6) A discussion of other relevant competitive factors such as ease of entry and excess capacity held by competitors.
(7) A description of how the applicant's rates compare to the competitors.

For instance, point 7 allows the company to cite any higher FERC-approved rate used by a competitor to justify the rate increase. The company, to the extent it controls its cost more scrupulously than the competitor, may in effect earn a higher return on capital than if it only charged according to a cost-of-service rate peculiar to the company.[o]

[m] See Market Based Rate Standards (2020).

[n] The HHI is the sum of the squares of the market share of each firm. Thus, a monopoly would be indicated by $HHI = 100^2$ or 10,000. A duopoly would be indicated by $HHI = 50^2 + 50^2$ or 5000. An HHI of 1800 could, for example, indicate a market with approximately five firms each having a 19% market share; or approximately four firms each having a 21% share; etc. Of course, there is no reason to assume that all firms in a market must have equal market shares. There is also no reason to assume that an HHI of 1800 or higher in and of itself indicates a serious restraint of trade.

[o] For a full discussion see Cook (2014).

Issues and problems going forward

Consider the tension that exists among for-hire carriers competing for market share and profits. Also, consider the market effects affording through achieving economies of scale and, by overreaching, having to deal with diseconomies of scale. Achieving the appropriate balance requires careful planning of transportation networks and monitoring operations along with them. Regulations, despite their intended effects, may be seen as operational constraints by for-hire carriers. At any rate, the structure of regulations can affect network design and routing decisions. Compliance with regulations certainly increases operational costs. Changes in market conditions and changes in the government's attitude to regulation are continuous activities. No for-hire carrier can afford to be complacent when it comes to dealing with these forces.

References

Coase, R.H., 1974. The lighthouse in economics. J. Law Econ. 17 (2), 357–376.

Cook, A., 2014. The oil and refined products pipeline business. In: Prokop, D. (Ed.), The Business of Transportation. Vol. 1: Modes and Markets. Praeger, Santa Barbara, CA, pp. 122–131.

IMO 2020-Cutting Sulphur Oxide Emissions. (2019). London: UK: International Maritime Organization. https://www.imo.org/en/MediaCentre/HotTopics/Pages/Sulphur-2020.aspx.

Kahn, A.E., 1998. The Economic of Regulation: Principles and Institutions. The MIT Press, Cambridge, MA.

Market Based Rate Standards. (2020). Washington, DC: Federal Energy Regulatory Commission. https://www.ferc.gov/industries-data/natural-gas/intrastate-transportation/market-based-rate-standards.

National Transportation Statistics. (2017). Washington, DC: U.S. Department of Transportation.

Prokop, D., 2014. International transportation management. In: Prokop, D. (Ed.), The Business of Transportation. Vol. 2: Applications. Praeger, Santa Barbara, CA, pp. 70–89.

Skousen, M., 1990. The Structure of Production. New York University Press, New York, NY.

State Transportation Statistics, 2015. U.S. Department of Transportation. Bureau of Transportation Statistics.

Transportation Statistics Annual Report (2020). Washington, DC: U.S. Department of Transportation.

CHAPTER 3

Transportation and supply chain management

Supply chain efficiency

In Chapter 1, footnote e, the term efficiency was divided into productive efficiency and allocative efficiency. Basically, a business should allocate resources to their best use in order to fulfill some goal. The goal could be profit maximization, increased liquidity, increased market share, etc. Out of all possible goods and services the firm could produce and sell, once it has decided on which one or combination of them to produce, it should do so in the least costly way. In that sense, productive efficiency strives to eliminate waste.

Both productive and allocative efficiencies have a symbiotic relationship. What is the purpose of producing something at least cost if there is no market for it? On the other hand, what is the purpose of allocating resources to produce a product that is in high demand but the production process has so much waste in it that the product is priced too high once costs are accounted for? Of course, this is how to look at efficiency within a single organization. What if there were multiple organizations and the efficiency in one were dependent on another? This is where supply chain management comes in.

No business would knowingly be a part of a supply chain that would sap its efficiency. Businesses outsource activities to upstream vendors when it is not cost-effective to produce certain inputs in-house. Similarly, businesses choose which downstream consumer markets to enter based on the level of competition that exists and the ability to deliver goods and services to those locales. Each of these decisions is about keeping resources allocated properly while not letting costs get out of control. Thus, supply chain management is about linking organizations such that they are more efficient together than being independent and uncoordinated.

Mergers and acquisitions are one way to link organizations from resource extraction and production all the way to retail distribution and final consumption. Another way is through contractual agreements. Leaving aside the different merits of these two methods, what they have in common is that different tasks need to be allocated among the supply chain partners.

Transportation Operations Management
https://doi.org/10.1016/B978-0-12-815415-1.00010-0

Should transportation be handled in-house? Should a for-hire carrier be used and if so, which of the other supply chain partners ought to be the consignor? Basically, a supply chain starts with extraction of raw materials and ends with a last-mile delivery to a final customer who is ready to enjoy the good or service as part of personal consumption. Everything in between involves production activities with all players being, in effect, intermediaries between the raw material extractors and the final customer. Organizing all the intermediaries is what supply chain management is all about. Building trust among these players, sharing information, and adding value as production moves downstream are what keeps supply chains viable. An efficient supply chain therefore has allocated resources to the player best able to add value. All partners are working to minimize cost along the supply chain in order to stay competitive. In this way, supply chains compete with one other. Most of the consumer products Walmart and Target sell are identical; however, it is their chosen set of vendors, distributors, and for-hire carriers that is where the competition to allocate resources and control costs are occurring. Boeing and Airbus Industrie produce similar medium and long-range commercial aircraft but it is their supply chains that make these two companies a competitive duopoly. They compete with each other through supply chain management rather than establish independent corners of the aircraft market.

The role of the consignor

In between raw material and retail items comes the value-adding processes handled among the different partners along the supply chain. As long as these partners are separated by some distance, the raw materials, subassemblies, and finished goods need to be transported from one partner to the next.

Who should bear the burden of being the consignor of freight? In other words, who should be the party to contract with the carrier of the freight? If the buyer or seller of the item to be transported owns a private fleet capable of performing the haul, then transportation is a simple internal exercise. All the calculations the supply chain partners make with respect to planning and costing in production carry over to transportation as well. In fact, transportation is part of the production process itself.

More often a for-hire carrier would be used to facilitate transportation. This introduces another player into the supply chain. Either the buyer or the seller of the item will take responsibility for arranging for transportation with the chosen carrier. Of course, if neither is willing, then a third-party logistics provider (3PL) would be hired—basically, one intermediary hired to oversee another intermediary. Whether it be a direct relationship with a for-hire carrier or a 3PL, either the buyer or the seller will have to sign a contract of carriage (i.e., the carrier's bill of lading) or a service contract to hire the 3PL. Between the buyer and the seller of the item to be transported, one of them is undertaking an extra transaction for the benefit of both.

Apart from who has the most experience, it makes sense to allocate costs to those players best able to bear them. Who has the extra time and money necessary to arrange for transportation? The idea is to keep costs down as tallied along the entire supply chain as opposed to forcing costs on those parties that may feel constrained. Just like some family members take on extra responsibilities to help their relatives, the intent is to promote family unity. The same logic carries into supply chain management. Since for-hire transportation is a transaction cost that must be incurred to promote value-added activity, some supply chain partners may be more adept at dealing with it than others.

The rule is very simple: allocate transaction costs to those parties best able to deal with them and not necessarily to those responsible for generating them. An infant spills something on the floor and the parent wipes it up. Parenting is not about what is fair but what is expedient. A company closes down a plant in a country overburdened with regulations and moves operations to another. The decision had little to do with the productivity of the workers in each country, yet the workers left behind may feel the decision was unfair to them.

The spot market

In a supply chain management context, consignors and for-hire carriers need to decide between an informal transactional linkage or a more relational and strategic one. Basically, transportation could be arranged in the spot market—akin to a one-time stock market transaction. Bids and asks for various levels of carrying capacity and routes are traded in the spot market for several types of conveyances. Alternatively, a given consignor and for-hire carrier could negotiate specific terms of transportation. Simply put, negotiate for certainty but use the spot market for flexibility. This is a trade-off. One likes certainty when the alternative is a lower return; however, the temptation to seek flexibility at the expense of certainty may be so great that contracting may be less popular. In some situations, contracts may not even be honored as will be discussed ahead.

The term strategic, as opposed to transactional, applies to a steady, long-term interaction which is typically codified in a well-defined service contract. A transactional situation deals with one sale at a time meaning short-term interactions are subject to change at the pleasure of either party. An automobile manufacturer likely thinks in a strategic way when it seeks steel and glass vendors for its assembly line. It more likely thinks in a transactional way when it seeks to fill a shortage of paper clips and bags of coffee for the clerical staff who work in the back office. The more strategic the item in the supply chain, the more certainty is sought.

Consignors and for-hire carriers may interact in strategic or transactional ways. Using the spot market to facilitate a one-time shipment is certainly transactional. Establishing a contract for a stream of services over time is more strategic. Dedicated transportation and beneficial cargo owners (BCOs) are good examples of this because they necessarily involve more negotiation between consignors and carriers. However, whether the two parties envision a stream of shipments over time or just one, a bill of lading is required by law. Of course, the terms within the bill of lading and the freight rate to be charged are open to negotiation if both parties care to do so.

Motor carriers may hire independent owner-operators to top up their services. These interactions could be strategic or transactional as well. The flexibility that owner-operators provide to the motor carrier sector is one of the reasons why it is so competitive. Of course, some modes are less flexible than others. Consignors and carriers may for different reasons seek spot market flexibility when freight rates and capacity are perceived to be moving in a favorable direction. Alternatively, they may seek the certainty of longer term service contracts when rates and capacity changes are perceived to be unfavorable. Naturally, consignors (as the buyers of transport) and for-hire carriers (as the sellers of transport) take opposite views as to what directions are favorable for them. This sets up a perennial tug-of-war. And the degree of market power in the tug-of-war is never the same over different transport networks, routes, etc. Consignors want routes that service their customers. In particular, those consignors providing e-commerce want to do this evermore quickly. Carriers want to move their capacity to where the demand is growing. In other words, each is looking for profit. The price to be paid for market flexibility is market volatility.

The ocean vessel mode has its own unique challenges. Whether strategic or transactional, this mode makes a practice out of container no-shows and so-called blank sailings as a means to adjust. Importers adjust to downstream order cancellations while carriers adjust schedules to fill capacity. Importer and carrier actions may also affect spot rates. They rise or fall depending on which of the two parties has more power to disrupt. Container no-shows and blank sailings represent one party's adjustment without giving much notice to the other. Furthermore, importers not providing scheduled containers on time leave carriers with excess capacity. On the other hand, blank sailings make it harder for importers and ports of call to allocate their time and resources to plan out their operations. Containers are moved to other vessels with different travel schedules which can disrupt supply chains. Containers waiting to be loaded onto vessels or moved inland after unloading at destination ports simply exacerbate demurrage charges. These account for the costs borne by a port when a container languishes in the terminal yard. This terminal space is valuable and yet the port is tied up providing extra security and dealing with the congestion.

The coordination problem goes even deeper and can lead to cascades. Container no-shows may result from blank sailings and vice versa. An importer, mitigating against the risk of running up against a blank sailing, could always book container capacity on two or more vessels. Such overbooking means at least one vessel is going to face a no-show. Carriers experiencing (or simply expecting) enough no-shows can do a blank sailing that delays the delivery of the other containers that were duly tendered. These containers will be delayed and become, in effect, a no-show downstream along the supply chain.

Volatility could, of course, be stopped by such things as freight rate regulation and territorial licenses. By and large, deregulation of transportation has served the economy well, spurred globalization, etc. The churn of consignors and carriers deciding between being strategic or transactional is better than a regulator deciding for them. On the other hand, each side trying to wiggle out of contracts because they do not have nonperformance penalties is rational only in a narrow sense. It is not an example of the sort of good faith behavior that engenders trust. To end the incentives to wiggle, each side needs to put teeth into their service contracts. Coming to terms with volume and capacity commitments, freight rate fixity, fuel surcharges, demurrage and detention, and dispute resolution procedures is necessary.

Many industry watchers have wondered why the ocean vessel sector plays games that would not be tolerated in, for example, the airlines. It is true that a plethora of oversold fights and traveler no-shows without penalties on either side would lead to chaos on the ground—though not in the skies since a lot of planes would simply not be flying. Passengers are "freight that complain." Containers, on the other hand, seem easier for regulators to tolerate as they languish at ports or loading docks. Of course, this is no excuse to avoid improved contracting procedures. However, just like each mode of transport is different, apparently so are the levels of regulatory tolerance.

Supply chain linkages

It is a common saying that a chain is only as strong as its weakest link. But that phrase presupposes one very important thing—all the other links are perfect (i.e., 100% reliable). If two or more links are not 100% reliable, then the chain is even weaker than the weakest link. How can that be? If every link is 100% reliable but the one weak link is, say, 80% reliable, then the chain itself is 80% reliable. This means it has a 20% chance of failing. However, if two of the links were 80% reliable, the reliability of the chain is only $0.8 \times 0.8 = 0.64$ or 64%. Thus, the likelihood of the chain failing rises from 20% to 36%. The difference is 16 percentage points or a percentage increase of 80%. In other words, the likelihood of failure increases by 80%.

A system of 100 independent parts, each of which is 99% reliable, is only 37% reliable (i.e., 0.99^{100}). Imperfections over two or more independent parts/nodes/organizations/etc. are magnified over the whole system. The more independent parts there are to a system, the more vulnerable the system is to failure. One way to overcome this problem is to build in redundancies. Basically, it is about not keeping all one's eggs in one basket. It is about having a plan B in place when a shock to plan A occurs. Supply chain managers working to readjust their vendor partnerships from one country to another are, in effect, implementing redundancies. Consignors who have options with two or more carriers if something happens to the carrier of choice are implementing redundancies. The spot market for freight is also an example of this.

Just like presupposing that most links in a chain are 100% reliable, there is a danger when businesses presuppose that risk does not rise when items are shipped over longer distances and from different countries. For example, a good relationship with an international for-hire carrier is put to the test when considering all the external logistical events that can impact a shipment in transit. Likewise, a good relationship with a vendor in another country can be strained given all the external political and economic events that can impact that country. In other words, relationships are not on a level playing field when these external events alter the rules of the game. Risks from exchange rate fluctuations and different legal and regulatory systems are prominent examples.

The intent here is not to make a case against global supply chains; rather, it is to say that the longer the physical distance and the more international borders the supply chain crosses, the more important the built-in redundancies become. What if a link that was 80% reliable had a backup link that was also 80% reliable? This means that if/when the first link fails (which is expected 20% of the time), the backup link will be used. This link's 80% reliability is expected to be needed 20% of the time. So the first link's reliability is, in effect, topped up by $0.8 \times 0.2 = 0.16$ or 16 percentage points. As noted above, given that a system of two links is only 64% reliable when each is 80% reliable, if both had a backup link of equal reliability, the system reliability would rise to $0.96 \times 0.96 = 0.92$ or 92%. Is this increase in reliability worth the extra cost and maintenance of backups? In other words, what is an acceptable level of supply chain risk? This is what supply chain managers need to grapple with as they devise their plan B.

Risk is often assessed in terms of probabilities. The probabilities themselves are often calculated under the assumption of a bell-shaped (i.e., normal) distribution. This distribution assumes that extreme events are not likely. But, as the COVID-19 pandemic of 2020 demonstrated, "black swan" events are possible? These are events that are rare, highly impactful and, most importantly, seemingly obvious only after they have come to pass.[a] This third point is a clue as to how to deal with them. It comes back to building in redundancies. The amount of money and time devoted to building them should be commensurate with the level of risk assessed by the business.

During the early stages of the COVID-19 pandemic, Taiwan-based Wistron Corp. prepared to move half of its manufacturing capacity out of China. Wistron partners with Apple Inc. in making the latter's iPhones. One possibility it considered was moving more capacity to India where it is already making some iPhone components. Other choices for Wistron were Vietnam and Mexico. Pegatron, another Taiwan-based partner of Apple's, also moved production out of China to Vietnam. These companies, however, were not completely abandoning China due to its reliable labor supply and large domestic market. They were simply building alternative supply paths should one of them become impacted by travel restrictions.

What is fortunate for the electronics manufacturers is that their largest customers (e.g., Apple and Microsoft) offer products that are in high demand whether the user is on the job or working remotely. These large companies

[a] For a full discussion, see Taleb (2007).

are resilient but it is their upstream supply chain partners that are the weaker links in the process of customer fulfillment. Also, their intermediaries in the transportation industry were necessarily forced to adjust their routes, capacity, and freight rates as global supply chains started recalibrating their relationships with China and Far East Asia in general. Readjusted port-of-entry activities led to bottlenecks as shipping containers were cleared to meet pent-up consumer demand. Airports and land borders saw similar problems. Basically, all links in a supply chain do not shut down and turn back on at the same time. Inevitably, the faster links will cause bottlenecks at the slower ones. In the short run, all links come under some degree of stress.

Cooperation and coordination

Supply chain partners want to cooperate with one another to some degree. The partnership is supposed to create a win-win outcome. Despite their best efforts, however, cooperation may be curtailed by constraints in the form of coordination problems. Many players need to coordinate because a faster move from point A to point B can exacerbate congestion at point B if the subsequent move from point B to point C is not well coordinated. In other words, logistical planning must be system-wide for it to be effective. Another example of this problem can be seen in how the US economy struggled to reopen over various state and local jurisdictions as the COVID-19 pandemic struck.

The US economy was never really closed during the pandemic. Essential workers were still on the job, restaurants were offering pickup and drive-through options, and seniors were able to shop for their groceries at special hours before younger folks. Amazon Prime was keeping up with ecommerce deliveries and Instacart allowed many homebound people to outsource their grocery shopping to gig workers. Financial markets were still trading as well.

Under the Defense Production Act (1950), some manufacturers were retasked to making medical supplies and some alcohol distilleries produced hand sanitizers. Happily, despite the retasking, these companies were still paying their workers who stayed on the job. But much of the US economy was, in effect, closed down or slowed to a crawl. From Boeing facing order cancellations to local fitness centers and barber shops closed due to an inability to guarantee social distancing, it took months for those businesses to gear up despite $2 trillion being doled out via the Coronavirus Aid, Relief and

Economic Security (CARES) Act. A further $1.9 trillion of fiscal stimulus was made available through the COVID-19 Relief Package in March of 2021.

There was certainly a lot to coordinate. After all, every organization has a supply chain. The only organization that does not would be one with all of its suppliers, production facilities, and customers in one location. This, of course, is a fantasy. But what is not a fantasy is that all supply chains in the United States cross over a patchwork of cities, counties, states, etc. which had their own definitions of essential workers and criteria for shutdowns and sheltering in place.

Effective supply chain management requires trust among partner organizations. Trust is a matter of intent. From there comes a willingness to cooperate. Of course, beyond intent and willingness comes action that turns these good intentions into actual gains. This action is called coordination. Without solid coordination plans in place, cooperation, despite the best of intentions, will not lead anywhere. For-hire carriers know this all too well. They are agents for consignors who have agreed to coordinate the process of buying transportation services. Whether the consignor is the buyer or the seller of the item to be shipped, one of them needs to take care of this for the benefit of both. For-hire carriers wait for the consignors to approach them with an offer to tender freight and then sign the bill of lading.

Coordination was the real challenge as the US economy returned to a normal business routine. It reopened in different jurisdictions at different times. There were some supply chain partners who were ordering faster or slower than their upstream vendors could deal with. On the other hand, vendors may be able to deliver while buyers are not willing or able to take possession. This is a coordination problem, pure and simple.

In the motor carrier sector, there was plenty of carrying capacity available but bottlenecks arose in the transport of items deemed essential because carrier arrival times and load/unload times were not well coordinated. Of course, drivers and/or dock workers falling ill or self-quarantining after suspected exposure to COVID-19 was a fact of life that required a lot of flexibility from both sides. Despite the relaxed hours-of-service (HOS) regulations, when a truck was detained while awaiting access to the loading dock and subsequent load/unload by dock workers, the driver's workday became less productive and, by extension, so did customer fulfillment.

Governments at the federal and state levels orchestrated this economic shutdown and they had to orchestrate a timeline for reopening. COVID-19 responses also brought out intergovernmental disputes. On the one hand, it is not clear that the president's Article II powers under the constitution could supersede those of governors in state affairs. On the other hand, the Commerce Clause (Art. I, Sec. 8, Cl. 3) gives the US Congress the right to regulate interstate commerce. The president, of course, has the right to enforce the Interstate Commerce Act (1887). For the most part the White House acquiesced to the governors, given that they were closer to understanding the needs of their populaces. This is reasonable coordination.

Lack of coordination, however, can be seen in the legislative branch where the brinksmanship of the Republicans and Democrats led to the draining of the nearly $350 billon set aside for small businesses under the Paycheck Protection Program (PPP). This gave firms with less than 500 employees access to forgivable loans so long as they continued to pay their furloughed workers. Of course, both political parties wanted to cooperate and provide more PPP funds but they wanted to coordinate the dispersal of funds in different ways. Thus, PPP expired in August 2020.

Coordination problems are easier to overcome when there is a rule or social convention that all parties know and follow. For example, if two cars are coming along a narrow road, each will swerve to the curb on their right (in the United States) or on their left (in the United Kingdom) and avoid a collision. Game theorists call this a stable result so long as the rule/convention is common knowledge among the players. The president and the governors were apparently better at coordinating because of the rules of the constitution. Legislators, without such rules in place, were left to negotiate and play politics, which always takes more time and ends up with results that are harder to predict. This is like the drivers of the two cars, knowing that one is from the United States and the other is from the United Kingdom. Both want to swerve but whose rule should adapt to whom? The result is not stable, especially if the political brinksmanship leads to the perverse result of agreeing not to cooperate at all and just letting the voters decide in a subsequent election who was right in allowing the legislation to die.

Purchasing and transportation

As noted above, the relationship between the consignor and the for-hire carrier could be simply transactional or it could be strategic and therefore more complicated. The level of importance of the freight being moved is decisive when making this distinction. If the buyer and seller of the item to be shipped consider it important, then no matter which of them takes on the role of consignor, the relationship with the for-hire carrier is important by extension.

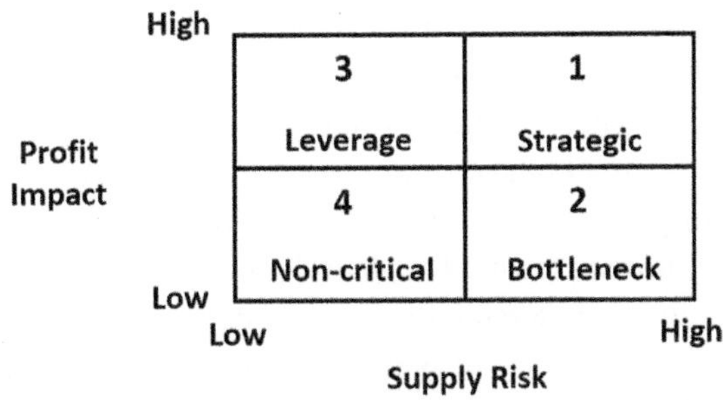

Fig. 3.1 The Kraljic matrix. *(Derived from Kraljic, P., 1983. Purchasing must become supply management. Harv. Bus. Rev. 61 (5), 109–117, exhibit II.)*

The Kraljic matrix shown in Fig. 3.1 is a useful tool in differentiating between transactional and strategic purchases of items from vendors.[b] The profit impact is assumed to be positively related to the volume of the product purchased. If the product is an input used in production of a final output, the profit impact would be positively related to the degree of value-add the input contributes to the production process. Supply risk is negatively related to the product's availability, its substitutability, and the stability of the logistical infrastructure which facilitates transportation. The cells numbered 1–4 show a descending degree of importance. This means oversight at the highest level (i.e., the C-suite) of the company descending downward to the lowest manager.

Cells 1 and 2 suggest the need for long-term contracts or mergers and acquisitions in order to deal with a high level of supply risk. A lot of buyer-seller coordination would be needed. Cell 3 suggests short-term contracts, or if enough vendors are available to elicit a competitive environment, the buyer could establish a reverse auction.[c] In other words, a competitive market should be leveraged by the buyer in order to keep costs down. Cell 4 suggest a purely transactional relationship between the buyer and the seller. The product is simply bought off the shelf and only as needed.

[b] Kraljic (1983).

[c] Also known as procurement auctions, reverse auctions differ from standard auctions (e.g., bidding for a rare painting) in that vendors are bidding for the right to supply a stream of products and support services over some time period. Other than buyers vetting vendors through a request for information about the product and support services, both reverse and standard auctions require thought as to the bidding rules, methods of communication, etc. Good introductions to auction design can be found in Klemperer (2004) and Milgrom (2004).

The Kraljic matrix looks at a buyer-seller relationship without a direct accounting of the consignor-carrier relationship that is implicit between the buyer and the seller. If the consignor-carrier relationship is strained due to a poorly designed bill of lading, or there are infrastructure problems affecting the transport route, a delivery may be late. Supply risk, in other words, may be systematically higher than the buyer-seller relationship alone indicates. In this way, the Kraljic matrix may collapse to just the right-hand column, thus making risk management even more important.[d] Just like diversifying supply sources is a way to mitigate supply risk in the buyer-seller relationship, the same is true in the consignor-carrier relationship. Logistically, this means a consignor should not rely on only one for-hire carrier, one transport route, one mode or transport, one storage facility, etc.

The COVID-19 pandemic brought about a case of what could be called *reverse* supply risk. In this case, certain buyers of crude oil not only had too much supply on hand but also were forced to take delivery of more than they could handle. A binge shopper's dream would be to find a merchant offering 100% off all prices. The nightmare would be knowing there is no place to store any of the items that were purchased for free. This is what the futures price for West Texas Intermediate (WTI) crude oil did on April 20, 2020, just 1 day before its May contracts expired. The price fell below zero for the first time in history. It fell to a negative $37.63 per barrel by the close of trading. The price started the day at $18.27 per barrel, which translates to a 306% drop.

Imagine a store front with a sign reading "306%-off Sale Today!" This signals the level of desperation that hit part of the crude oil futures market. There were murmurs of such an event from the previous month. The market for Wyoming Asphalt Sour, a special type of crude oil used in bitumen, saw Mercuria Energy Group Ltd. bid a negative 19 cents per barrel. At the same time, while Saudi Arabia and Russia ended their crude oil price war with a truce on April 9, 2020, the agreed to cut in production did not begin until May 2020.

In effect, WTI buyers—those who could not sell their futures contracts in time—morphed simultaneously into buyers of storage space. In other words, those stuck with long positions in the market (i.e., they owned the underlying asset specified in the contract) were facing contract expirations that would require them to take physical possession of WTI. So many

[d] For a discussion of the Kraljic matrix in the presence of intraorganizational coordination problems, see Tesfay (2019).

people wanted to avoid their impending oil deliveries badly enough that they were willing to pay to give it away rather than burn it or dump it. Since doing either of these things on a large scale is illegal, not to mention very tough on the environment, they were better off signaling a willingness to give it away and, in addition, offer a cash incentive per barrel for any buyer's trouble. Farmers, of course, were in a different situation during the pandemic since they could simply let their crops rot in the fields, dump their milk into rivers, etc.

Interestingly, WTI futures contracts cannot be closed out with negotiated cash settlements in place of physical delivery. By contrast, Brent Crude futures, another world benchmark, do allow for it. Moving cash electronically is certainly much easier than finding scarce storage capacity. While WTI is better suited for refining gasoline, Brent is more appropriate for diesel. Each product tends to have its own market with different demand and supply activities.

The US Department of Energy has been examining options to treat crude oil producers somewhat like farmers. The Agricultural Adjustment Act (AAA) of 1933 handled crop surpluses by paying farmers subsidies, gathered from taxes levied on food processors, as an incentive not to grow anything. In a way this was easier for the government than allowing surpluses to build and then having to buy up excess crops in order to maintain a healthy market price for the farmers who still had to cover their costs of fertilizing, irrigating, harvesting, etc. Of course, to maintain the higher price, the government had to store the food and let it rot lest it reenter the market and depress prices. Though found to be unconstitutional in 1936, because of the scheme of directly taxing Peter to subsidize Paul, AAA was revised in 1938 to better comport with the Commerce Clause of the US Constitution. Since then, federal government intervention in agriculture has been the norm.

One option for the Department of Energy is to pay oil exploration companies to keep their reserves untapped. In effect, the oil would stay in the ground and not have to be extracted and added to the US Strategic Petroleum Reserve as way of keeping it off the market. In 2021, this reserve contained over 600 million barrels with a capacity for a further 200 million. But it is up to Congress to designate funds to purchase crude oil to add to the reserve. Of course, the real question is whether or not any untapped reserves would ever become viable in a world of lower oil prices.

Another way to, in effect, pay a buyer to take on the unwanted WTI is to rent out space on oil tankers or in pipelines—again signaling a negative price.

Logisticians call slow-flow pipelines "inventory in transit." Of course, the use of oil tankers as floating storage facilities is certainly a new twist. It is also possible that some investors with long positions might even make a profit by paying someone else to store their WTI. In late April of 2020, with the forward price for WTI being higher than the spot price, so long as the rental cost per barrel was less than the price spread per barrel, it paid to buy the oil and simply sell it later. Again, the proviso was that sufficient storage capacity was found somewhere.

The negative price for May 2020 WTI futures was a legitimate signal, albeit a strange one. It was strange because the market for crude oil was still functioning but it was doing so with government-imposed bottlenecks. Only essential workers and businesses were allowed to operate during the pandemic. This meant that they demanded only as much oil-based energy and products as they needed. Everyone else was, in effect, shut out of the market. The futures contracts apparently did not factor in the logistical realities of the shelter-in-place orders lasting so long and being so widespread. Investors can miscalculate but logistical infrastructure is fixed in the short run. Investor expectations simply hit a logistical wall. The constraints of time, physical space, and location are governed by the unchanging laws of physics.

Still, the market did the best it could in the area of supply chain management. Trying to pass along the storage of a product to a party better able to handle it is sound business practice. Negative price signals showed that it took a lot of coaxing within the market because the aggregate demand for crude oil was at record lows at the time. The supply is hard to curtail because it is expensive to shut down an operating oil well. In effect, it was easier for the producers to operate at a loss in the short run. This exacerbated the capacity crunch.

New technology has led to more oil discoveries and increased the amount pumped into the market. Yet, at the same time, fuel efficiency and improved transportation planning have meant that oil consumption per passenger and per ton-mile has fallen. This explains the structural fall in oil prices since 2014. Technology provides the opportunity while logistics puts up constraints.

Inventory control and transportation

Transportation is one of several logistics activities; that is, activities that promote flows along a supply chain. Procurement of products, storage in inventory, production and assembly, and distribution are logistics activities that require elements of transportation. In addition, every logistics activity requires support activities such as exchange of information and order processing. Packaging and handling also take place along the supply chain. Since typical supply chains facilitate production, these logistics processes follow some schedule. This brings about issues of quality control and customer service to ensure consistency as flows of inputs are procured and outputs are distributed.

It is ironic that transportation is not always visible in some supply chain models. Setting it aside means the model is essentially missing the logistical constraints of time, physical space, and location. Locating centers of production and distribution at point A and point B, respectively, does not reveal much unless some appreciation is given to distance, the available options for transportation, and the support infrastructure. Of course, modeling those variables can be done in ways that range from arbitrary to complex. As such, useful models tend to be situational.

A standard model of inventory control is known as the economic order quantity (EOQ). It presents two cost elements in a trade-off with the goal of minimizing their sum. The trade-off is between making small orders with frequent delivery and large ones with less frequent delivery. In the real world, the holding of inventories is part of the logistical process in the sense that customer demands are never certain and are seldom uniform over time. Of course, holding inventories to meet demand contingencies will incur a cost. Yet, inventory accumulation allows for a steady level of production runs in the face of nonuniform demand; that is, inventory buildups occur during off-peak demand followed by inventory drawdowns during peak demand. Fig. 3.2 illustrates the problem.

The challenge with maintaining level production at quantity Q is that supply chain managers must try to find a level which allows inventory buildup to match what is needed during the drawdown period. However, even if the result is excess inventory at the end of the 6-week cycle shown in Fig. 3.2, there are other benefits. Level production maintains a steady workforce including workers hired to manage the storage and drawdown of inventory as required over the cycle of production. It may also generate economies of scale over the long run if the rhythm of production over time is large enough for average costs to fall.

In contrast to Fig. 3.2, three simplifying assumptions are made in the standard EOQ model: (1) production involves only one product with a fixed price; (2) the quantity of the product demanded by consumers is fixed over a

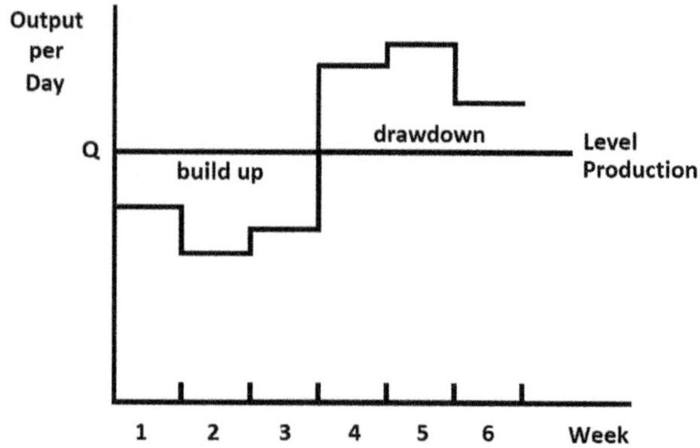

Fig. 3.2 Production and inventory.

time period (T); and (3) stock is replenished by the vendor the moment it runs out based on a uniform (i.e., linear) drawdown. While there may be a lead time from order placement to order receipt, it is also fixed in duration. Successive time periods trace out a sawtooth function as seen in Fig. 3.3.

Fig. 3.2 illustrates production while Fig. 3.3 illustrates inventory drawdown. For Fig. 3.2 to be compatible with the EOQ model, customer demand would have to be equal to the quantity chosen for level production. Customer demand would be constant instead of erratic.

If the chosen stock size increases, inventory carrying cost rises in a linear fashion while ordering cost declines at a decreasing rate. Why? A larger stock order quantity (Q) means less frequent ordering over the time period to satisfy a given quantity demanded of the item. But a larger inventory means higher carrying costs in the form of warehousing, handling, insurance, spoilage, and potential obsolescence. On the other hand, there are fixed costs of ordering that are independent of the stock order quantity; for example, delivery charges and bookkeeping. A larger stock order quantity allows those fixed costs to taper off on average. Thus, a cost trade-off exists. The

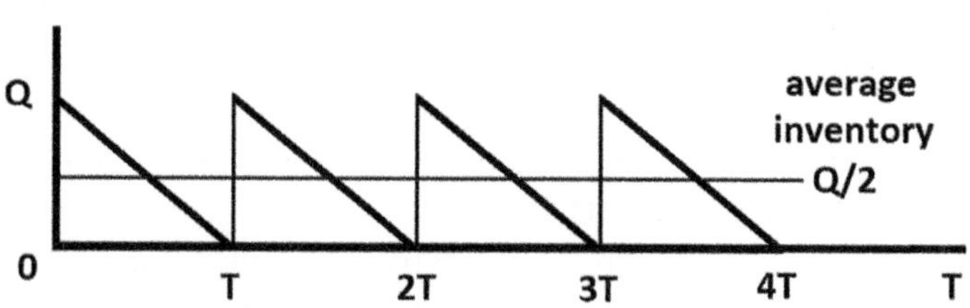

Fig. 3.3 EOQ drawdown and replenishment.

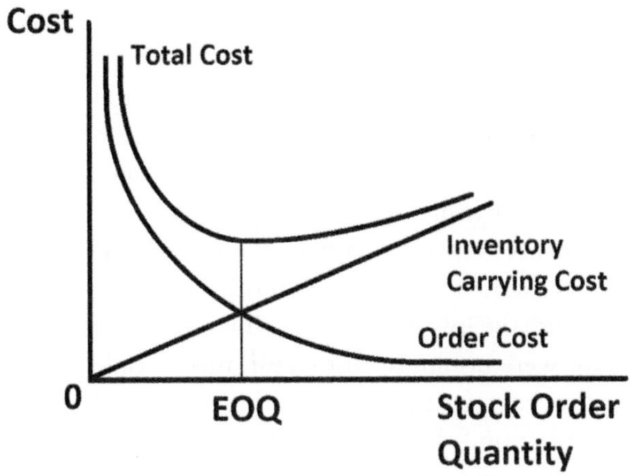

Fig. 3.4 The economic order quantity.

vertical summation of these two cost curves gives the total cost of the stock order quantity. The EOQ is the minimum point on this total cost curve as seen in Fig. 3.4.

Mathematically, the EOQ may be written as

$$(2DK/H)^{1/2} \tag{3.1}$$

where D is the quantity demanded (assumed fixed) over a given time period; K is the fixed storage cost from placing an order (independent of the quantity in each order); and H is the inventory carrying cost per unit in stock per time period.

The EOQ is simply the first derivative of total cost (TC) with respect to stock order quantity (Q), set equal to zero.

$$\mathrm{TC} = (DK)/Q + DV + (HQ)/2 \tag{3.2}$$

where V is the variable storage cost per unit ordered.

TC is derived in the following manner. The total cost for placing an order is.

$$(K + VQ) \tag{3.3}$$

Each stock order is depleted at time $T = (Q/D)$, and with the *average* inventory carried over the time period being (Q/2), the total carrying cost becomes:

$$(THQ/2) \tag{3.4}$$

Total inventory cost per time period held is $(1/T)[(K+VQ)+(THQ/2)]$, which when $T=(Q/D)$ is substituted in gives Eq. (3.2).

The first term in Eq. (3.2) indicates a nonlinear order cost curve with a slope of $-(DK/Q^2)$ and the third term indicates a linear inventory carrying cost curve with a slope of $(H/2)$. In fact, the order cost curve is a rectangular hyperbola, and as such the inventory carrying cost, being a ray from the origin, would intersect it perpendicularly to the order cost's tangent line. The implication is that EOQ in this simple model will always be at the stock order quantity where the lower two curves intersect. Of course, if the inventory carrying cost were nonlinear, the implication would only be true if the marginal cost of inventory carriage equaled the marginal cost of ordering at the point of intersection.[e] The simple symmetrical, sawtooth function for inventory depletion over time is what brings about the linear inventory carrying cost because average inventory size is always $(Q/2)$. Of course, a more complicated pattern of inventory depletion is always possible.

Building the cost of transportation into the EOQ model will necessarily shift the total cost curve upward. Of course, the EOQ would not change if unrealistically transportation cost was fixed (i.e., a horizontal line). The total cost curve would simply shift upward by the value of the fixed cost and its minimum point would be unchanged. However, it would be more appropriate to use a cost function with realistic attributes.[f]

A more realistic transportation cost function would be downward sloping.[g] It would also have one or more discontinuities to suggest a discount on the freight rate for tendering a larger shipment. The stepwise function

[e] A more realistic model could have the inventory carrying cost curve rise exponentially as Q increases. The curve would asymptotically approach the maximum capacity of the warehouse where inventory is stored. Discontinuities could be introduced where more warehouse space is built or leased once capacity is reached.

[f] Examples of building transportation into inventory models can be found in Baumol and Vinod (1970) and Carter and Ferrin (1996).

[g] By contrast, the total cost functions in Figs. 1.4, 2.1, and 2.2, for example, are upward sloping because, in standard microeconomics, total cost functions are measured in monetary units relative to quantity produced per some fixed period of time. More production in a given year necessarily raises total cost. The EOQ model has a subtle difference. The horizontal axis represents a range of possible order sizes while the vertical axis represents costs per period of time. Smaller batch orders are drawn down faster than larger ones and this necessarily means more orders over a given year. This is why order cost is high for small batches but inventory carrying cost is low. Small batches require frequent orders but there is less to store in inventory. Likewise, small batches mean more transportation over a given time period, although shipments are of less weight and volume.

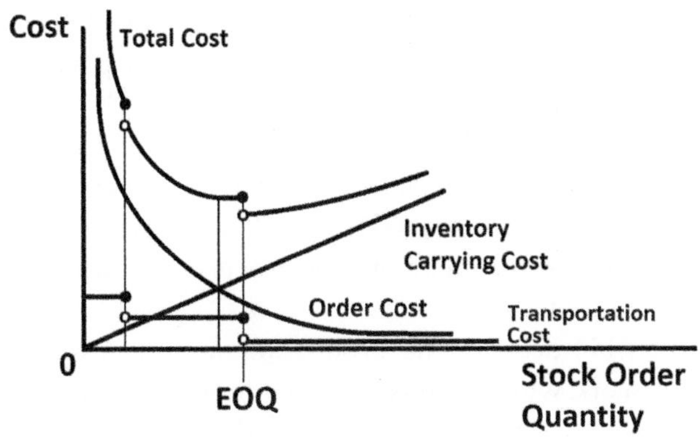

Fig. 3.5 The economic order quantity with transportation.

shown in Fig. 3.5 also allows for indivisibilities in carrying capacity. In other words, each step has a fixed cost of transport over a range of stock order quantities.[h] In order to demonstrate these points while keeping the figure manageable, certain attributes were either exaggerated or diminished. For example, a more realistic cost curve would have more steps and each would be shorter. Also, transport cost was kept low so that the total cost curve did not rise too much in comparison to Fig. 3.4. Realistically, transport cost would be much higher than order cost. But, in each case, the result is the same: the EOQ would be larger than when there are no transportation costs. This makes intuitive sense because the transportation cost declines with larger batches, which therefore adds pressure to increase the EOQ.

Just-in-time operations

The EOQ model was concerned with cost control. Inventory carrying costs were assumed to be linear and faced no storage capacity constraint. Certainly, this is not very realistic. Fig. 3.2 highlighted the benefits of level production if customer demand was erratic. In contrast, if the firm has confidence in its weekly demand forecasts, it may wish to "chase" demand rather than maintain level production. If these forecasts were accurate, the production cycle would follow the step function shown over the 6-week cycle. Of course, chasing customer demand means that not only production is erratic, but also workers might be hired or laid off as required. However, one option is to carry a

[h] Another possibility is that costs fall within each descending section. See Battini et al. (2014, Fig. 2).

minimum labor force conducive to producing the lowest level of weekly demand. Other weeks would be topped up by temporary workers as required. In this situation, the firm is trading off the need to hold inventory for a more flexible labor force. The firm needs to make sure that the product in question does not suffer quality control problems due to erratic production, a limited pool of temporary workers, etc. Basically, if inventory management is too costly, the firm may opt for procuring inputs and producing outputs only as needed.

Just-in-time (JIT) delivery and production are attractive to companies that are able to work with vendors and for-hire carriers to arrange precise and reliable schedules. There are financial and physical benefits to be had when items spend less time on a company's books and in its warehouse. Of course, there is more risk involved as well. There is an artful balance to be made in managing the trade-off between buying in bulk (i.e., in the hope of securing lower transport costs per ton or per unit) and buying in small amounts with more frequent shipments (i.e., in the hope of lowering inventory carrying costs). Customers like it when tighter cost control translates into lower prices, but they do not like it if mistakes in scheduling lead to stock-outs.

When there is uncertainty in the US economy and in trade relations across the globe, it suggests departing from JIT in favor of building up safety stock. The feeling may be that JIT is not appropriate when there is so much flux in global supply chains. It is true to say that there is never a one-size-fits-all answer in logistics management, let alone in inventory management. Therefore, some companies may still find JIT to be their best choice.

The automobile industry, though comprising less than 10% of total US trade flows, is the most prominent example of JIT. US exports and imports of new passenger vehicles and light trucks in 2019 totaled $59 billion and $197 billion, respectively. Volume-wise, this amounted to 1.9 million vehicles exported and 8.2 million vehicles imported. For automobile parts, the export and import values were $85 billion and $156 billion, respectively. About half of each of these numbers is accounted for by trade with Canada and Mexico. Certainly, the economic integration and proximity of these two countries help facilitate JIT. The United States-Mexico-Canada Agreement (USMCA) further codifies the relationship.

While the automobile industry was struggling like many other industries during recent recessions and the COVID-19 pandemic, it is not likely that it will be giving up JIT anytime soon. Improvements in customs documentation and customs clearance through electronic interfaces will enhance the visibility of smaller, more frequent orders. These improvements could potentially speed trade flows so long as congestion at border crossings is handled properly.[i]

Additive manufacturing (i.e., 3D printing) applied to parts of increasing size and complexity will serve to switch the activity from JIT delivery to JIT printability. General Electric was an early adopter of this technology. Its Catalyst engine, used in turboprop aircraft, saw the total number of parts reduced from 855 to 12. The engine was also 100 pounds lighter. In this way, the engine requires less maintenance and is more fuel efficient. Basically, the nature of the automobile industry is that large, expensive items such as engines can be ordered to match the scheduled daily or weekly rate of output along the assembly line.

To the extent that electric vehicles begin to displace some of the market share of those with internal combustion engines (ICEs), it is the case that electric engines have fewer moving parts. This means a lower aggregate safety stock is needed. Should one of those components break or prove defective, there are fewer stock keeping units (SKUs) to track. An electric vehicle essentially has the engine's shaft as the primary moving part. Tesla's electric engines are made up of only 17 moving parts with a single transmission, meaning no extra gears. ICEs, on the other hand, use pistons, rods, crankshafts, valves, etc., which add up to hundreds of moving parts per vehicle.

There are two requirements for successful JIT programs. The first is to have excellent customer demand forecasts. The second is to have an excellent relationship with the vendor who is providing JIT fulfillment. Of course, whether it be the automobile manufacturer or the vendor who is the consignor of the JIT freight, an excellent relationship with the for-hire carrier must also be established. In this way, time constraints are dealt with collaboratively and systematically.

Ecommerce speed over capacity utilization

When considering how to increase efficiency, it does not seem sensible to ship empty space. In other words, why not fill a box, shipping container, etc. completely? The less-than-truckload (LTL) segment of motor carrier operations strives to avoid empty space. By combining small shipments from multiple consignors, these for-hire carriers try to fill their trailers as well as they can.

[i] For a complete review of these electronic interfaces and the responsibilities that for hire carriers have, see Prokop (2017), Chapter 4.

More revenue is earned to cover the cost of shipping a given box, container, etc. when more capacity is utilized. Ironically, automation has increased the amount of air shipped from origin to destination. Those who are regular users of retail ecommerce have no doubt received an item tucked away in a much larger box insulated with overly generous amounts of bubble wrap. Sometimes the individual bubbles of air are just as large as the single item in the box. Is it wasteful to ship all that air and extra volume? Basically, if capacity utilization is the goal (i.e., maximizing revenue-earning items per unit of carrying space), it would be wasteful. But ecommerce giants like Amazon do not mind shipping air in this way because its overarching goal is speed to the customer. Also, these companies ship so much and so often that they receive favorable freight rates.[j] In that regard, tossing an item into a comparatively large box with a bed of bubble wrap and another layer tossed on top is quick and easy for workers at fast-paced distribution centers. Elegant and tightly packaged items take more time.

There are more subtle reasons to ship air. For example, consider how an HP inkjet cartridge is packaged. It has a thin flap at the top that is used to allow the package to hang nicely from the hooks on retail display shelves. The package is also angular, which means that the solid rectangular inkjet cartridge inside shares sections of empty space. Why ship these bubbles of air and why not make the package form-fitting? The reason is that that these larger and awkwardly shaped packages are harder to shoplift via a quick drop into one's side pocket. HP and their retail partners devote more risk avoidance to pilferage than to ease of shipping.

Transportation for production and distribution

Until an item reaches a final customer for final consumption, transportation is a value-adding process—from the first mile involving resource extraction to the last mile involving delivery to retail shelves or to the customer's front

[j] Amazon has set up its own private fleet of air freighters in order to take part of the transportation function in-house. By leasing these air freighters, Amazon can plan its fleet operations while avoiding most of the fixed costs of fleet ownership. It hopes to have dozens of branded freighters in place over the next couple of years. In 2019, Amazon began developing its own air cargo hub at Cincinnati/North Kentucky International Airport. Currently, Amazon Air serves 40 domestic airports. Through its freighter leases and alliance with Sun Country Airlines, it has access to about 70 aircraft. This is on top of the ecommerce business it tenders to FedEx and UPS.

door. One can make a distinction between production and distribution. Production involves resource extraction, refining, subassembly, and final assembly along with the transportation processes which facilitate those activities. Distribution involves the transportation of finished products which are ready for final usage or consumption at the retail level.

This distinction is important from a transportation perspective. Since production involves activities between vendors, it is governed by demand forecasts and the physical constraints of the production process (i.e., limits on storage, productivity, etc.). In other words, inputs are required based on the final item's bill of material and in amounts that conform to the vendor's production plan. Distribution is based on demand forecasts as well, but final purchase is based on customer preferences and their purchasing power rather than the physical limits of a production plan. As long as the bill of material and the production plan conform with allocative efficiency, there is a better chance that first-mile inputs will end up as part of last-mile deliveries.

Bulk transport (e.g., crude oil, gravel, grain, livestock, etc.) are more appropriate for some modes of transport over others. The same may be said for retail transport (e.g., fresh flowers, toys, pharmaceuticals, etc.). Because of the value-adding process along a supply chain, bulk items tend to be less expensive per unit of weight than retail items. Imagine the value of, say, one ton of grain versus one ton of breakfast cereal; or one ton of lumber versus wooden furniture. Of course, these comparisons involve durable products that are relatively easy to ship. When the finished product is more fragile or voluminous, extra care in transport is part of the value-adding process. For fragility, consider ground or powdered glass versus mirrors and vases made from it. For volume, consider farmed cotton versus irregularly shaped stuffed toys.

One way to appreciate the modal differences in bulk versus retail transport is to consider the value-to-weight ratio of shipments as seen in Table 3.1.

A higher value-to-weight ratio tends to imply higher value-added shipments. Since a pipeline is an exclusive source of bulk transport, it should be no surprise that it has a relatively low ratio. Water and rail carry both bulk freight and containerized finished items, but bulk freight dominates so as to keep the ratio relatively low. It should also be no surprise that air has the highest ratio. Air transport has the advantage in speed but since it is also more expensive, it makes sense that high value-add items are shipped that way. Fragile, time-sensitive, and ecommerce retail characterize air transport.

Table 3.1 Value-to-weight by transport mode.

	Shipments within the United States (2018)		
Mode	**Value (billions of 2012 dollars)**	**Weight (millions of tons)**	**Value-to-weight (2012 dollars per ton)**
Truck	12,975	11,920	1089
Rail	782	1782	439
Water	545	838	650
Air and truck-air	593	6	98,833
Pipeline	1533	3346	458

Calculated from Pocket Guide to Transportation 2021, 2021. Bureau of Transportation Statistics. United States Department of Transportation, Washington, DC, Table 3-1.

Issues and problems going forward

Supply chain efficiency requires coordination. Of course, coordination can be difficult when shocks to the system occur. Economic downturns, natural disasters, etc. can disrupt plans by both consumers and producers. The COVID-19 pandemic was responsible for three types of coordination problems that made supply chain management particularly difficult. Products suffered precipitous drops, spikes, or surges in demand.

Travel bans grounded most air travel and therefore all the support activities that come with it. Hotels, restaurants, convention centers were closed. Sheltering in place meant a drop in oil and gas refining, building spare parts for airplanes, etc. The initial stage of lockdowns prompted demand spikes (i.e., hoarding) of necessities like canned food, medicine, bathroom products, etc. Surges in purchases for home entertainment, books, face masks, etc. were the new requirements for sheltering in place.

Since structural drops/surges and temporary spikes wreak havoc with supply chains, the question becomes what to do? Can they be planned for or are they "black swans" which are impossible to predict? Whether it be in normal business activities or under the stress of emergencies, the COVID-19 pandemic has shown that the transportation industry needs to improve how it leverages and shares information among its supply chain partners.

The continued rise of ecommerce activities means that increasing speed will be a sought-after attribute in transportation. The various modes of transport and their different support infrastructure will see increased pressure in order to provide customer fulfillment. This will necessarily require improvements in supply chain resiliency and cooperation along the supply chain.

References

Battini, D., Persona, A., Sgarbossa, F., 2014. A sustainable EOQ model: theoretical formulation and applications. Int. J. Prod. Econ. 149, 145–153.
Baumol, W., Vinod, H., 1970. An inventory theoretic model of freight transport demand. Manag. Sci. 16 (7), 413–421.
Carter, J., Ferrin, B., 1996. Transportation costs and inventory management: why transportation costs matter. Prod. Invent. Manag. J. 37 (3), 58–62.
Klemperer, P., 2004. Auctions: Theory and Practice. Princeton University Press, Princeton, NJ.
Kraljic, P., 1983. Purchasing must become supply management. Harv. Bus. Rev. 61 (5), 109–117.
Milgrom, P., 2004. Putting Auction Theory to Work. Cambridge University Press, Cambridge.
Prokop, D., 2017. Global Supply Chain Security and Management: Appraising Programs, Preventing Crimes. Butterworth Heinemann, Cambridge, MA.
Taleb, N., 2007. The Black Swan: The Impact of the Highly Improbable. Random House, New York, NY.
Tesfay, Y., 2019. Central applications of Tesfay coordination in transportation supply chain: case of airline industry. J. Traffic Transp. Eng. 6 (5), 514–525.

Further reading

Prokop, D., 2000. The microfoundations of logistics: an economist's perspective. J. Transp. Law, Logist. Policy 67 (4), 348–366.

CHAPTER 4

Location, networks, and congestion

The role of geography

The earth is round

To most people, it is obvious that the Earth is round and orbits the sun. However, most people may not make decisions as if the Earth is round. Basically, most people passively act as if the Earth is a flat surface. For example, if a person were asked to point to the North Pole it is highly likely he would point to the north since most people reside south of the Arctic.[a] Of course, if one literally followed a *straight line* from this person's fingertip it would diverge away from the Earth's curved surface and head into outer space. It is, therefore, taken for granted that the person means to follow a path from his fingertip with the Earth's gravitational pull taking care of the rest. If, however, the person was standing on the North Pole itself he would have pointed straight down to the ice-covered Arctic Ocean underneath his feet.

There is a difference between pointing directly at something and pointing to the path used to get to it. With that in mind, consider someone standing on the South Pole in Antarctica. If asked to point to the North Pole the person could point to the north thereby suggesting a path to the North Pole. Of course, since *every* direction from the South Pole is northward, he has 360 degrees worth of options. However, there is one more option. He could point straight down. While he is pointing to the solid ground that is underneath the South Pole,[b] he is also pointing to the North Pole which is also below his feet, though straight through the Earth. He would be literally pointing to the North Pole without consideration of the path to get there. People also follow this convention when pointing to things that are considerably closer. For example, consider a person standing on a street next to his apartment block. If he lived in the penthouse he would point directly to the

[a] This example refers to the geographic North Pole as opposed to the North Magnetic Pole.
[b] Technically, the South Pole sits on land which is about 300 ft above sea level. Above that is another 9000 ft of ice. The North Pole, by contrast, is on the ice at sea level.

Transportation Operations Management
http://doi.org/10.1016/B978-0-12-815415-1.00001-X

top of the building if asked where he lives. He would not point to the front door to the building which is the beginning of the path to get to the penthouse.

A round earth presents logistical challenges. It is not homogenous in its climate, water resources, topography, and subsurface resources. With billions of people unevenly distributed throughout this diverse world, an understanding of key issues in geography will improve logistics management. Fig. 4.1 shows that the Earth's axis is tilted about 23.5 degrees relative to its orbital plane around the sun. This is the reason why there are four seasons per year.

Using the North Pole as a point of reference, the counterclockwise rotation of the Earth about its axis can be verified by noting that the sun "moves" from east to west in the sky. One rotation takes about 24 h. The Earth orbits around the sun in a clockwise fashion as well. One revolution takes about 365 days. The North Pole is hit by sunlight during the Summer Solstice in June but not during the Winter Solstice in December. The sun is as high as it can be in the northern hemisphere during the height of summer. At that time, things are opposite in the southern hemisphere which is why it is in deep winter. During the equinoxes in March (Vernal) and September (Autumnal), the sun hits the equator directly meaning that both hemispheres share equal amounts of daylight.

If the northern hemisphere were entering fall the southern hemisphere would be entering spring. There are logistical implications of simultaneously opposite seasons in the two hemispheres. Certainly, spring planting in one hemisphere corresponds with fall harvesting and deliveries in another.

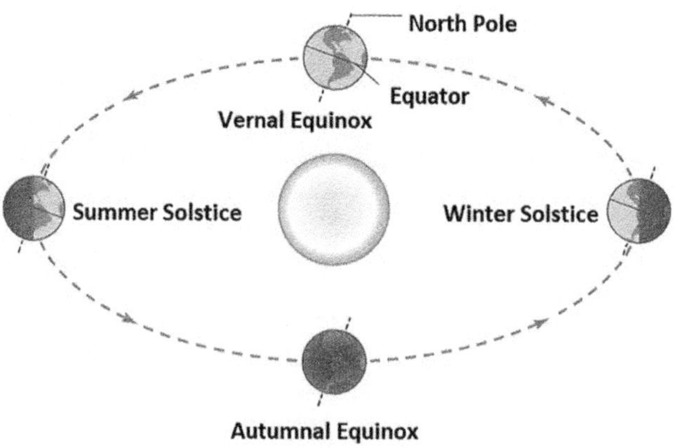

Fig. 4.1 Earth's four seasons.

For example, soybean seeds harvested in the US Midwest are often flown to warmer South America locales for storage and processing before returning to the United States for spring planting the following year. This is a method used to improve seed fertility.[c] Seasonality also affects transport modes in different ways. For example, the 27-mile Welland Canal connects Lake Erie with Lake Ontario. As such it allows cargo vessels plying the Great Lakes to reach the Atlantic Ocean via the St. Lawrence Seaway. However, the canal is typically closed from January through March due to seasonal ice. This means that long-haul or international shipments of iron ore, coal, and grain via the Great Lakes are seasonal unless moved by rail to different ports of exit in the United States or Canada.

Orthodromes

Since transportation takes place on round earth the concept of great circles or orthodromes is important. Basically, a great circle shows the shortest distance between two points on a sphere. It is often said that the shortest distance between two points is a straight line. The problem is that flat-earth projection maps give the viewer a misleading impression. In fact, all such maps have built-in distortions. This is because it is impossible to spread a round, three-dimensional surface onto a two-dimensional one without distorting something. To really appreciate the routes taken by airplanes or ocean vessels it is better to measure them with a string on a globe rather than viewing a map on a wall.

The great circle routes from the Port of Yokohama to the Port of Seattle, the Port of Portland, the Port of San Francisco, and the Port of Long Beach are shown in Fig. 4.2.

The left-hand panel is a flat-earth projection map. The shortest distances between Japan and the four ports in the contiguous United States are northerly curved lines. This is because heading across the Pacific Ocean in a straight line would be akin to traveling around a bulge as opposed to a

[c] When airline passenger load factors were at record lows during the COVID-19 pandemic in 2020, American Airlines broke a weight record by shipping soybean seeds on a Boeing 777-300 passenger plane. This all-cargo flight traveled from Buenos Aires to its hub in Miami. The company's record-breaking flight on April 16, 2020 hauled over 115,000 pounds of palletized seed bound for the US Farm Belt. The airline has been in this business for over a decade. Apart from soybean seeds the haulage of essential equipment to fight the COVID-19 pandemic was one way the airlines validated keeping their passenger planes in the air.

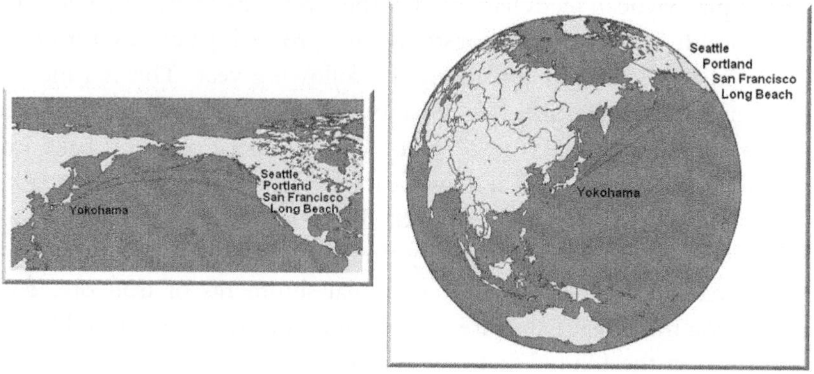

Fig. 4.2 Flat-earth routes and orthodromes.

tapered route to the north. The right-hand panel shows the same four routes if these were traced out along a globe. Looked at from above they would appear as straight lines.

Natural choke points

Since international trade takes place on an Earth that is not topographically consistent it is natural to expect that trade lanes are subject to congestion. Areas that experience a lot of trade activity incentivize the building of infrastructure that tries to build loyalty and attract even more traffic. These network effects can lead to agglomeration as discussed below.

Singapore's importance in trade began in the early 19th century when the British East India Company established it as a port of call in the spice trade. It has worked hard to maintain its center of gravity in container trans-shipping. Being on the tip of the Malaysia peninsula alongside the Malacca Strait, Singapore is the only major port at this chokepoint in the shipping lanes connecting Europe and the Middle East with Far East Asia. The Malacca Strait is just over 1.5 miles wide at its narrowest point. Trade between Europe and Far East Asia also passes through the Suez Canal alongside the politically volatile Middle East.

Simply looking at a map reveals the choke points in ocean vessel activity. Similar to criminals trying to catch their victims at vulnerable points, it should not be surprising that the hot spots for maritime piracy are either at choke points or along the coasts of failed states as seen in Fig. 4.3.

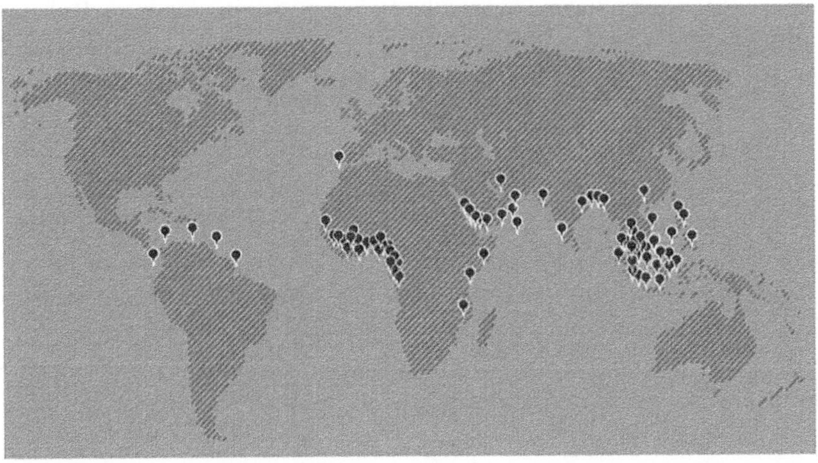

Fig. 4.3 Natural choke points. *(Source: Prokop, D.J., 2017. Global Supply Chain Security and Management: Appraising Programs, Preventing Crimes. Butterworth Heinemann, Cambridge, MA.)*

Location theory

Agglomerations

Agglomerations or clusters of interrelated companies in a town or region act like a magnet attracting other companies or service providers. They can also incentivize the creation of key infrastructure (i.e., roads, airports, water ports, etc.) to add further vitality to the cluster. For example, if the government builds a public freeway to allow better access to a major factory, not only does it speed input and output transport it also encourages other companies to build nearby to take advantage of the new shipping opportunity.

Memphis is the global headquarters of FedEx. As such, many vendors locate nearby because of the global air cargo connectivity FedEx offers them in order to reach their customers in a timely fashion. Similarly, all of the largest (i.e., Class I) US railroads pass through Chicago. They long recognized the value of that location as a transport hub due to the large presence of commodity producers in need of bulk transport to domestic and international customers. The hub-and-spoke model was introduced in Chapter 1. In this context, the hub can be examined as an agglomeration within a transportation network. Chicago's rise was induced by geography and agriculture while FedEx-Memphis rose as a result of preexisting infrastructure. Rail networks follow routes dictated by supply of and demand for bulk commodities. Airports, by contrast, have relatively more flexibility in locale.

Certainly, some clusters are based on the need for close proximity to key resources such as oil fields, minerals, arable land, fisheries, etc. Some clusters are based on regional proximity. For example, the Maquiladoras region of northern Mexico offers low-cost labor in manufacturing. But it also offers access to the United States and Canada via its membership in the United States-Mexico-Canada Agreement (USMCA). Though USMCA replaced the North American Free Trade Agreement (NAFTA) in 2020, both specified certain "rules of origin." These determine how much value-add must take place in one USMCA country for duty-free export to the other members of the trade bloc.

Some clusters are based on specialized knowledge. For example, Bangalore's prominence in call center activity relates to low-cost labor and English proficiency. Other prominent business clusters which are not dependent on physical geography include Detroit for automobiles; Las Vegas for gaming; New York City for finance; and Silicon Valley for computer technology. Local institutions may add value to these clusters. From universities, think tanks, and lobby groups—each can offer services targeted to the cluster's niche.

Still, effective logistics management is the reason why so many of today's clusters need not be self-sufficient zones of business. Before improvements in global connectivity due to the internet and more efficient transportation, a lot of attention was paid to proximity to vendors and customers—and striking the right balance between the two. Access to abundant information and multiple means of transportation has made agglomeration more of an exercise in supply chain connectivity rather than spatial concentration.

Gateways

A gateway is an access point to a city, region, or country. It may have resulted from an agglomeration of business and/or key transportation infrastructure. It may also be due to geography. For example, the Panama Canal is a gateway from the Pacific Ocean to the Atlantic Ocean and vice versa. Of course, geography played an important role when it came to choosing the site. The relatively short distance between the two oceans in that part of Central America added to the feasibility of the project.

Alaska is another example of a geographically induced gateway. The Port of Alaska (originally called the Port of Anchorage[d]) came to prominence after a magnitude 9.2 earthquake hit southcentral Alaska in 1964. The quake destroyed the state's original gateway, the Port of Seward. The Port of Alaska, about 75 miles away from the epicenter, was left intact. Alaska's logistical center of gravity shifted north from Seward to Anchorage. It was not the shaking that destroyed the Port of Seward, it was the resulting tsunami waves. Also, the Port of Alaska's locale along Cook Inlet's shallower and narrowing waters make it tsunami proof. On the other hand, those waters have the second-highest tides in North America; are fed by silty glacial run-off; and are burdened by numerous winter ice floes. The Port of Alaska, for its size, may be the most dredged port in the world, including the need to dredge during icy winter months. This is the reason why the port is in need of major repairs to its support pilings.

There was also an infrastructure-induced move from Seward to Anchorage. The Alaska Railroad has its southern terminus in Seward but it travels through Anchorage to its northern terminus in Fairbanks. The railroad began as a private company in 1903. Through the Alaska Railroad Act of 1914 the US Congress authorized the purchase of the railroad from its struggling private owners and voted to fund construction northward through Anchorage up to Fairbanks. The project was completed in 1923 when President Harding drove the final (golden) spike at the town of Nenana where the railroad connected with the Fairbanks-based Tanana Valley Railroad (also bought by the federal government). Alaska's only commercial railroad would remain under federal control until it was transferred to the state in 1985.

Before state ownership, the rail network had not changed very much. But perhaps the biggest addition was the construction of the Port of Whittier in 1943 to support the war effort. In order to reach the rest of the state, two massive rail tunnels were blasted through Maynard Mountain and Begich Peak (both a part of the Chugach mountain range) in order to lay a rail spur from the port to the railroad's mainline. At 2.5 miles long the Anton

[d] The Anchorage Assembly decided on the name change in 2017. It can be argued that this was a polite signal to the state government in Juneau that while the port may be under a city government's control it really is an important piece of infrastructure for the state. Since the Port of Alaska is in need of repairs that Anchorage itself cannot easily finance there was a political impetus to the name change.

Anderson Memorial Tunnel is one of the longest in the United States. In 2000 the tunnel was fitted to allow for a single toll lane of vehicular traffic in alternating directions. Naturally, vehicles are not allowed in the tunnels at the same time with the trains. Unlike the vehicular traffic, however, the trains must proceed through the second, 1-mile-long tunnel through Begich Peak before reaching the mainline. Since 1962 the Port of Whittier has been the means by which rail cars are barged to and from the Port of Prince Rupert, BC, and the Port of Seattle. This is part of the longest rail haul in the United States. The interline service from Panama City, FL to Fairbanks covers over 4800 miles. Though the rail barge services work fairly well, arrivals and departures can be impeded by erratic and harsh marine weather.

With about half of Alaska's small but widely dispersed population centered in Anchorage and Fairbanks, the Port of Alaska has become the only reliable gateway for large volume freight deliveries to those cities. About 90% of Alaska's inbound freight arrives by water. The Port of Alaska's share of this serves about 85% of Alaskans. Importantly, of the amount that arrives in Anchorage, only half is for the local residents. The other half is for residents outside of the city northward along the highway and railroad up to Fairbanks.

For the contiguous United States, there are several ocean ports along the US West Coast. Yet, the nearby ports of Los Angeles and Long Beach attract the largest volumes of containerized imports from Asia. Most of these imports are not destined for Southern California; rather these ports serve as a gateway to the contiguous United States. After clearing US Customs and Border Protection at these ports, most of the containers are placed on motor carriers or trains heading for the Midwest and East Coast. This makes sense since most of the US population lives on its eastern half. About 15% of the population lives in West Coast states while 36% (i.e., more than double) lives in East Coast states. With most of the consumer market residing eastward, any cargo arriving at a West Coast port must be moved inland via motor carriers or rail in order to reach those locales. About 60% of US imports from Asia via ocean vessels head to West Coast ports and about two-thirds of what enters moves inland to the Midwest and East Coast.

Ted Stevens Anchorage International Airport is another gateway to the contiguous United States. In this case, it is a gateway for Asia-sourced air cargo. About 80% of this traffic lands at the airport for refueling. Why should that be when these air cargo planes are quite capable of overflying Anchorage? It comes down to what the airport's management team calls keeping their airport "sticky." Anchorage has both geographic and operational advantages that are unique along the great circle between Asia and the contiguous United States. Geographically, Anchorage is just about the distance (i.e., 4400–4800 nautical miles) a fully loaded jumbo or wide-body US-bound air cargo plane can go from, say, Hong Kong. So, if the intent is to fill the planes in Asia with more revenue-earning cargo and less cost-inducing fuel, it makes sense to land and refuel in Anchorage. It also helps that the airport managers work hard to keep its landing fees and fuel charges low by industry standards.

The airport is centrally located and within 9.5 h of flying time to 90% of the industrialized world. This makes it an excellent air cargo trans-shipping point. This operational advantage is accentuated by the airport's innovative air cargo transfer program.[e] Belly-to-belly transfer of US bound cargo between a foreign air carrier's planes or between those of two different foreign air carriers would be illegal at any other airport in the contiguous United States. In fact, the airport's management team has had to work hard to convince skeptical Asia-based carriers that this quasi-cabotage activity is quite legal. What makes it hard to believe at first is why the United States would offer such a unilateral trade benefit to countries such as China and Japan. Basically, Alaskans can thank the advocacy of the late Senator Ted Stevens when he wrote this unique operation into a re-appropriation bill for the Federal Aviation Administration (FAA) in the mid-1990s. The airport's managers know that their air carrier customers can literally fly away so they have to be imaginative in order to maintain their logistical center of gravity against other US and Canadian airports looking to attract Asia-US traffic.

Transportation networks

The collection of routes connecting various points of origin, interlining, intermodal transfer, and destination over land, water, and air is called a transportation network. While networks may have formed systematically (e.g., a gridded set of streets in a business district) they may also have arisen out of passive respect for tradition (e.g., a maze of curved streets in older European cities). In any case, networks are intended to provide connectivity in order to promote mobility for business, leisure, or military purposes.

Various networks are shown in Fig. 4.4. Each shows the maximum number of pairwise connections given the number of nodes in the network.

[e] For more detail see Prokop (2002) and Prokop (2008).

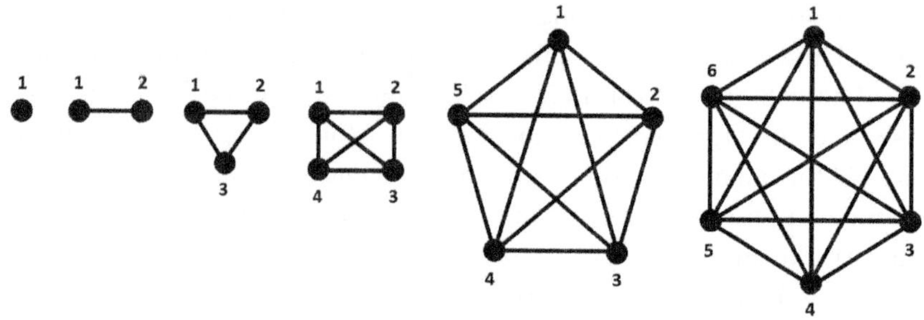

Fig. 4.4 Transportation networks with maximum connectivity.

Naturally, a single node with no connections provides no mobility. Two nodes offer the possibility of one connecting route (called an edge in graph theory). This one route provides a mobility benefit which may simultaneously increase the value of the two nodes. This one route provides two possible origin-destination pairs. Three nodes which are not in a row but exist triangularly can offer the possibility of two routes emanating from each of them. Thus, an extra node has doubled (i.e., increased by 100%) the other two nodes' mobility possibilities. Four nodes which are not in a row but exist rectangularly can offer the possibility of three routes emanating from each of them. Thus, an extra node has increased the other three nodes' mobility possibilities from two to three (or a 50% increase). Five nodes which are not in a row but exist in the shape of a pentagon can offer the possibility of four routes emanating from each of them. Thus, an extra node has increased the other four nodes' mobility possibilities from three to four (or a 33% increase). Finally, without belaboring the logic too much, a six-node network in a hexagonal shape offers each node a total of five routes of connectivity. Logically, therefore, the maximum number of uniquely paired routes is $(n-1)$ for each node (n) in the network. So, with n nodes in a given network, the total number of routes emanating from all of them is

$$n(n-1) \tag{4.1}$$

But Eq. (4.1) counts a route twice (i.e., a line from node 1 to 2 and the same line from node 2 to 1). Therefore, the number of connector lines or edges in a network of size n is:

$$n(n-1)/2 \tag{4.2}$$

While it is true that the percentage increase in routes diminishes as the number of nodes increase, it is only because the base number is getting larger. This is why adding one road to a network of two roads is a larger proportion (i.e., 50%) than adding one road to a network of 20 roads (i.e., 5%). The point is that the value of the network, as a whole, is growing because of the mobility options it offers. There is a caveat, however. Since valuation is a subjective term, there is no objective way to say what the magnitude of the increase in the network's value is. In fact, one could argue that some nodes should not be connected due to increased social and/or military tensions. They may apply when nodes are in different countries. Again, what constitutes valuable mobility is subjective.

It is also possible to argue that some nodes are more valuable than others. This means that any increase in value among the connected nodes is not equally distributed. For example, the first two nodes to be connected have more time to enjoy the benefits of network effects than say, the nineteenth and twentieth nodes. In a business sense, it is like an older company having more experience in building trusting relationships and generating profits from its network of vendors, customers, and for-hire carriers. In other words, there was more time for supply chains and agglomerations to form. In a transportation sense, a for-hire carrier with a longer presence in the network gains more experience traversing the different nodes, avoiding chokepoints, etc.

Fig. 4.4 illustrates all possible connections among pairs of preexisting nodes. Of course, it is possible that some connections could beget more nodes. The rectangular, pentagonal, and hexagonal-shaped networks have several routes that intersect. These have the potential to be interline and/or intermodal transfer points. If such activities lead to the formation of a stationary populous of employees and their families it is possible that another node may form. The transformation of villages or towns into centers of trade due to being at crossroads, railroad junctions, or confluences of rivers is an example of this. Istanbul, Frankfurt, and Chicago are prominent examples from ancient, medieval, and modern times, respectively.

If, for simplicity, it is assumed that each node has equal value or, at least, equal effect in terms of having enough capacity to meet the mobility demands of all users, then the value or effect of the network is proportional to the square of the number of nodes added to the network. This is known as Metcalfe's law.[f] If the network's value is simply its effect (i.e., the ability of one node to reach every other node in a timely and safe manner) then Eq. (4.1) expresses this effect. If looked at in terms of people (or users) rather than nodes, if each person in a 2-person network valued his connection to

[f] Shapiro and Varian (1999, p. 184).

the other at \$1, then the network is worth \$2. If each person in a 10-person network valued his connectivity to the nine other people at $\$1 \times 9 = \$9$ the network is worth \$90 which is a bit less than the square of 10. If the network doubled to 20 people then each person values his connectivity at $\$1 \times 19 = \$19$. Therefore, the value of the network is \$380. In other words, doubling the people or nodes raises the value or effect from \$90 to \$380. This is a bit more than a fourfold increase (which is close to the square of the twofold increase in the network size). Similarly, if the network tripled from 10 to 30 the network valuation rises from \$90 to $\$1 \times 29 \times 30 = \$870$. The network value increased a bit more than ninefold (which is the square of 3). Obviously, for larger increases, the effect asymptotically approaches the square. In other words, as the network becomes large, Eq. (4.1) asymptotically approaches the value n^2.

Metcalfe's law was first applied to communications networks starting with the fax machine in 1980 to the modern internet. Network effects in communication are sought after and relatively easy to handle since the marginal cost of adding an extra user on, say, a social media platform is near-zero. Connecting users with everyone else is much easier than having all US cities connected by roads in unique pairs. Therefore, transportation networks are rarely topologically complete. Redundancies in routing are also not the norm. Therefore, network resiliency in transportation infrastructure is a major challenge. The same cannot be said for a communications network. Data moving at the speed of light through cyberspace is governed exclusively by the laws of physics. Commuters traversing a transportation network, on the other hand, are affected by physics and psychology. Adding broadband capacity to communications networks is easy compared to adding enough miles of road to stay ahead of congestion in densely populated areas. The mobility opportunities offered by large transportation networks may also generate social costs that are difficult to overcome.

Design options

With limited time and material, it is unrealistic to expect a given network to offer all possible pairwise connections. Out of necessity compromises must be made. Taking the hexagonal network from Fig. 4.4 as an example a few options can be developed as shown in Fig. 4.5.

Option 1 offers minimal connectivity and forces a long backhaul to the point of origin if it were at node 1 or 6. If the point of origin were at nodes 2–5 it would require some degree of doubling back if all nodes are to be visited.

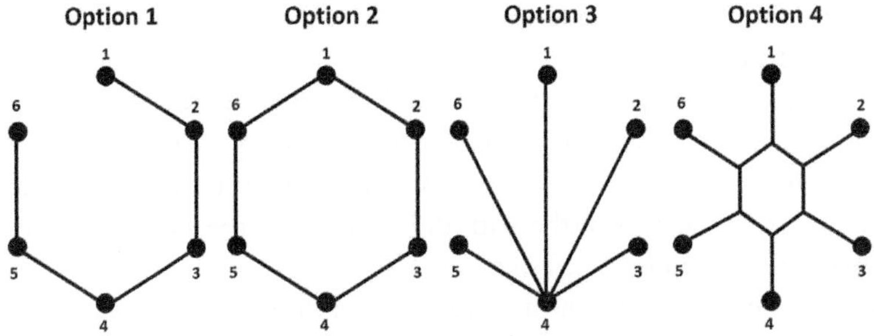

Fig. 4.5 Options for less mobility within a six-node network.

While this configuration has relatively low material cost it may add to social costs since funneling traffic along only one route makes it susceptible to congestion. Option 2 offers clockwise and counterclockwise routing along the perimeter of the network. Option 3 funnels all traffic into a hub at node 4. As noted in Chapter 1 there may be benefits to a hub-and-spoke configuration. Option 4, in contrast to option 2, offers an inner perimeter. This requires a shorter distance to traverse since the goal is to be some distance away from each node without having to go through them. From a pick-up and delivery perspective, option 2 is preferred when stops at all nodes are definite and necessary. On the other hand, option 4 is preferred when stops are not definite. Option 2 takes on the extra travel cost along with the revenue to be earned from stops at each node. But if revenues are subject to probability the inner perimeter allows the for-hire carrier to be in a reasonable vicinity should pick-up opportunities arise.

An option not shown in Fig. 4.5 is a set of connections that achieves a solution to the so-called traveling salesman problem.[g] Basically, a roundtrip is possible within any network of two or more nodes. The challenge is to find one that does not require doubling back past a previous node or connector. Some graphical distinctions which are important to make at the outset are:

- Node circuit: starts and ends at the same node while touching all those nodes along the way only once (i.e., a roundtrip).
- Connector circuit: starts and ends at the same connector while covering all those connectors along the way only once (i.e., a roundtrip).

[g] For a complete analysis see Applegate et al. (2006).

- Node path: starts at a node and touches all those nodes along the way to the end node only once (i.e., not a roundtrip). Of course, if the end of the path did go back to the starting node it becomes a node circuit.
- Connector path: starts at a connector and covers all those connectors along the way to the end connector only once (i.e., not a roundtrip). Of course, if the end of the path did go back to the starting connector it becomes a connector circuit.
- Hamilton circuit: a circuit that touches every node in the entire network just once (though the start node is touched twice because it is also the end node) (i.e., a roundtrip over the whole network).
- Hamilton path: a path that touches every node in the entire network just once (e.g., option 1 in Fig. 4.5).
- Euler circuit: a circuit that covers every connector in the entire network just once (though the start connector is reached by the end connector) (i.e., a roundtrip over the whole network).
- Euler path: a path that covers every connector in the entire network just once.

In summary, circuits are about roundtrips while paths need not be. Node circuits/paths are about touching a node only once. Connector circuits/paths are about covering a connector only once. Hamilton circuits/paths are about touching every node in the entire network only once. Euler circuits/paths are about covering every connector in the entire network only once.

The traveling salesman problem involves finding a Hamilton circuit. While there may be more than one the problem is to find the Hamilton circuit that minimizes travel cost, typically in terms of distance traveled. Of course, apart from distance traveled other forms of cost may include time in transit and stop-start congestion. There may also be asymmetries in the cost of a connector between two nodes. For example, traveling a given road into a central business district is more costly during the early morning peak than during the late afternoon peak. Seasonality may also be a factor. For example, it is more costly to travel to ski resorts during the winter months. In other words, timing may be an important consideration when choosing a circuit.

Looking at Fig. 4.4 for guidance and choosing node 1 as the point of origin, a two-node network offers only one roundtrip route (albeit by doubling back). The three-node network offers two roundtrip routes: one clockwise and the other counterclockwise. The four-node network offers six roundtrip routes as shown by the arrows in Fig. 4.6.

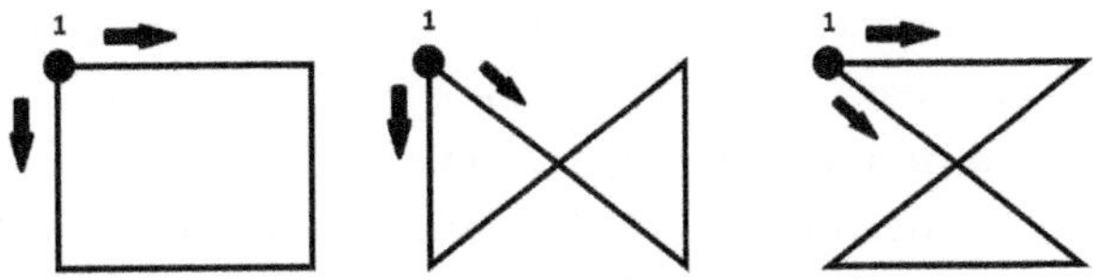

Fig. 4.6 Roundtrip options within a four-node, fully connected network.

Naturally, the number of roundtrips becomes very large when there are many nodes and pairwise connections.

If a given network offers all possible pairwise connections, it is straightforward to calculate the total number of possible roundtrips without any doubling back. If the number of nodes in the network is n, then starting from the chosen node of origin there are $n-1$ ways to get to a second node. From the second node, there are $n-2$ ways to get to a third node. From the third node, there are $n-3$ ways to get to a fourth node, and so on. Therefore, the total number of possible roundtrips is

$$(n-1)! \tag{4.3}$$

For example, the hexagonal network in Fig. 4.4 offers $(6-1)!$ or 120 possible roundtrips. A network of 10 nodes offers $(10-1)!$ or 362,880 possible roundtrips. Finding the cost-minimizing roundtrip, especially when there are many nodes and many types of cost constraints, requires either an algorithm for a precise answer or a heuristic method for an approximation.

The traveling salesman problem involves reaching each node just once. A different problem requires the traveler to traverse every connector only once as a sort of leisurely tour of the entire network but without any backtracking along a connector already traversed. In this case, some nodes may be reached more than once. For this to work planners must make sure that the network offers either an Euler path or an Euler circuit. Basically, an Euler path exists when all nodes are connected and there are no more than two nodes with an odd number of connectors. An Euler circuit exists when there are no nodes with an odd number of connectors.

Though graph theory offers formal proofs of the Euler path and circuit theorems, each can be reasoned intuitively. Consider a set of nodes with no connectors. Placing connectors like toy railroad tracks between nodes shows that the starting node has one connector leading to the second node. The second node will have two connectors (i.e., one for entering and one for exiting) as it proceeds to the third node. The third node will have two connectors as it proceeds to the fourth node, and so on. When the *n*th node's connector proceeds back to the first node it gives the latter its second connector. The roundtrip Euler circuit is completed with every node having an even number of connectors (i.e., two in this case). But what if there was one more node that popped up near the starting node? The starting node will have a third connector going to it. At this point, the network is an Euler path because there are two nodes with an odd number of connectors (i.e., three for the starting node and one for the pop-up node). Placing a parallel connector between these two nodes gets a traveler back to the starting point and reestablishes the Euler circuit. Of course, there would no longer be any nodes with an odd number of connectors. There would now be four connectors at the starting node and two at the pop-up node.

Do Hamilton circuits/paths coexist with Euler circuits/paths? Not necessarily. For example, the triangular network in Fig. 4.4 traces out both. However, tracing the perimeter of the rectangular network in Fig. 4.4 is a Hamilton circuit but there is no Euler circuit/path that can deal with both of its diagonal connectors without doubling back on another connector. Fig. 4.7 uses a rectangular network to show all four possibilities for circuits. Networks A and C offer Hamilton circuits by simply tracing the perimeter. Networks B and D do not because it is not possible to get back to the starting node (e.g., node 1 or 5) without crossing one node previously touched.

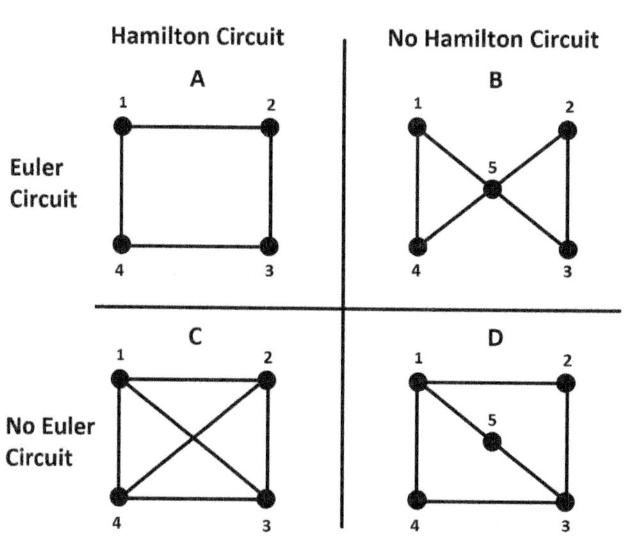

Fig. 4.7 Hamilton and Euler combinations.

Networks A and B are Euler circuits because the connectors are easily traced and there are no nodes with an odd number of connectors. Networks C and D are not because each has a node with an odd number of connectors. However, since network D has only two nodes with an odd number of connectors it does offer several Euler paths. Tracing the perimeter first gives: 1–2–3–4–1–5–3 and 1–4–3–2–1–5–3. Tracing two triangles gives: 1–2–3–5–1–4–3 and 1–4–3–5–1–2–3. These four options started with node 1. Four similar options can be traced out by starting with node 3.

The existence of Hamilton circuits/paths does not provide any insight into the existence of Euler circuits/paths and vice versa. Also, establishing the existence of an Euler circuit/path is simply a matter of looking for either zero or two nodes with an odd number of connectors. Unfortunately, there is no simple method which applies to establishing the existence of Hamilton circuits/paths.

Managing congestion

All five modes of transportation are subject to congestion. While motor carriers, locomotives, and gases/liquids in a pipeline travel along man-made pathways even airplanes and water vessels travel within limited bounds along specific air and water routes. All five modes may reach choke points along their routes. Some routes may be more popular or expedient than others. Whether the pathways are privately owned (e.g., railroads) or publicly provided (e.g., common use roads) each is subject to congestion. Conveyances and their cargo may need to be queued in order to facilitate loading when the point of origin has limited space. Queuing before unloading at the point of destination may also be necessary.

Modeling transportation networks is particularly complicated because there are so many variables. Operators are constrained by the physical limits of their conveyances. This applies to their speed, range, and maneuverability. Operators are also affected by their physical health (e.g., responsiveness, perception, and stamina) and psychological attitudes (e.g., mood) while commuting. Environmental factors like the weather affect the visibility and surface quality of roads, runways, etc. From a safety perspective transportation networks are not consistent. For example, differences in road width, number of curves or sharp turns along the way, traffic control devices used, etc. require operators to adjust accordingly. For some operators, this relieves boredom while for others it may increase the risk of accidents.

To handle the analysis of complex transportation networks, certain simplifying assumptions are made regarding commuters:

- each operates an identical vehicle (i.e., size, speed, cargo onboard, etc.);
- each has perfect information about the structure and usage of the network;
- each impacts the same amount of traffic; and
- each wants to travel between the same origin and destination, at the same time, and complete the trip in the shortest (and safest) amount of time.

Assuming identical vehicles avoids other considerations when planning trips. For example, a driver with a small car may not want to use roads frequented by slower-moving trucks since they obscure vision, generate more exhaust, etc. Similar inconveniences apply when following school buses and public transit vehicles because of their frequent stops.

The assumption of perfect information is used so that each commuter is able to gauge the time cost of each alternative route and thereby make individual (i.e., self-interested) decisions. Onboard technology and smartphones offering real-time information about traffic patterns make this assumption a reasonable one.

A lone commuter certainly does not impact other commuters. Two commuters are assumed to impact each other equally meaning that each is responsible for one-half of the traffic. However, in a one-lane road, one of them is in the lead without facing any traffic ahead. One thousand commuters mean each is responsible for a one-thousandth share of the traffic. The more commuters there are the smaller each one's impact is. In congested traffic, the typical commuter is the "average" commuter who is part of the congestion problem but has a small impact on it. In large traffic flows the individual impact is negligible in size; but the whole group is collectively impactful. Of course, a single commuter who breaks the rules of the road or has a lapse in judgment which causes an accident could be very impactful. It, therefore, makes sense to assume that all commuters act responsibly at all times. While accidents can magnify congestion the concern here is congestion due to overwhelming the infrastructure.

All commuters are assumed to want to complete their common trip in the shortest amount of time without worry for safety. Again, it is assumed that no commuter would drive recklessly. When alternative routes between a given origin and destination exist, the network will be in equilibrium when all possible routes take the same amount of time for a given commuter.[h] In other words, travel time would be independent of the number of commuters on a given route. The socially optimal distribution of traffic is the one that brings about this result. The implication is that if a route allows for greater speed it is only because the distance from the origin to destination is longer. Conversely, if a route is shorter in length it will attract more commuters thereby creating congestion which slows the pace (i.e., the distance covered per unit of time). This same argument applies to routes with varying surface quality. A bumpy road will be less popular than a smooth one. However, the smooth road will become more congested as a result and this slows the pace of traffic.

Construction and expansion of network infrastructure tend to lag behind user demand. For example, if a destination can be reached by only one route, a government or private entity would not consider upgrading or building an alternative route until there is evidence of systematic and unresolvable traffic congestion on the current route. Why should there be such a lag? Apart from confirming that the congestion problem is truly systematic, and likely not to dissipate on its own, there is the problem of indivisibility. It makes little sense to expand infrastructure on the basis of just one of a few commuters beginning to cause delays.

Suppose managers at an airport with a single runway notice that not all airplanes entering their air traffic control area can automatically be cleared for landing like they used to. How many airplanes should be placed in holding patterns in the sky on a given day before the time comes to consider building another runway? How many ocean vessels should be moored offshore before port managers decide that it is time to build another dock? In the same vein, how much congestion is acceptable before it is time to widen a road or build an alternative one? There is no easy answer; and, where the government is concerned, such decisions will be influenced by politics.

Construction taking place in a frequent, yet piecemeal, fashion is more expensive than doing it less frequently but in a larger setting. This is due to

[h] For simplicity time is taken to be the only relevant cost in commuting. This makes sense when looked at from a commercial perspective. In the real world, however, some leisurely commuters may make choices that deliberately take more time because the intent is to sight-see. Also, if the time differences are not too great some motor carriers may take longer routes because their favorite truck stops are along the way. They may also prefer more time-consuming, free-flowing routes since they do not involve the annoyance and vehicle maintenance costs involved in start-stop travel through congestion.

the economies of scale that come from bulk purchases and usage of construction materials. The larger the project the larger this effect. Of course, one must be careful not to wait until the project becomes too big and unwieldy. There may be shortages when demanding a lot of material all at once. There may be problems staging all the necessary material and delivering it in a timely fashion. This is when diseconomies of scale set in. Therefore, timing is an artful balance of these two forces.

Once an alternative route is available to relieve congestion along an older one, commuters will have to make a choice between them. It turns out that a Nash equilibrium would be reached after a while whereby the travel time between the common origin and destination would be equal over both routes no matter how much wider, smoother, and less congestible the new route is.[i] A Nash equilibrium, by definition, means that no commuter would change routes so long as no other commuter does.[j] In fact, if the two routes incentivized people from outside the network to relocate their businesses to the origin and/or destination the level of congestion could be even higher than in the *status quo ante*. If the infrastructure is not privately owned (i.e., not subject to entry restrictions) it should not be seen as a closed system with fixed populations, commuters, etc.

The Nash equilibrium means that the alternative route will offer the same travel time. This also means that, in the absence of any congestion, the free-flowing travel times will be equal. On the other hand, if there is still some degree of congestion, any delay on one or both routes will still factor into the travel time for both. As noted above the Nash equilibrium is not instant. The fact that it takes some time is part of the reason why this system does not have what game theorists call a dominant strategy. In other words, a commuter could decide the route to take simply by flipping a coin

[i] Harper (1982) provides evidence for a Nash equilibrium among ducks in a pond. When two people at opposite ends of the pond tossed out breadcrumbs at fixed but different intervals the 33 ducks sorted themselves out such that each was able to eat the same amount. Naturally, more ducks settled around the person tossing out more breadcrumbs per minute; but there was no consumption advantage as far as any single duck was concerned. Even when one or both people changed their tossing frequencies a new equilibrium would come about within a couple of minutes.

[j] Reference is being made to the "average" commuter. In the real world, there is no doubt that some commuters choose to drive faster or slower than others and these choices would affect travel time. Slower drivers can interfere with those wishing to go faster. A group of fast drivers may, in their attempts to get ahead of each other, create chokepoints ahead as they all race to their exit ramps, points where the road narrows, etc.

in order to test the options.[k] Contrary to the assumptions outlined above, what if a very slow-driving commuter existed, was known by all, and pre-committed to route 1 instead of route 2? It should not change the sorting out the process even if route 1 was a one-lane road with the slow driver in the lead. Enough commuters would switch to route 2 until it became as time-consuming as following the slow commuter along route 1.

Pigou (1920) provided the seminal analysis of commuter choice and its social implications. Known today as the Pigou-Knight-Downs Paradox, building a faster but congestible alternative route with the same origin and destination as an older, slower route will not reduce average commute time so long as the original (and noncongestible) route continues to be used by at least one commuter.[l] The new route takes some proportion of traffic off of the older route but, whatever that proportion is, it will lead to the same travel time as along the older route. This paradox, therefore, suggests futility in expanding a transportation network, even if the new addition is seemingly more efficient than preexisting routes.

To start with a problem with an obvious solution, suppose routes 1 and 2 are identical in terms of length, surface quality, number of lanes, etc. Each route is subject to congestion since the travel time (t) on it rises in a linear fashion with the number of commuters (N) using it. Trial and error will lead the commuters to eventually divide themselves up evenly between the two routes going from the origin (O) to destination (D) as seen in Fig. 4.8.

[k] A contrivance to demonstrate what a dominant strategy looks like would be if all commuters but one announced their choices between routes 1 and 2. If they all chose route 1 then it is obvious that the silent commuter should take route 2. Of course, if any of the other commuters were allowed to change their minds the game would revert to the original form since the announcement was not binding. This is why binding commitments in isolation can lead to inefficient results. Either the independent, self-interested commuters must be allowed to sort themselves out in their own way or an authority figure must intervene and control all commuters' actions by regulating access, speed, lane usage, etc.

[l] Under a similar scenario the Downs-Thomson Paradox applies to the choice between private commuting and public transit. If the carrying capacity on a road network is expanded between a given origin and destination it may incentivize public transit users to switch to their own private cars. Thus, it is possible that traffic congestion could increase rather than decrease in the face of the expanded network. Worse, the fall in public transit ridership could force the transit authority to raise fares in order to cover its operating costs. This may create a vicious circle of increasing congestion combined with lower quality, yet higher priced, transit services. Basically, the positive pecuniary externality of reduced traffic congestion conferred by using public transit is ignored by those willing and able to switch to cars. In other words, self-interest and the freedom to choose how to commute have social implications.

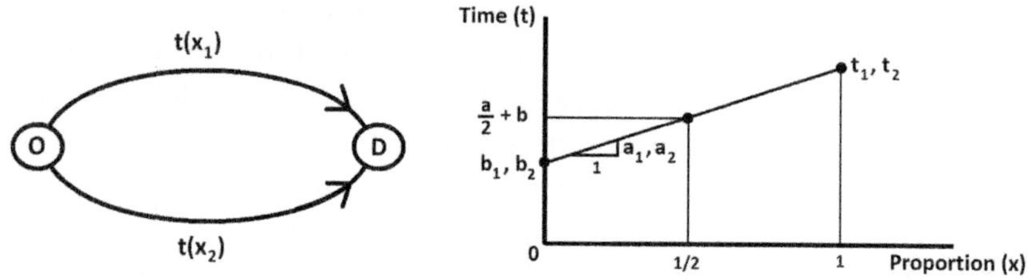

Fig. 4.8 Travel time on a network of two identical roads.

The optimization problem is to minimize the total cost (TC) of travel time along the two-route network:

$$\text{Minimize TC} = x_1 t_1(x_1) + x_2 t_2(x_2); \text{where } 0 \leq x_i \leq 1 \text{ and } x_1 + x_2 = 1 \tag{4.4}$$

Routes 1 and 2 will have a proportion (x) of commuters (N) choose to travel on them. Each commuter will incur a time cost that will be the same over both routes in equilibrium:

$$t_1(x_1) = t_2(x_2) \tag{4.5}$$

For simplicity, assume that time is a linear function with respect to the proportion of commuters. Therefore, Eq. (4.5) becomes

$$a_1 x_1 + b_1 = a_2 x_2 + b_2; \text{where } a_i, b_i \geq 0 \tag{4.6}$$

Parameter (b) is the base level of travel time with unobstructed traffic while parameter (a) indicates the extra time (i.e., delay) each extra commuter causes across the route. Of course, these parameters offer various modeling options. For example, a lower (b) could indicate a shorter road and an exponent on (a) could indicate a more rapid (i.e., nonlinear) increase in congestion.

Given that $x_2 = 1 - x_1$ it can be substituted into Eq. (4.6) in order to solve for x_1:

$$x_1 = (a_2 + b_2 - b_1)/(a_1 + a_2) \tag{4.7}$$

Since both routes are identical, $a_1 = a_2$ and $b_1 = b_2$ meaning that Eq. (4.7) equals 1/2. Both routes will share an equal proportion of commuters. Another way to show this is to use Eq. (4.6) and $x_2 = 1 - x_1$ in order to expand Eq. (4.4) and find its minimum:

$$x_1[a_1 x_1 + b_1] + (1 - x_1)[a_2(1 - x_1) + b_2]$$

$$d\text{TC}/dx_1 = 2a_1 x_1 + b_1 - 2a_2 + 2a_2 x_1 - b_2 = 0 \text{ at the minimum point of TC} \tag{4.8}$$

Solving Eq. (4.8) for x_1 leads to the same result as Eq. (4.7) (i.e., $x_1 = 1/2$) so long as both routes are identical. Eq. (4.7) is useful for calculating the traffic proportions if the two routes differed in their rates of congestion. For example, let route 2 be twice as congestible as route 1. This means $a_2 = 2a_1$ and by plugging this into Eq. (4.7) the result is $x_1 = 2/3$. This makes intuitive sense because the efficiency of route 1 is double the efficiency of route 2; therefore, its share (at 67%) is double the route 2's (at 33%). The Nash equilibrium is also Pareto optimal since there is no other arrangement of traffic that lowers travel costs. This means that the equilibrium achieved by self-interested commuters has no inefficiencies. However, other scenarios are not as neat and tidy.

To demonstrate inefficiency characterized by the Pigou-Knight-Downs Paradox all that is necessary is to have one noncongestible route matched by a new route that is congestible. This is shown in Fig. 4.9.

Suppose route 1 is so wide that any and all commuters would be able to travel between O and D for a fixed amount of time. This means

$$t_1(x_1) = b_1 \text{ where } b_1 \geq 0 \tag{4.9}$$

Route 2 is the new alternative. It is subject to congestion; but it is shorter in length than route 1. This gives route 2 an apparent time advantage and it will continue to attract commuters from route 1 until congestion increases travel time to b_1 on it as well. Using Eq. (4.9) to rework Eqs. (4.6), (4.7) gives

$$x_2 = (b_1 - b_2)/a_2 \tag{4.10}$$

Route 2 will attract commuters so long as $b_1 > b_2$ which means that its initial time cost must be less than that for route 1. Also, the equilibrium proportion of commuters attracted to route 2 increases the lower a_2 is. This means, given its shorter length, it is even more attractive the less congestible it is. For example, if a_2 equals $(b_1 - b_2)$ then Eq. (4.10) equals 1. In other words, route 2 would take

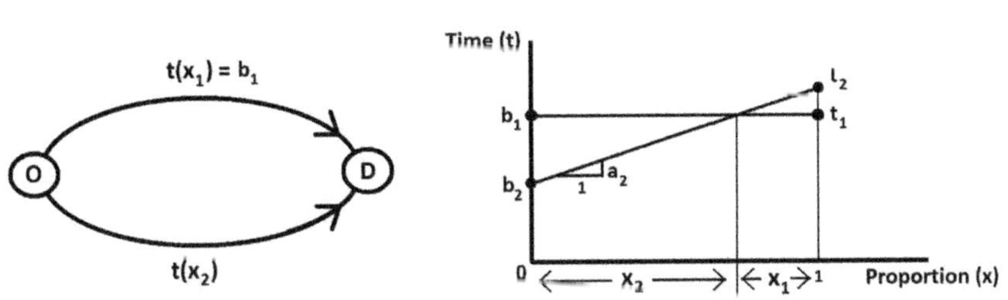

Fig. 4.9 A network exhibiting the Pigou-Knight-Downs Paradox.

a 100% share of the commuters. This effect could be seen in Fig. 4.9 by pivoting line t_2 down to intersect the end point of line t_1.

While Eq. (4.10) shows the share to route 2 under a Nash equilibrium it is not Pareto optimal. To see this take Eq. (4.9), plug it into Eq. (4.4), and solve for x_2 under minimum TC. This gives

$$(1 - x_2)[b_1] + x_2[a_2x_2 + b_2]$$

$d\mathrm{TC}/dx_2 = -b_1 + b_2 + 2a_2x_2 = 0$ at the minimum point of TC. This means,

$$x_2 = (b_1 - b_2)/2a_2 \tag{4.11}$$

Eq. (4.11) is half the size of Eq. (4.10). This means route 2 is overused from a collective or societal standpoint when commuters make their own self-interested decisions. Taking half of the commuters using route 2 under the Nash equilibrium and reallocating them to route 1 would keep their time costs equal to b_1 but the remaining half of the commuters on route 2 would see their travel times fall by half. Instead of an average travel time of, say, 60 min under the Nash equilibrium, it would fall to 45 min under Pareto optimality. This is because half are traveling for 60 min on route 1 while the other half are traveling for 30 min on route 2.

A challenge in striving for the Pareto optimal solution is that government regulation is required to force any reallocation away from self-interested choices. Why? Any commuter moved to route 1 has an incentive to move back to route 2 and try to reduce travel time from 1 h to slightly more than 30 min (i.e., "slightly" because this commuter adds to the traffic already on route 2). This is the reason why the socially optimal result is not a Nash equilibrium.

The distinction between self-interested behavior and a socially optimal outcome can be expressed as a ratio:

$$\text{Price of anarchy} = (\text{Average travel time under self-interest}) / (\text{Average travel time under social optimality})$$

The fact that half the commuters on route 2 would need to be reallocated to route 1 in order to achieve Pareto optimality leads to the following weighted average of travel time:

$$0.5t(x_1) + 0.5[t(x_2)/2] = (3/4)t(x) \tag{4.12}$$

In other words, whatever the proportion (x) of commuters (N) that choose route 2 under self-interest, a reallocation to achieve Pareto optimality means that average travel time across the network decreases to three-quarters of what it would be under self-interest. This also means that the price of anarchy ratio is

$$[t(x)/(3/4)t(x)] = 4/3 \tag{4.13}$$

Eq. (4.13) indicates that the price of anarchy is a degree of overusage equal to 33% and, worse, travel time does not improve even though the network was expanded from one route to two.[m]

The congestion problem rests on the idea that an individual commuter knows that entry onto a busy roadway might delay him. However, the commuter rarely considers the delay his entry causes to others (i.e., the negative pecuniary externality due to his actions). It also rests on the fact that transportation infrastructure tends to be underprovided rather than overprovided. Attempts by the government to overprovide it tends to run into the politics of providing voters with politically expedient short-term benefits rather than the promise of future benefits through infrastructure projects. Similar attempts by private providers run into the problem of short-term profitability and ensuring an acceptable return on investment. It also does not help that infrastructure provision, as noted above, is subject to indivisibilities. While building piecemeal is not preferable, sometimes it cannot be avoided. For example, suppose the origin and destination are separated by a road spanning 20 miles. If the congestion problem leads to a decision to widen the road it is not likely that it would be handled within a single project. Only portions of the road will be widened, and lulls could occur because of seasonal weather, securing further funding, etc. An unintended consequence of roads that widen and narrow is that a potential chokepoint is created as commuters are able to drive faster toward it. It is possible that the commute times could actually rise if the traffic is not controlled properly.[n]

Transportation planners must be alert to chokepoints and the congestion they cause. Even in a closed system where improvements do not attract outsiders, the result can lead to unintended congestion. Schelling (1978) illustrated this point by considering a long line of skiers waiting their turn to

[m] In fact, when the time delays are expressed as linear functions, the price of anarchy cannot be larger than 4/3. For further discussion see Roughgarden and Tardos (2002).

[n] Imagine a large room with 50 people all racing to get through a single exit door at once. The inevitable chokepoint is a result of the absence of traffic control. The question, however, is how should the traffic be controlled? Should there be priority access for some? Should there be staggered access to keep things orderly? In the context of roads, this is like offering priority access based on high vehicle occupancy or to those willing to pay a toll.

jump onto a ski lift. It sounds intuitively appealing to increase the speed of the ski lift in order to shorten the line. The problem is that it will lengthen the line. Why? The closed system has three steps: (1) wait in line for a ski lift chair; (2) ride the ski lift to the top of the mountain; and (3) ski down the mountain and get back in line. The time for step 3 is unchanged because it is independent of the ski lift's speed. Step 2 is faster of course. This also means that the combination of steps 2 and 3 is faster. In other words, those who get onto the ski lift are back in line faster; but they are not jumping onto the ski lift any faster. With less skiers in steps 2 and 3 of the cycle at any given moment of time, there is only one other place for the rest of them to be and that is standing in line. The situation gets worse if the ski lift moves so fast that skiers actually have to take more time to get into the right position to jump onto a fast-moving ski lift seat. Obviously, the extreme case is that the ski lift moves so fast that no skier feels safe jumping on it. In that case, every skier in the system would be waiting in line.

From a network perspective, the lesson is that partial improvements to a transportation system may actually reduce the efficiency of the system as a whole. This is a problem when funding, the material on hand, and timing require that only a partial improvement to a network can be undertaken. Waiting for the opportunity for a system-wide improvement means that the congestion problem may continue to worsen.

Another example of unintended and counterintuitive consequences in traffic planning across a network arises when Braess' Paradox is present. Simply put, under certain circumstances building more roads can lead to even more congestion across a network and, conversely, closing down roads can reduce it. The best example of the latter may have been when traffic improved after New York City shut down 42nd Street to celebrate Earth Day in 1990.[o] It should be noted that Braess' Paradox is not the result of outside commuters being attracted to an improved network or existing commuters being repelled by one that is being pared back. The paradox is that the same number of commuters (N) in a closed system can end up acting in a suboptimal way after the route options are increased.

Braess' Paradox can crop up in unexpected situations. Suppose that routes 1 and 2 are parallel and connect an origin (*O*) and a destination (*D*). The two routes also have a one-way connecting road along the way. The two routes are identical except for their congestible and noncongestible

[o] See Braess et al. (2005) for an English translation of his original 1968 article written in German. For the 42nd Street example, see Kolata (1990).

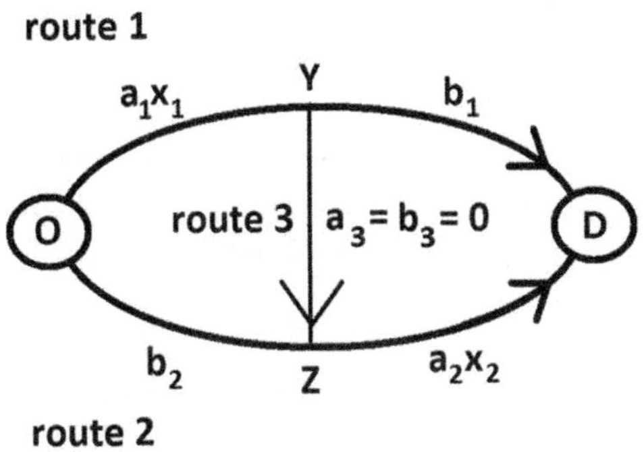

Fig. 4.10 A network exhibiting Braess' Paradox.

sections being reversed as shown in Fig. 4.10. The one-way connecting road is marked by points Y and Z which are also the inflection points along routes 1 and 2. For example, the first section of route 1 is congestible but it is very short and has no time cost when used by only one commuter (i.e., $b_1 = 0$ in that section). In contrast, the second section of route 1 is not congestible but it is longer and, therefore, has a fixed time cost ($b_1 > 0$) in using it.

The total costs for each section of routes 1 and 2 are

$$\begin{aligned} TC_1 &= a_1x_1 + b_1 \\ TC_2 &= a_2x_2 + b_2 \end{aligned}$$

where $0 \le x_i \le 1$ and $x_1 + x_2 = 1$.

Noting that $x_2 = 1 - x_1$ and equating the two total cost functions gives

$$x_1 = [a_2 + b_2 - b_1]/(a_1 + a_2) = 1/2 \text{ since } a_1 = a_2 \text{ and } b_1 = b_2 \tag{4.14}$$

Thus, without a connecting road, the Nash equilibrium has $x_1 = x_2 = 1/2$ as expected.

The connecting road is significant because it allows traffic to go in a direction that avoids the longer sections that take a fixed amount of time, $b_1 = b_2$. For simplicity let route 3 have $a_3 = b_3 = 0$. But the connecting road incentivizes commuters to use the congestible sections of routes 1 and 2 which magnifies the problem caused by self-interest. Perhaps the intent was to relieve congestion on route 1 by offering the chance to switch to route 2. Basically, this allows a commuter the option to change his commitment to one of the routes in mid-commute. These all sound like reasonable intensions. However, if enough commuters take this option, travel time may increase.

If the short and congestible sections take less time than the noncongestible but longer ones, route 3 is a dominant strategy meaning that a 100% share of the commuters will use it (i.e., $x_3=1$). To see the time difference, suppose $a_1=a_2=0.01$; and $b_1=b_2=45$. Let N be 4000 commuters. Plugging Eq. (4.14) (i.e., $x_1=½$ or 2000 commuters) into the total cost functions for routes 1 and 2 shows that each route takes

$$0.01(2000)+45=65\,\text{min}.$$

However, route 3 induces all commuters to take the connector with a total time cost of

$$0.01(4000)+0+0.01(4000)=80\,\text{min}.$$

The price of anarchy is 80/65 or 23%. Recall that Eq. (4.13) states that the price of anarchy with linear time delays cannot exceed 4/3. If $b_1=b_2=40$ then routes 1 and 2 would take 60 min while using route 3 still takes 80 min. Thus, the 4/3 ratio is maintained. But what if $b_1=b_2=39$? Would not the price of anarchy increase? The problem is that route 3 at 80 min would no longer be a Nash equilibrium. One commuter could stay on route 1 throughout and travel $0.01(4000)+39=79$ min or switch to route 2 and travel the same amount of time (i.e., $39+0.01(4000)=79$ min).

In addition to being a dominant strategy route 3 is also a Nash equilibrium because switching to either route 1 or 2 in full would take a commuter $0.01(4000)+45=85$ min. Of course, the existence of Braess' Paradox is based on the size of the delay parameters. For example, if $b_1=b_2\geq 60$ then routes 1 and 2, with 2000 commuters each, would take at least 80 min in equilibrium and Braess' Paradox would not occur. Building route 3 in this case would offer an equal or less time-consuming option. Similarly, if $a_1=a_2=0.0075$ and $b_1=b_2=30$ then all three routes would take 60 min in their respective equilibria.

Another form of the Braess' Paradox is shown with all three routes as general linear functions:

$$\begin{aligned}\text{TC}_1 &= a_1x_Y+b_1\\ \text{TC}_2 &= a_2x_Z+b_2\\ \text{TC}_3 &= a_3x_{(Y+Z)}+b_3\end{aligned}$$

where $0\leq x_i\leq 1$ and $x_1+x_2+x_3=1$ and $b_3<b_1$, b_2 since the connector is a short road.

For simplicity, routes 1 and 2 are identical.

The Y and Z nodes in Fig. 4.11 are best understood as chokepoints. Instead of route 1 having an inflection point as in Fig. 4.10, the inflection

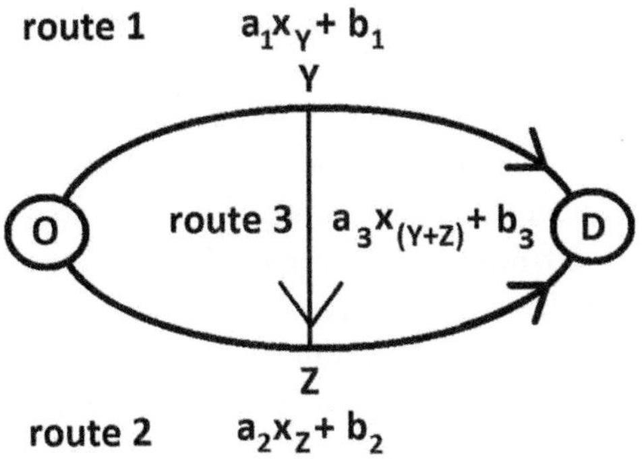

Fig. 4.11 Generalized version of Braess' Paradox.

point is where route 1 turns and becomes the connecting road. For example, making TC_1 a function of x_Y recognizes that it is affected by the proportion of commuters who choose route 1 straight to D and the proportion of commuters who choose route 1 merely to use the $Y-Z$ connector as part of route 3. Thus

$$x_Y = x_1 + x_3$$
$$x_Z = x_2 + x_3$$
$$x_{(Y+Z)} = (x_1 + x_3) + (x_2 + x_3) = x_1 + x_2 + 2x_3$$

The total cost for all three routes must be equal in a Nash equilibrium:

$$a_1(x_1 + x_3) + b_1 = a_2(x_2 + x_3) + b_2 = a_3(x_1 + x_2 + 2x_3) + b_3 \tag{4.15}$$

Looking at the first two sides of Eq. (4.15) and noting that $b_1 = b_2$ and $a_1 = a_2$, means

$(x_1 + x_3) = (x_2 + x_3)$ or $x_1 = x_2$ in equilibrium. This makes sense since both routes are identical.

Looking at the second and third sides of Eq. (4.15) and noting that $x_1 = x_2$ means

$$a_2(x_2 + x_3) + b_2 = a_3(2x_2 + 2x_3) + b_3 \text{ or}$$
$$(b_2 - b_3)/(2a_3 - a_2) = (x_2 + x_3) \tag{4.16}$$

Since $x_1 + x_2 + x_3 = 1$ Eq. (4.16) becomes

$$(b_2 - b_3)/(2a_3 - a_2) = (1 - x_1) \text{ or}$$
$$x_1 \text{ and } x_2 = 1 - (b_2 - b_3)/(2a_3 - a_2) \tag{4.17}$$

Thus,

$$x_3 = 1 - 2[1 - (b_2 - b_3)/(2a_3 - a_1)] \tag{4.18}$$

With the shares on routes 1 and 2 being equal and the share on route 3 being double those, the only solution is where 50% of the commuters choose route 3 and 25% apiece choose routes 1 and 2. Since $x_3 < 1$, route 3 is not a dominant strategy, but trial-and-error leads to the Nash equilibrium.

In effect, the connecting road is meant to be a shortcut and commuters, acting in their own self-interest, are attracted to it. But when every commuter thinks likewise there is collective overuse that leads to a longer travel time for all. This result is a Nash equilibrium that is not Pareto optimal. If traffic returned to the allocation of commuters with their commitments to either route 1 or 2 exclusively, it would be a Pareto-improvement. Of course, because the shortcut exists, that allocation is no longer a Nash equilibrium. Why? Because a driver always has an incentive to switch roads and use route 3 without considering that others will do the same.[p] Only an authority acting for the benefit of all commuters could effectively stop this behavior which is akin to an incentive to cheat. Either entry quotas or tolls would have to be enacted.

Fig. 4.12 is a subtler illustration of Braess' Paradox. Junction node (*J*) in between *O* and *D* obscures the idea that, say, switching from route 1 to 4 at *J* is the same thing as using the $Y-Z$ connector in Figs. 4.10 and 4.11.[q] In fact, treating $Y-Z$ as costing zero travel time in Fig. 4.10 is akin to simply making it a node. Fig. 4.12 looks like two versions of Fig. 4.9 fused together and this carries over into the Nash equilibrium. Commuters would use routes 2 and 4 up to the point that the time cost equals routes 1 and 3 with $b_1 = b_3$. In effect, all four paths will take the same amount of time. Of course, moving half of the commuters using the congestible routes 2 and 4 to the noncongestible routes 1 and 3 would be Pareto optimal. If (*J*) does not have properties leading to Braess' Paradox or if (*J*) only allowed connections between routes 1 and 3 and between routes 2 and 4 then the socially optimal result is possible without an authority intervening.

[p] This scenario is similar to the Prisoners' Dilemma. The Nash equilibrium of mutual cheating has a lesser payoff for all concerned when compared to the Pareto-improving decision to mutually cooperate. The problem is that the latter is not a stable choice since a player would be better off cheating amidst all the other cooperative players. In effect, the shortcut road is akin to cheating on the intended effect of making a choice for route 1 or 2 and sticking with it. While there are methods to engender cooperation in Prisoners' Dilemma games, they involve other players using multiple interactions to punish the cheater. For these methods, see Axelrod (1984). The problem is that it is difficult to envision a group of commuters working together to punish a renegade. Proper infrastructure planning and traffic control would be the preferred solution.

[q] For a similar figure and analysis see Roughgarden (2005, pp. 30–31).

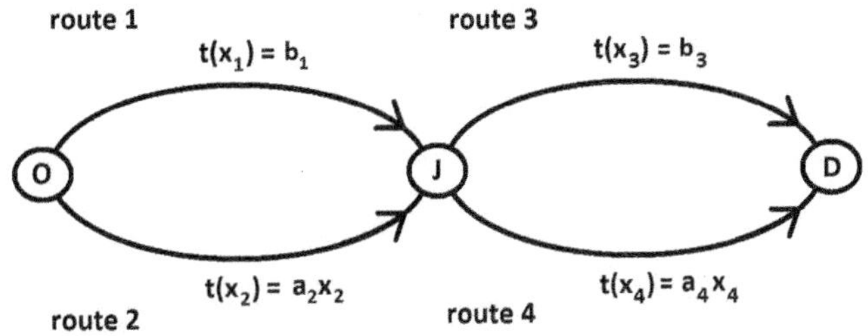

Fig. 4.12 Braess' Paradox in a junction.

Can Braess' Paradox be overcome? In real-world urban networks of multiple roads in a grid, or even a set of just a few intercity highways offering ways to get from city A to city B, one could only, at best, suspect that a less efficient route is being taken by the commuters. The problem with any network is that the removal of a single road (i.e., a localized solution) may cause a problem elsewhere in the network. Computer simulations of different scenarios showing the effects of different roads being removed might show evidence of Braess' Paradox through trial and error. In any case, it is a cautionary tale for network planners.

Issues and problems going forward

While transportation technology may improve over time, seasonality and the Earth's topography are basically fixed phenomena. Global climate change is the geographical exception. The degree and speed of this change is by no means fully understood or agreed to among various governments and businesses. To the extent that this filters into socio-political decisions, transportation networks and their support infrastructure will be forced to adjust.

Traffic planning, even within small networks with a fixed number of commuters, is very complex. There is a tension between self-interest and authoritative control when it comes to mitigating the congestion problem. Will emerging transportation technology resolve this tension in one direction or the other? Each mode of transport has different mixes of private control and government regulation. It cannot, therefore, be expected that each mode will adopt new technologies in the same way and at the same speed. The financial and political problems facing partial or system-wide improvements to a transportation network are likely to remain so long as funding and supplies are limited.

References

Applegate, D.L., Bixby, R.E., Chvatal, V., Cook, W.J., 2006. The Traveling Salesman: A Computational Study. Princeton University Press, Princeton, NJ.
Axelrod, R., 1984. The Evolution of Cooperation. Basic Books, New York.
Braess, D., et al., 2005. On a paradox of traffic planning. Transp. Sci. 39 (4), 446–450.
Harper, D.G.C., 1982. Competitive foraging in mallards: 'ideal free' ducks. Anim. Behav. 30, 575–584.
Kolata, G., 1990, December 25. What if They Closed 42d Street and Nobody Noticed? New York Times.
Pigou, A.C., 1920. The Economics of Welfare. Macmillan, London.
Prokop, D., 2002. The logistics of air cargo co-mingling at Ted Stevens Anchorage International Airport. J. Air Transp. Manag. 8 (2), 109–114.
Prokop, D., 2008. Air cargo's cutting edge: transfer flexibility in anchorage. Can. J. Transp. 1 (Pt. 2), 99–110.
Roughgarden, T., 2005. Selfish Routing and the Price of Anarchy. MIT Press, Cambridge, MA.
Roughgarden, T., Tardos, E., 2002. How bad is selfish routing? J. ACM 49 (2), 236–259.
Schelling, T.C., 1978. Micromotives and Macrobehavior. W.W. Norton, New York.
Shapiro, C., Varian, H.R., 1999. Information Rules: A Strategic Guide to the Network Economy. Harvard Business School Press, Boston, MA.

Further reading

Downs, A., 1962. The law of peak-hour expressway congestion. Traffic Q. 16 (3), 393–409.
Downs, A., 2004. Still Stuck in Traffic: Coping with Peak-Hour Traffic Congestion. Brookings Institution Press, Washington, DC.
Knight, F.H., 1924. Some fallacies in the interpretation of social cost. Q. J. Econ. 38 (4), 582–606.
Prokop, D.J., 2017. Global Supply Chain Security and Management: Appraising Programs, Preventing Crimes. Butterworth Heinemann, Cambridge, MA.
Thomson, J.M., 1977. Great Cities and Their Traffic. Victor Gollancz, London.

CHAPTER 5

Transportation fleet management

Private fleet vs for-hire

From a transportation perspective, the choice between a company maintaining its own fleet and using a for-hire carrier is the choice between insourcing and outsourcing. The choice to outsource is easy if the transportation services required are not too specialized or customized and there is enough competition among for-hire carriers to keep freight rates relatively low (i.e., at a reasonable margin above costs) while offering sufficient carrying capacity. The decision for the company becomes harder if control of the transportation process is critical. In other words, while the company must take on fixed costs associated with maintaining a private fleet, it does have command-and-control over the transportation function as opposed to having to play the spot market or negotiate the bill of lading and the freight rate with a for-hire carrier. Here, the company wants to control scheduling and routing. It also wants sufficient access to any specialized conveyances that the company requires.[a]

Of the five modes of transportation, all but pipelines can be assembled into fleets of conveyances. Of the four modes remaining, only rail is not appropriate for a private fleet because all of the support infrastructure must be built by the company as well. This represents a lot of fixed cost taken on before inhouse services can begin. In other words, there is a lot of risk the company would take on. This leaves air, water vessel, and motor carriers as possible choices for a private fleet.

[a] There is no a priori answer as to the net effect of a private fleet on a company's operations and finances. Furthermore, the transportation function has spillovers into other areas of the business, which further complicates such calculations. Owning transport assets (i.e., conveyances and infrastructure such as terminals, garages, repair shops, etc.) expand the company's balance sheet for good or bad. On the other hand, while customer fulfillment improves, these extra costs of service will raise prices. At the same time, private motor carriers' logos emblazoned across the sides of trailers, provide effective advertising to motorists on shared roadways. Are customers willing to pay more because of the company's stronger control of transportation? Does the extra advertising induce them to buy more than otherwise? Some of these positive and negative cost effects are summarized in Farris and Pohlen (2008), Table 1.

Transportation Operations Management
https://doi.org/10.1016/B978-0-12-815415-1.00005-7

As noted in Chapter 3, Amazon has been building its own private fleet of air freighters. The intent is to enhance its own last-mile services while being less reliant on the air cargo integrators, FedEx, and UPS. Other prominent examples of private air freighter fleets are Boeing's set of four 787–400 conversions and Airbus' set of five A300 conversions. These freighters enhance their respective company's manufacturing of aircraft by specializing in transporting large and awkward subassemblies such as wings. Boeing's fleet, known as "Dreamlifters," are extra-large aircraft developed in the mid-2000s to speed the transfer of large components along the company's multi-country supply chain which it developed for its 787 Dreamliner aircraft. Being the world's longest air freighter, the Dreamlifter saved the company from relying on slower ocean vessel and ground transport. Airbus' freighters, known as "Belugas," perform similar duty among the company's European production facilities. A new generation of freighters, called BelugaXL, has been developed. The first two of a projected fleet of six freighters went into service in 2020. With production of Airbus' double-decker freighters, the A380, ending in 2022, the Belugas will be used to transport subassemblies for the company's largest remaining model, the A350.

Fixed costs for commercial water vessels are not as large a proportion of operating costs as rail. Yet, they can be expensive because of the need to be large enough to validate their use as a private fleet in order to facilitate production and distribution. In other words, there are no economies of scale if a company wishes to move less than a few hundred shipping containers by vessel or barge. In comparison, ocean vessel companies consider 1–2 thousand twenty-foot equivalent unit (TEU) vessels to be small.[b] These would likely be built with enough regularity to make shipbuilding costs manageable. But if a company were looking to own a vessel to make voyages with under 1000 TEUs, it is likely to require a special build.

A good example of private water vessels is global energy companies, which carry their own crude oil, natural gas (compressed or liquified), and various refined fuels. Several of these companies maintain their own tanker fleets (e.g., BP, Chevron, Exxon, and Shell). Of course, these can be chartered by other companies as well. This sharing of capacity helps validate the investment in a private fleet given that these large companies are dependent on a commodity with a variable supply, subject to world prices, and vulnerable to socio-political shocks. However, most of these companies' products are transported by independent tanker companies under charter

[b] For a review of the small vessel market, see Barnard (2017).

agreements. These charters can be arranged for a single voyage or for a longer time period (typically on a monthly basis) over which the company can run multiple voyages. Time charter agreements can range from requiring the company to pay only for costs related to the voyages (i.e., fuel, dockage fees, etc.) all the way to paying all maintenance costs associated with the vessels. These so-called bareboat charters basically require the company to hire the crew and operate as if it owned the vessel.

Events such as the spike in oil prices in 1973 due to the OPEC crisis, the oil price collapse in the mid-1980s, and the regulatory effects of the Exxon Valdez oil spill in 1989 highlight the fact that fleet ownership adds another level of risk on top of those related to the oil company's core business of energy exploration and extraction.[c] In US waters, the extra cost of regulatory mandated double-hull vessels and escort vessels shifted the advantage to the independent tanker companies.

Commercial trucks, whether private or for-hire, must be registered with the Federal Motor Carrier Safety Administration (FMCSA). FMCSA regulates all interstate motor carrier transport; and it also licenses vehicles engaged in intrastate transport. In 2021 there were 1.8 million registered motor carriers. Of these, 51% operated as for-hire carriers, 39% as private fleets, and 8% as both.[d] Of the 8.4 million drivers employed in the motor carrier sector, 39% worked for private fleets. Of the 7.6 million vehicles used in the motor carrier sector, 40% were used in private fleets. Naturally, most of the companies maintain small private fleets. In fact, 93% of them had fleets of 10 vehicles or less. However, fleets exceeding 100 vehicles were maintained by 2000 companies. Of these companies, 112 maintained fleets of at least 1000 vehicles.

The largest fleets made up of straight trucks as opposed to tractors and trailers were dominated by companies specializing in construction, utilities, and waste management. Of course, these tend to be highly specialized vehicles. The largest fleets using tractors and trailers were dominated by food and beverage companies (e.g., Coca-Cola, Kroger, PepsiCo, and Sysco), retail (e.g., Wal-Mart), and agri-food (e.g., Nutrien Ag Solutions).[e]

[c] For a complete review of the causes and regulatory aftermath of the Exxon Valdez oil spill, see Alaska Oil Spill Commission (1990) and Ott (2005).

[d] The remaining 2% is classified as "other." This is defined as "Companies registered to transport property and/or passengers and characterized as one or more of the following: migrant, US mail, federal government, state government, local government, Indian tribe, or other." See Federal Motor Carrier Safety Administration (2021).

[e] For a detailed list of the top 500 private fleets, see FleetOwner 500 (2021).

The operators of private conveyances are an extension of the company and, as such, may be trained in performing duties that a for-hire carrier would not perform. At a minimum, these operators have direct access to the company's resources (e.g., the sales team), which may be useful when dealing with dock receivers and managers at the point of destination. On the other hand, any damage that occurs during transport is the direct responsibility of the company. By contrast, using a for-hire carrier would shield the company in its role as consignor while the consignee, for-hire carrier, and the cargo insurance company investigate and settle any damage claims. While the company may carry its own insurance to mitigate against large claims it will no doubt be seen by its customer as directly responsible for any damages. This means there are brand and reputation issues to consider.

Of course, even the customer service and fulfillment options are limited to inputs and outputs shipped directly to and from the company. It cannot control the transportation used by other companies further upstream and downstream along the supply chain unless it owns those companies as well. And it faces a back-haul problem since it likely can only carry items it owns. To do otherwise would turn the private conveyance into a for-hire carrier making it subject to a variety of federal and state regulations, which add to compliance costs. Of course, hours-of-service (HOS) regulations and electronic logging device (ELD) mandates apply to both private fleets and for-hire carriers. Basically, companies that move enough products to ensure capacity utilization and wish to use command-and-control to ease inventories, improve customer fulfillment, etc. are good candidates for private fleets.[f] The more specialization required in handling the product (e.g., fragility, perishability, etc.) adds to this.

Avoiding fixed costs

Own vs lease

Companies with private fleets and for-hire carriers each have the choice between owning a conveyance and leasing it over a period of time. Ownership gives full control while leasing offers more flexibility. Conveyances such as trucks, ships, and airplanes can be leased. Pipelines and railways, on the other hand, are built and owned by the service provider. In a leasing

[f] In fact, large companies like Wal-Mart can use their private fleet of thousands of straight trucks, tractors, and trailers as leverage when they need to negotiate more standardized services with for-hire carriers. See Schulz (2010; p. 30).

arrangement, the lessor wishes to receive a suitable return on invested capital; that is, a return on the outlay of funds used to purchase the conveyance. The lessee, on the other hand, is trying to avoid the cost of owning the conveyance while generating suitable sales revenue from operating it. The lessor's activity is about investment while the lessee's activity is about operations and how to finance them.[g]

A good example of the leasing option is found in the air carrier mode. There are two prominent types of operating leases. With a dry lease, the lessor provides only the aircraft to the air carrier. The air carrier is required to perform all necessary maintenance and carry insurance on the aircraft. A wet lease includes the aircraft and at least one crew member (typically starting with the pilot) and the lessor also provides the insurance. Of course, the air carrier must still pay all operating costs (i.e., aviation fuel, fees for airport landing slots, etc.). From the lessor's perspective the dry lease gives it less risk since it does not have to hire and take responsibility for the operational expertise of pilots and other crew members. Lessors who prefer this option tend to be banks and other finance companies that prefer to own assets rather than develop expertise in operations. However, leases made among air carriers are more convenient as wet leases since the lessor-air carrier has all necessary operational expertise. These are also useful when the lessee-air carrier is looking for a quick way to handle a shortage of carrying capacity during an emergency or a spike in demand for carrying capacity.

Another advantage air carriers derive from leasing is that the turnover in aircraft keeps the fleet relatively new and, therefore, able to take advantage of new and emerging technology. Air carriers which purchase aircraft have an incentive to keep them in service for many years so as to validate the purchase cost, the investment in maintenance equipment and spare parts, etc. The drawback is the fleet can become less efficient relative to available technology on newer aircraft. Of course, with flexibility from leasing comes the risk of volatility in lease financing costs if cargo demand grows faster than leasable capacity.

From the perspective of the for-hire carrier as lessee, the economic choice between leasing and owning is made by comparing the net present cost (NPC) of the two options. From the point of view of the lessor, it would be comparing the mirror image, the more familiar net present value (NPV)

[g] A hybrid of the lease and ownership options is the capital lease, which is an operating lease with an option to buy at some discounted price at the end of the lease. For an application of this in the context of aircraft financing, see Chen et al. (2018).

of issuing a lease or selling the conveyance outright. It is assumed that a given conveyance will generate the same level of sales revenue per time period for the for-hire carrier under either a lease or ownership. The for-hire carrier would have to calculate the following:

$$\mathrm{NPC}_{\mathrm{lease}} = IO + \sum\nolimits_{i=1}^{n} [LP_i/(1+r)^n] \tag{5.1}$$

$$\mathrm{NPC}_{\mathrm{purchase}} = IO + \sum\nolimits_{i=1}^{n} [LP_i/(1+r)^n] - RV_n/(1+r)^n - (IO - RV_n)/n \tag{5.2}$$

where *IO* is the initial outlay; *LP* is the lease or loan payment as applicable; *RV* is the residual value at end-time (n); r is the interest rate or opportunity cost of capital invested.

Eq. (5.2) applies to a loan as a way to finance the purchase. If, instead, the conveyance was bought outright with cash then the equation would reduce by losing the second term. The fourth term shows straight-line depreciation expressed as the difference between *IO* and *RV* divided evenly over the duration of the loan (n). Of course, accelerated depreciation may be allowed in some jurisdictions. Since the for-hire carrier would be entitled to the residual value of the conveyance once the loan is paid off and is also entitled to depreciate the asset, the third and fourth terms are subtracted. These are benefits derived from ownership; hence, they are negative costs. Only if Eq. (5.1) is less than Eq. (5.2) is leasing preferred since it imposes a lower cost on the for-hire carrier over the time period.

RV in Eq. (5.2) is affected by the duration (n) of the loan. It is also affected by market conditions at the end of the loan period. How useful is the conveyance in this future time period relative to the latest available technology? In other words, while *RV* and the ability to write off depreciation from taxes are important benefits from ownership, they do come with risk of obsolescence, higher maintenance costs, etc. Eqs. (5.1) and (5.2) may also differ in other forms of tax treatment. If lease or loan payments are tax deductible, LP_i needs to be multiplied by the tax factor $(1 - t)$ to lower the size of the cash outflow for the lease or loan as applicable. The tax rate (t) is assumed to be a flat rate. Of course, if the tax regime is progressive then higher rates apply as the fleet earns higher sales revenue.

Motor carrier owner-operators

From the perspective of a multivehicle, for-hire motor carrier, topping up an established fleet with owner-operators is a good way to increase routing, service options, etc. without taking on any fixed costs associated with ownership, loans, and leases. The owner-operator, comprised of an independent driver with a straight truck or tractor-trailer, acts as an agent of the for-hire carrier which, of course, does confer responsibilities on the latter vis-à-vis the consignors who will be dealing with the owner-operator at the time of pick-up or delivery.

While owner-operators add to the flexibility of the motor carrier sector, there is a debate over their true status in a business. The question boils down to: are they really agents or are they more like employees of for-hire carriers? The question is important and recently it was looked at seriously in California. Basically, while motor carrier pricing and routing has been deregulated since 1980 at the interstate level and since 1994 at the intrastate level, owner-operator status has the potential to add further regulations on the labor side of operations.

The California law, referred to as AB5, uses an "ABC" test to determine the owner-operator and independent contractor status. AB5 became law in 2019. The law amended the California Labor Code and Unemployment Insurance Code as they relate to employees and independent contractors. There are restrictions on a business from hiring independent contractors to top-up its operations unless certain criteria are met.

A preliminary injunction against the law's enforcement in the motor carrier sector was issued in early in 2020 by a US District Court (i.e., a federal court). An appeals court overturned the injunction later that year. While the California Trucking Association issued a further appeal, it seems likely that the motor carrier sector will not be exempt from the new law.

Why the need for this regulation? The intent is to give contractors in the gig economy some degree of protection and access to benefits that are typically provided to employees. Such benefits are minimum wage, workers' compensation, paid leave, sick days, and the right to unionize. Of course, the Teamsters Union supports the new law since it provides an opportunity to organize drayage vehicle operators at ports if enough of them feel misclassified as independent contractors by the companies which hired them.

Thus, Uber and Lyft drivers in California must be treated as employees of these companies and the same will likely be the case for owner-operators working as agents for other for-hire motor carriers. Any newly designated employers would be taking on costs that would not normally be a part of a service contract. An agent's contract does not have to be renewed. In parallel manner, can a worker in California be laid-off as easily? How would background checks be dealt with under these different cases?

AB5 includes an "ABC" test to allow businesses to determine if they are de facto employers hiring de facto employees or simply businesses outsourcing activities to an agent. This test was based on guidance from a 2018 California Supreme Court ruling which penalized Dynamex Operations West, Inc. for misclassifying its delivery drivers as contractors rather than employees. There are three questions:

(A) Is the agent free of control and direction by the business?
(B) Is the agent's work outside of the business' usual work?
(C) Does the agent customarily perform this work as part of an independently established trade or occupation?

Naturally, question (B) runs against the frequent practice of a motor carrier hiring an independent motor carrier (i.e., an owner-operator) to perform haulage on its behalf. Basically, under AB5, contracting for someone who practices a company's core business needs to be treated as an employee.

The question is: Does it make sense to treat motor carrier drivers who own their own conveyances in the same way as other forms of labor? Although not covered by the original federal injunction, the same question could apply to those who use an app on their smartphone to turn their private cars into ride-sharing vehicles. Are gig drivers and owner-operators in need of an employer-provided safety net of benefits? Does the agent/worker owning the conveyance set him apart from other forms of labor? If the work is seen as a "gig" by the service provider, why block the hiring party and the agent from their ability to negotiate a service contract? Are businesses exploiting the gig economy or are both parties simply taking advantage of the flexibility they have? These are important questions to consider now that the California law has been scrutinized by other states.

Pollution is an example of a market failure because it affects parties who are external to the transaction between the buyer and the seller. The transaction, though beneficial to the two parties, generates pollution as a byproduct. This is where the word externality comes from. Pollution regulation is designed so that the two parties in the private transaction are made to consider the third-party (or societal) effects of their activities. But attempts to reclassify labor are not about external effects. There is no third-party who is harmed by the gig economy or by hiring owner-operators.

The independent owner-operator is a legitimate business model that requires upfront investment in trucks or tractors and trailers as well as the necessary licenses. They want the flexibility, and tax benefits, of an agency relationship. In many ways, this sets motor carriers apart from other modes of transportation. Is that mode less stable than others? Often it is. But by being more competitive, it incentivizes a level of cost control that is ultimately good for the consumer at the end of the supply chain.

Interstate motor carriers were deregulated through the Motor Carrier Act (1980) in terms of freight rates and routing. These terms would no longer be considered by the government when determining public convenience and necessity. Intrastate motor carriers were subsequently deregulated in 1994 thereby leaving states only with jurisdiction over safety (e.g., truck configuration, weight, and insurance coverage). It came from an unlikely source. The Federal Aviation Administration Authorization Act (1994) provided that "a State, political subdivision of a State, or political authority of two or more States may not enact or enforce a law, regulation, or other provision having the force and effect of law related to a price, route, or service of any motor carrier." (49 U.S.C. § 14501(c)(1)). Of course, exceptions exist for motor carriers affiliated with direct air carriers and motor carriers hauling property (i.e., moving companies).

Economist Ronald Coase once asked a simple but powerful question: Why do firms exist? In effect, why do we have employers and employees? His answer was that it was a way to control transaction costs. Sometimes command-and-control is better than negotiating and contracting out. Regarding owner-operators, what is the difference between working under contracts with other motor carriers and being employees of motor carriers? Question (B) of the ABC test turns the well-established theory of the firm on its head. Question (B) implies that hiring within one's core competency is akin to taking on an employee. Yet, it is relatively easy to establish a service contract in this case because both parties know fairly well what that service is and how it should be performed.

Firms are best understood as organizations formed to avoid the problem of "incomplete" contracts. In this regard, employees normally do not have all of their duties codified in a service contract because it would be impossible to predict what these would be given all the possible changes in the internal and external conditions affecting a firm. It would also not make sense to open negotiations on a new contract every time one party wanted another to adapt to, say, the latest changes in technology. Command-and-control works better when the hiring party needs a long-term relationship while the range of required duties is in a state of flux.

The ABC test implies that independent contracting is a market failure. On the contrary, spot markets and gig workers are examples of markets working quite well. But is AB5 an inadvertent attempt to reregulate motor carriers? Its hiring cost would certainly have an indirect effect on freight rates. Also, at the federal level, the House of Representatives passed the Protecting the Right to Organize Act in 2019 and again in 2021 under a new Congress. It includes AB5's ABC test in the legislation. Although not likely to pass the Senate due to the filibuster rule, the debate over access to employee benefits and the right to unionize is by no means over in the transportation sector.

Front-haul vs back-haul

As noted in Chapter 1, for every front-haul there is a back-haul because it is assumed that the carrier wishes to return eventually to its point of origin or domicile. If freight is available on the back-haul the carrier would earn revenue to offset some of the sunk costs of the return trip. What are the costs incurred on front-hauls and back-hauls? Appropriate cost allocation would suggest the following:

- Front-haul costs = cost to move freight on the front-haul + cost to return empty
- Revenue-earning back-haul costs = cost to move freight on the back-haul − cost to return empty

Why is the cost to return empty allocated to the front-haul's costs? If there is no revenue-earning back-haul it makes sense to say that the front-haul propagates all costs incurred over the round-trip. These would be the costs the carrier would allocate to the front-haul consignor. But if there were a back-haul consignor the only costs it propagates are those extra costs of actually carrying the freight. The cost of an empty back-haul remains inseparable from a font-haul. This is why the cost to return empty is deducted from revenue-earning back-hauls. Over a given round-trip, the marginal cost of a front-haul is always higher than the marginal cost of a back-haul.[h]

There is also the possibility that carrier A's back-haul route is carrier B's front-haul route. Carrier B, in other words, is domiciled at carrier A's destination. What would happen within these seemingly mirror-imaged markets? There are four possibilities: (1) perfect competition forces freight rates down to carrier A's lower marginal cost; (2) a lack of competition keeps freight rates from falling below carrier B's higher marginal cost; (3) conflict

[h] For a discussion of front-haul and back-haul pricing when all carriers move in the same direction, see Prentice and Prokop (2016; pp. 145–148).

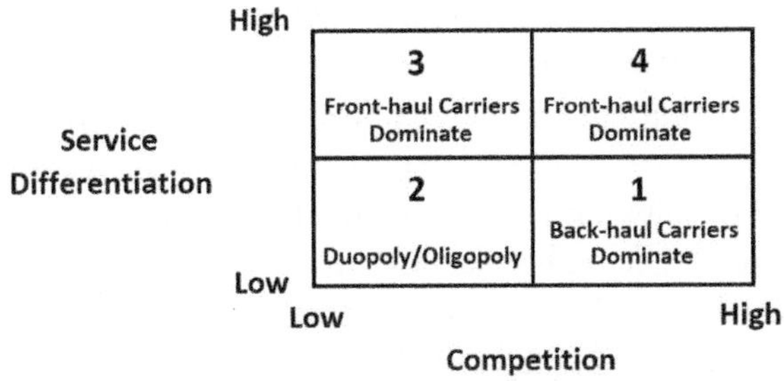

Fig. 5.1 Matrix of outcomes among front-haul and back-haul carriers.

is avoided because of logistical constraints; or (4) conflict is avoided because of preestablished supply chain relationships. Fig. 5.1 compares these four possibilities in terms of levels of competition and service differentiation.

Consider the perfect competition case under possibility 1. Carriers A and B would be matched closely in their hauling services and available capacity. Carrier B has to compete against the discount that carrier A would offer to consignors in order to try to fill its back-hauls. Since competition typically implies many carriers, it makes sense to assume that carriers A and B are representatives of several more carriers within their respective front-haul and back-haul markets.[i] Competition would pressure carrier B to lower costs, and therefore its freight rate, to try to compete with A or else cede the market and look to establish a viable front-haul route elsewhere. Transport networks would sort themselves such that carriers' moves were roughly in the same direction so as not to have higher cost front-haul routes run parallel with lower cost back-haul routes.

Possibility 2 suggests that the freight market may not be competitive due to carriers facing barriers to entry. Alternatively, there could be a limited number of consignors wishing to tender freight. In this case, the freight market could literally have just two carriers (i.e., a duopoly) on the supply side. If a lack of competition did not incentivize cost control there may, instead, be incentives for carrier A not to discount its back-haul and simply match carrier B's front-haul freight rate, which covers the latter's marginal cost. This would be akin to duopolistic behavior whereby carrier A knows that there is more profit to be had in splitting the market rather than "race to the bottom"

[i] Another assumption in the standard model of perfect competition is unlimited product demand at the equilibrium price. This means that individual firms face a demand curve that is infinitely price-elastic. In the freight market, this implies that there are more than enough consignors available to allow carriers to equate their marginal revenue with marginal cost.

via tit-for-tat competitive discounts on freight rates.[j] For this to work, carrier A must feel there are enough back-haul shipments available to be shared in this way. Given the limited number of consignors, both carriers will charge a freight rate equal to carrier B's marginal cost and split the market. The equilibrium number of shipments carried would be less than in possibility 1 and the freight rate would be higher. Just like in the highly competitive case, the carriers are not differentiated by haulage services and available capacity. However, if market splitting did not allow carrier A to fill all of its available back-hauls it has an incentive to lower its freight rate just below B's marginal cost and capture some or all of the latter's market share. In this way, the market is ceded in part or in full to carrier A just like in the perfect competition case.

Possibility 3 is more realistic than possibilities 1 and 2 because it views transportation as time and place sensitive. It also recognizes that the front-haul is the driving force when a carrier plans its routes. So, while carrier A would like to have a consignor for the back-haul it may not arrive in time for the required pick-up. Alternatively, it might arrive too early and prefer not to wait around for the required pick-up time. In other words, carrier A's front-haul consignor's time and place requirements may not match well with those of some or all back-haul consignors. Perhaps the front-haul and back-haul consignors require specialty haulage which are not compatible (e.g., bulk tanker vs palletized freight, general freight vs hazardous material, etc.). These logistical constraints, in effect, cede carrier A's back-hauls to carrier B. The two markets are not compatible and carriers A and B have no conflict of interest. These logistical constraints are barriers to entry and serve to limit the level of competition in the freight market.

Possibility 4 also adds more realism compared to possibilities 1 and 2. Instead of carriers A and B feeling they are competing for the same consignors each has the incentive to differentiate themselves rather than submit to near-perfect competition with its concomitant homogeneity of services. Carriers A and B may try to establish a strategic rather than a transactional relationship with the consignors at or near their respective domiciles. In other words, they offer customized services that build loyalty and create

[j] This scenario deviates from the standard duopoly model, which assumes a homogeneous product and equal marginal costs for the two firms. Of course, since marginal costs on the back-haul are always lower than those on the front-haul, carrier B cannot set a freight rate below its marginal cost to try to match A. The equilibrium in the standard duopoly model has price equal to marginal cost for both firms, which is the same result as under perfect competition. It is also a Nash equilibrium.

certainty in deliveries along the supply chain they are serving. This means that carriers compete not just on time, place, and available capacity but also on the quality of support services.[k] If a consignor sees a carrier as a supply chain partner akin to a vendor of critical inputs, it may be willing to pay a premium for a particular carrier's services. Since the front-haul propagates the round-trip, it makes sense for a given carrier to differentiate itself to the benefit of potential front-haul consignors. Back-haul consignors would only be a secondary consideration. In effect, carrier A must take on empty back-hauls because a discount on carriage is not important for the consignors domiciled near carrier B. The only back-hauls carrier A could attract would be those available on the spot market—meaning consignors with occasional shipments. Unlike the logistical barriers to entry noted in possibility 3, carriers do face a high level of competition. Service differentiation is an attempt to stand out from the competition.

Of course, it is not unheard of for back-haul opportunities to be refused. For example, demand for containerized imports from China to the United States was so strong in late 2020 that some ocean vessel carriers did not leave empty containers on hand to facilitate US exports back to Asia. The reason was that the carriers wanted to keep the containers (which they, in fact, own) for empty back-hauls to Asia in order to maintain the lucrative cycle of imports. When there is a shortage of vessels and/or containers to maintain a front-haul, such things can happen. In the ocean vessel mode, however, US regulators keep a watchful eye on the activities of the carriers since the majority of them are foreign-based.[l]

Fleet management

The concepts of interlining and hub-and-spoke networks introduced in Chapter 1 were examples of fleet management. As applications of economies of scale they demonstrate that attention to routing and how different-sized conveyances are deployed (e.g., using smaller aircraft on spokes) can enhance efficiency.

Once it is determined which party will own the fleet it should be managed by the users to promote longevity of the equipment as well as efficiency

[k] Support services could include: dedicated carriage (i.e., only the consignor's freight is onboard), state-of-the-art freight tracking, logistical support services (e.g., warehousing), etc.

[l] See Gallagher (2020).

in pick-up and deliveries. The former means handling maintenance and repairs as they come up. In other words, a good relationship with the original equipment manufacturer (OEM) is essential. If the for-hire carrier does not own the conveyance it needs to know how strong the lessor's relationship is with the OEM. What works in a supply chain relationship is also necessary in a lessor-lessee relationship. Basically, what situations are likely to come up and is the OEM able to deal with them in a timely manner? Working with the OEM also helps when deciding on the time to replace the conveyance due to age, new technology, etc.

The conveyances used should be appropriate to the marketplace. Similar to deploying different-sized aircraft on hubs-and-spokes this means distinguishing between rural and urban conditions for motor carriers, lengths of runways for aircraft, and dockage space for water vessels. In other words, look for the most challenging parts along the transportation infrastructure and make sure the conveyances can deal with them. Since conveyances need operators, the users need to make sure that wages and benefits are attractive enough to retain qualified operators.

There is no need to assume that the fleet is made up of identical conveyances. Some may be of different carrying capacity, fuel usage, etc. depending on market characteristics and regulations in the jurisdictions involved. A drawback is limited substitutability across routes. For example, a trailer with refrigeration equipment can substitute for a trailer without it but not vice versa. Nonsubstitutable equipment should be treated as subfleets and targeted to their specialty market. On the other hand, modes with common storage vehicles (e.g., truck trailers, rail cars, and shipping containers) offer more flexibility than tractors, locomotives, and water vessels alone. Storage vehicles can be prepositioned and re-positioned along a network; and some may even be shared among different carriers.[m]

In any case, conveyances should be allocated so that their capacity is utilized to the fullest extent. The following equations layout the problem:

$$\sum_{i=1}^{m}\sum_{j=1}^{n} H_{ij} = P_i \quad \text{for every } i = 1, 2, \ldots, m \text{ and } j = 1, 2, \ldots, n \qquad (5.3)$$

[m] Similar to owner-operators moving another for-hire carrier's trailer or container on a flatbed, several railroads have established carpools to share their rolling stock along their interconnected networks. Unlike the motor carrier sector, the less competitive nature of the rail sector means that carpool agreements are subject to oversight by the Surface Transportation Board. For a review of the mathematical models used to formulate rail carpools see Milenkovic and Bojovic (2020), pp. 24–27.

$$\sum_{i=1}^{m}\sum_{j=1}^{n} H_{ij} \leq M_j C_j \quad \text{for every } i=1,2,\ldots,m \text{ and } j=1,2,\ldots,n \quad (5.4)$$

where n is the number of different types of conveyances available; j is a particular type of conveyance out of 1, 2, …, n; m is the number of different types of hauls required (measured in ton-miles); i is a particular type of haul out of 1, 2, …, m; H_{ij} is the number of haul type (i) actually performed by conveyance (j); C_j is the number of conveyance type (j) required; P_i is the predicted number of haul type (i) demanded over the planning period; M_j is the maximum number of hauls that conveyance (j) can perform over the planning period.

Eq. (5.3) states that the number of haul types (m) performed by the number of conveyances deployed (n) needs to be sufficient to meet the predicted demand by consignors for each of those haul types. Eq. (5.4) states that the number of haul types (m) performed by the number of conveyances deployed (n) cannot exceed the product of the number of conveyances (C) and the maximum number of hauls (M) they can carry over the planning period. With these constraints in mind the objective function is to minimize total cost:

$$\sum_{j=1}^{n} \mathrm{FC}_j\, C_j + \sum_{i=1}^{m}\sum_{j=1}^{n} \mathrm{VC}_{ij}\, H_{ij} \quad \text{for every } i=1,2,\ldots,m \text{ and } j=1,2,\ldots,n \quad (5.5)$$

where FC is fixed cost over all conveyance types (n). This occurs even if there are no hauls (m); VC is variable cost over all conveyance types (n) and hauls (m).

The problem is to find a value for the required number of conveyance types (C) to perform the requested hauls (H) so as to minimize Eq. (5.5).[n]

When it comes to routing decisions, it is straightforward to provide more attention to high-volume consignors. These should exemplify the highest level of customer service. Still, once a fleet is in place the classic transportation problem arises; that is, how to set up multiple routes in order to move multiple items from multiple origins to multiple destinations. The items moved could be inputs from multiple sources to multiple factories; finished goods from multiple factories to multiple distribution centers, and so on. With only one origin and destination it is a trivial problem if one conveyance has the capacity to haul enough supply to satisfy the demand. If more capacity is needed then two or more conveyances will be used. However, as noted

[n] Problems like these can be solved using heuristics or algorithms found in mathematical programming. The seminal work is Clarke and Wright (1964)

in Eqs. (5.3) through (5.5) the optimization problem becomes complicated as the ranges of (m) and (n) increase. To further complicate matters are sources of stochastic behavior. Apart from estimating P in Eq. (5.3) there is the "black box" effect of shared infrastructure among other carriers. Traffic and timing will impact variable costs over the planning period.

How would Eq. (5.5) be adjusted to consider sales revenue? In other words, the for-hire carrier wishes to maximize a profit function instead of minimizing a cost function. Eq. (5.6) shows this alternative objective function.

$$\sum_{i=1}^{m}\sum_{j=1}^{n} F_{ij} H_{ij} - \left[\sum_{j=1}^{n} \mathrm{FC}_j C_j + \sum_{i=1}^{m}\sum_{j=1}^{n} \mathrm{VC}_{ij} H_{ij}\right]$$

$$\text{for every } i = 1, 2, \ldots, m \text{ and } j = 1, 2, \ldots, n \qquad (5.6)$$

where F_{ij} is the freight rate charged on haul type (i) performed by conveyance (j).

Solving Eq. (5.6) subject to constraints amounts to maximizing the gap between sales revenue and total cost. An added dimension is that the freight rate (F) is likely endogenous. Recall from Fig. 5.1 that cells 1 and 2 describe conditions approaching perfect competition. While this exogenous price effect may apply to the motor carrier sector under certain conditions, the other four modes will most likely have carriers with some degree of market power.

Basically, the carrier needs to distinguish between the front-haul and the back-haul of a particular conveyance and which of the four cells in the matrix best describes its place in the market. Since the front-haul and back-haul are two distinct markets from the carrier's perspective, the appropriate parts of the round trip's costs can be allocated so as to have a front-haul and back-haul version of Eq. (5.6).

Issues and problems going forward

The choice of how to manage a conveyance—either by ownership or lease—and how to assemble them into fleets—either through private control or for-hire commerce—are choices between command-and-control in operations and flexibility in cost. This is a trade-off. The choice made will affect customer fulfillment and, therefore, the revenue side of the profit equation.

Given that the fleet management problem is complex when set in realistic terms, it should not be surprising that many consignors and for-hire carriers have looked to emerging technology to help ease the burden of trying to optimize fleet operations. Of course, computers and software able to handle large quantities of data and make calculations with increasing speed are useful. But what is required to make this process truly effective is the gathering of relevant and accurate data along with incentives to share it among supply chain partners. This is still a challenge in the transportation sector despite the potential value-add.

References

Alaska Oil Spill Commission, 1990. Spill: The Wreck of the Exxon Valdez; Implications for Safe Transportation of Oil. Final Report. State of Alaska, Juneau, AK.

Barnard, B., 2017. Small ships seduce shipowners. J. Commer. Nov. 1.

Chen, W.-T., Kuancheng, H., Ardiansyah, M., 2018. A mathematical programming model for aircraft leasing decisions. J. Air Transp. Manag. 69, 15–25.

Clarke, G., Wright, J.W., 1964. Scheduling of vehicles from a central depot to a number of delivery points. Oper. Res. 12, 568–581.

Farris, M.T., Pohlen, T.L., 2008. Evaluating the private fleet. Transp. J. 47 (4), 51–66.

Federal Motor Carrier Safety Administration, 2021. Analysis & Information Online. US Department of Transportation, Washington, DC. https://ai.fmcsa.dot.gov/RegistrationStatistics/CustomReports.aspx.

FleetOwner 500, 2021. Top Private Fleets 2021. https://www.fleetowner.com/.

Gallagher, J., 2020. Regulators Warn Container Lines to Stop Refusing US Exports (American Shipper Online. Dec. 16) https://www.freightwaves.com/news/news-alert-regulators-warn-container-lines-to-stop-refusing-us-exports.

Milenkovic, M., Bojovic, N., 2020. Optimization Models for Rail Car Fleet Management. Elsevier, Amsterdam, Netherlands.

Ott, R., 2005. Sound Truths and Corporate Myths: The Legacy of the Exxon Valdez Oil Spill. Dragonfly Sisters Press, Norwich, CT.

Prentice, B.E., Prokop, D., 2016. Concepts of Transportation Economics. World Scientific, Hackensack, NJ.

Schulz, J.D., 2010. Private fleet operations: maintaining the advantage. Logist. Manag., 28–32.

CHAPTER 6

The role of information technology in transportation

From steam to data

The modern economy has benefited from improvements in production. From steam power to the power of artificial intelligence the common theme has been automation in tandem with mass production. Ever since the invention of the steam engine (which displaced the Pony Express), for-hire carriage has been expected to become faster, more reliable, and offer a larger carrying capacity. Couple this with cheaper and faster access to information thanks to desktop computers connected to each other via the Internet.

Another theme that runs through these phases of production is displacement. Examples of this include the printing press (which displaced medieval scribes) through to the one-click-away Uber/Lyft drivers (who are now displacing traditional taxicab companies). In all these cases, markets became more efficient (i.e., using fewer inputs to generate higher-value outputs) in order to fulfill demand. As a result, jobs were lost and those remaining were retasked to utilize the latest technologies. These structural changes are rarely smooth but, at the same time, they are hard to stop.

If these new developments are to be taken advantage of, a new data-driven mindset is needed by all players in the transportation process. Generating products to be transported, providing transportation services, and receiving, storing, or consuming those products, all generate data. Any value-adding activity along a supply chain not only applies to physical movement of tangible items and passengers but also applies to communication among the various players. All of these activities generate data. Will it be useful data? Will it be generated through analyzing every interaction one of the player's feels is important? Will there be enough data generated to make informed decisions? This is the challenge to analogizing data to fuel used power vehicles. Is it the right blend in order to run an engine efficiently and will there be enough available at a reasonable price in order to ensure a goal is met? In other words, all players need to think of themselves as data generators and data refiners.

Transportation Operations Management
https://doi.org/10.1016/B978-0-12-815415-1.00011-2

Of course, one item that proceeds back and forth between supply chain partners is information. In this sense, information is one of the foundations that support all markets and the transactions that take place between buyers and sellers. Today, a lot of information is formulated using data as an abundant raw material. Following the fuel analogy, data is like oil—a gusher of numbers, signals, or other collected facts. The number of bytes (i.e., digital representations of a letter, a number, or a symbol) generated per day is in the quintillions. Where is the source of all this data? Basically, it is everywhere. It comes from every person with a smartphone. It comes from every item affixed with a barcode or a radio frequency identification (RFID) tag. It also comes from every vehicle, machine, and household appliance connected to the Internet. They all generate data—a virtual power source. The earlier industrial revolutions were powered by water, steam, electricity, and oil. Like oil, data is of little use unless it is refined (i.e., processed) into something valuable and actionable.

Data turned into information is akin to oil being turned into, say, fuel or plastic. Likewise, information turned into knowledge is akin to developing a deep understanding of the socioeconomic implications of how fuel facilitates the proliferation of transportation networks throughout the world or developing an understanding of how plastics have made both industrial and household activities more convenient and less costly at the same time.

In contrast to the fuel analogy, data is like sunlight. There are socioeconomic implications of that metaphor as well. Sunlight is a day-to-day phenomenon (except, of course, when there is cloud cover or an eclipse). Sunlight is abundant and "nonrival" in its use meaning that one person's enjoyment of it does not impede another's. And being intangible, the same data can be used over and over again. In this way, a data set analyzed on one user's computer does not impede other users from doing the same thing at the same time.

The marginal cost of sharing data is close to zero. If the data is computerized, emailing it to one, two, or thousands of people at a time takes just one click on the send button. Moving at light speed, it does not have the same cost differentials as mailing one letter, two letters, or thousands of letters through the postal service. However, like paper letters, data is "excludable." It is relatively easy for senders to block unintended users from receiving it. This is where the metaphor of data like sunlight breaks down; however, data like oil still holds up. Oil producers can block people from using their oil by simply affixing a price per barrel and reminding them that taking the oil without paying for it is a crime. In contrast, the abundance and reliability of sunlight make it a costly and futile exercise to bother trying to block someone from enjoying it. Data's nonrivalry (like sunshine) but price-excludability (like oil) makes it a price-excludable public good (also called a club good). Data is a blending of both private goods and public goods; hence, the socioeconomic implications.

Of course, refining oil is a costly and time-consuming technique; and the same goes for data. For data to be turned into information it needs to be standardized into apples-to-apples consistency. Will the software used to process video footage always be able to "tag" a pedestrian as a pedestrian? Can it recognize a moving vehicle in fog as well as on a clear day? What if snow totally, or even partially, obscures road markings and/or signage? Invoices, packing information, etc. used in container transport may come from multiple parties using multiple idiomatic formats. This is a problem; however, this is where digitization comes in.

Digitization and transportation

Electronic logging devices (ELDs), covered in Chapter 2, represent a government-mandated standardization of data. Of course, the private sector is also exploring options for evaluating data and refining it into actionable information. Digitization turns multiple formats of "mushy information" into one format of computer bytes. For example, optical character recognition software can be used to make handwritten documents computer-readable and, therefore, analyzable. If the data is in one format, it can be processed faster and consignors can manage their container bookings on ocean vessels, and other modes of transport, much faster than with traditional methods.

The promise of automation is that it removes people from mundane tasks but improves their accuracy. Apart from gathering data, there is the issue of sharing data. If one party shared its standardized data with all of its stakeholders all of them, presumably, would be better off. The more data that is collected by a manufacturer of self-driving cars from its buyers (who are also the software users), the more information it can share with them (i.e., its "club" members). The same can be said for ocean vessel ports. With enough participation from importers, container terminal operators, ocean carriers, motor carriers, railroads, and freight forwarders, congested ports could provide all users in the "club" with better information related to vessel arrivals, container availability, port clearance times, and intermodal transfers.

Of course, a given road network may handle self-driving cars made by different manufacturers. A given ocean shipping lane has two independent ports at its ends and maybe other ports in-between. Each of these independent organizations may not be willing to share its data let alone any information and/or knowledge they developed from it. A reason to worry about sharing data is cyber theft and computer hacking. Just like stealing oil is illegal so is stealing data. However, stealing oil from silos may leave telltale signs and certainly, an empty silo is left behind. In contrast, when data is stolen, or when computers are hacked, users may not discover the theft for some time—especially if the perpetrators merely copied the data over to their own computers. This is the downside of data being both valuable and "nonrival." A cybersecurity plan is needed. However, since money is limited—and time is money, after all—companies need to prioritize what data is worth gathering, digitizing, refining, and securing. This raises a series of questions:

- What are the company's most pressing issues that are open to data collection?
- Is there a technological platform that can facilitate data gathering, digitizing, refining, and securing?
- Is there internal buy-in across the company when it comes to this process?
- Can and should the data be shared among the supply chain partners? How about with the government and the general public?
- What decisions and/or policies should be made once the data is turned into actionable information and knowledge?

From a supply chain perspective, will data be shared among partners? Will datasets be compatible across different partners' data storage and analyzing procedures? For all its promise, digitization is not flourishing in the transportation industry. In fact, things seem to decelerate into guarded caution when it comes to its adoption. Success seems to be concentrated in the disruptors like Uber and Lyft in the taxi market and Flexport and Convoy in freight forwarding.

Is digitization simply a technology for technology's sake or is there long-term value-add in its adoption? If there is then why the hesitancy and is it justified? Perhaps it is, but tough decisions will have to be made over the next few years. Cyber innovations are moving supersized data sets (i.e., big data) at literally the speed of light. They have a role to play in for-hire transportation.

For-hire transportation involves deploying conveyances to move freight within a defined network along a reliable infrastructure. Those are the tangibles. The time utility and place utility that consignors and consignees derive from a well-done transportation job is an intangible service. These tangibles and intangibles are inseparable. To say otherwise would be akin to saying that 18th century flour mills were automatically more efficient when they moved closer to sources of waterpower. This would only be true if there was equal access to transportation. After all, what is the point of being more productive in milling flour if it could not be transported to market? Happily, flour millers made sure they had access to river barges. In other words, flour's value derives in part from transportation.

Production of services is distinguished from the production of tangible items in that services are dependent on interactions between the buyer and the seller. Buying a muffin from a vending machine is routine compared to ordering a muffin for dessert at a fine restaurant. The greater the buyer-seller interaction the less routine and more subjective the transaction becomes. It also becomes more experiential for both parties. This leads to the concept of VRIN which is an acronym for an input that is valuable, rare, inimitable, and nonsubstitutable.[a] Such inputs have strategic value. Is for-hire transportation a routine activity for the most part or is it more interactive requiring a lot of planning and negotiation? Of course, the answer would depend on a lot of things. But would there be value in digitizing information gathered from consignor-carrier interactions and those of their intermediaries?

Consider Uber and how its tech-driven ride-sharing business is necessarily more interactive than traditional, quasimonopolistic taxi services. It is not just about using smartphones to connect passengers and drivers in the ride-sharing market. Apart from the cost savings from low overhead and using gig drivers, Uber is trying to leverage the digital world to improve its services. For example, in 2019 its Uber Money division began offering digital wallets and mobile banking services to pay its drivers after each ride. With around 100 million rides per month that could add up to a lot of transactions. On the passenger side, it offers no-fee debit cards. Uber claims that 70% of its US-based customers are now using this "instant pay" service.

Apart from becoming a publicly traded company in 2019 Uber's big bet is on its digital/financial experiments building brand loyalty on both sides of the ride-sharing market. If these services build VRIN, then Uber is on the

[a] VRIN derives from the resource-based view of sustained competitive advantage as outlined by Barney (1991).

right track. Consider that Uber also offers its drivers no-fee $100 overdrafts as part of its digital wallet service. That might be very attractive to drivers in poorer locales who need to fill their gas tanks in the morning before heading out to earn their fares. On the other hand, Uber increased its "tax" on drivers who use its destination mode feature. This allows drivers to be paired with sequential passengers heading along the desired route—say, homeward for a driver nearing the end of the workday.

Flexport, the digital freight forwarder founded in 2013, has attracted a lot of venture capital. In fact, over 80% of the seed money that reached the maritime sector in 2019 went to the company according to Thetius, a supply chain intelligence firm.[b] Flexport offers secure, cloud-based visibility by connecting multiple parties involved in the movement of freight. Consignors, carriers, customs agencies, ports, and terminals can collaborate on its platform called Operating System for Global Trade. The intent is to get the paper out of import-export documentation and streamline e-communication through the standardization of documents.

As one might expect, Flexport uses machine learning (discussed below) to add value to its intermediary function. If consignors and for-hire carriers do not feel artificial intelligence (AI) is a core competency, then intermediaries may add value. Access to more of their data means more computer-based "learning" and "experiences." Yet learning is a particular challenge for Flexport because of the lack of standardization which is prevalent in domestic and international trade. Uber's use of smartphones in the ride-sharing market gives it much greater control over how information is received.

Invoices, packing information, waybills, etc. in container transport come in multiple formats from multiple parties. As noted above, digitization requires turning these multiple formats into one. Therefore, optical character recognition software must be used to make the documents computer-readable. If the data is in one format, it can be processed faster and, presumably, Flexport can manage its bookings on ocean vessels, air freighters, and trucks much faster than traditional freight forwarders. The same can be said for its OceanMatch portal which matches consignors of less-than-container-load (LCL) freight in order to fill excess container capacity. A challenge, typical in LCL traffic, would be in coordinating the types of shipments and their consignors' trade histories. This would reduce the chance of the container being stopped by customs officers due to odd-looking cargo manifests.

[b] See Johnson (2020).

Flexport's services combined with cloud-based visibility for its customers are quite similar to how Uber is VRIN-differentiated from a standard taxi company. As an intermediary, Flexport is offering digitization for users across multiple locales. Other organizations are less wide-ranging. The Port of Los Angeles, in collaboration with GE Transportation, developed a "single window" cloud-based system in 2016 called Port Optimizer. It is designed to gather information to be shared among users of the port. With enough participation from importers, container terminal operators, ocean carriers, motor carriers, railroads, and freight forwarders this often-congested port could provide them with better information related to vessel arrivals, container availability, and gate clearance times.

Improved predictability ought to improve how users of the Port of Los Angeles schedule their arrivals and departures. This can help lower drayage costs and environmental impact among other cost savings. But there are growing pains. Currently, the problem is in reluctance to share data. Typical reasons relate to the feeling that the information should remain proprietary or that if it is released it can be stolen. Supply chains made up of private organizations use contracts to enhance trust. Since big data management is so new to many of the players, they do not know how to use their own data let alone be willing to share it.

Social network giant Facebook once had a motto for its platform developers: "Move Fast and Break Things." That may be fine for the cyber world but it is hard to imagine a for-hire carrier adopting such a motto for its conveyances. Yet in 2014, Facebook, with an eye to improved service, changed its internal motto to: "Move Fast With Stable Infra." It is nice to know that Silicon Valley is trying to learn what haulers have known for centuries. In the meantime, however, will the promise of AI and big data in for-hire transportation become balkanized with a few "single windows" or will data be seen as the free-flowing waterpower of old? Whether data is free-and-shared or monetized-and-traded, these options are better than simply hoarding it.

Predictive analytics

Simply put, formulate a goal, assemble data, and create a model to generate a way to achieve the goal. Historical data covering past events are used to build a model (i.e., an inductive process) to make predictions about future events based on uncovering patterns and discerning behaviors. Since it is an inductive process it is also a form of data mining. For example, big data assembled from sensors on thousands of vehicles can model behavior of the drivers.

Algorithms (i.e., rules) can be designed for an autonomous vehicle to follow and thus mimic a human driver. Sensors on engines can be used in the same way to model engine operations and, from there, an algorithm can be designed for performing preventative maintenance. Once a given vehicle and/or engine is governed by predictive analytics others can be interconnected to achieve scale, create feedback across the network, etc.

Consider a binary case meaning an either-or situation. A consignor tenders freight to a for-hire carrier on the basis of the latter's stated ability to deliver on time. Of course, a lot of things in-between origin and destination can impact delivery time. The carrier may have invested in data collection and modeling to help it better understand its operations. It may also use it for marketing purposes.

Suppose the carrier claims that last month 86% of its shipments arrived on time. Furthermore, it adds that its predictive analytics are quite good given this high rate of consignor fulfillment. Unbeknownst to the consignor it simply calculated this from the fact that it handled 500 shipments and 430 of them indeed arrived on time. Thus, the 86% represents last month's reality and has nothing to do with predictability—unless, of course, the carrier feels that last month is an excellent indicator for the next month.

What the carrier really needs to provide the consignor with is a prediction for next month. Basing a prediction solely on past reality would be the equivalent of the carrier saying that it predicted that 100% of loads would be delivered on time—and it was 86% correct about that. Basically, 430 of the loads that arrived on time were predicted to do so. The rest of the loads were also predicted to arrive on time but did not. Are these 70 loads false positives? No, since there was no proper prediction made. Basically, the carrier ought to make a prediction about how many loads will be on time and compare it to what actually happened.

In this framework, prediction is compared to reality rather than using past reality to stand in for a prediction. Suppose the carrier did indeed make an internal prediction using its predictive model. It predicted that 408 out of the 500 loads to be carried would arrive on time. Of these, it is discovered that only 387 loads arrived on time while 21 were late. With 408 loads predicted to be on time, this means, in tandem, that 92 loads were predicted to be late. Of these late loads, the model was correct about 49 of them while 43 loads arrived on time after all. This information can be collected into a so-called confusion matrix.

All four cells add up to 500 loads. There are four possible classifications of each load. The cells are populated with the 500 loads tagged, say, load 1 through load 500. A separate prediction was made about each of these and the actual result either bore out the prediction or did not. The four classifications summarize what happened over these 500 loads.

The left-hand column takes the 408 loads predicted to be on time and breaks them into what actually happened. The right-hand column does the same thing with the 92 loads predicted to be late. The top row indicates that 430 loads indeed arrived on time while the bottom row indicates that 70 loads were late.

What can be said about the predictions? Stating 408/430 or 95% is not very meaningful because it is one-sided. A better measure is 387/430 or 90% which is also called the rate of true positives. It is also called sensitivity or recall. It is the proportion of true predicted positives to actual positives. The balance to this is 43/430 or 10% which is the proportion of false predicted negatives to actual positives. The model duly predicted the true positives and incorrectly predicted the false negatives. Stating 49/70 or 70% is the proportion of true predicted negatives to actual negatives. The balance to this is 21/70 or 30% which is the proportion of false predicted positives to actual negatives.[c]

A prediction based solely on past reality would have the confusion matrix reduced to just the left-hand column with values of 430 and 70 placed from top to bottom. In other words, this "prediction" overlooks the possibility of a type I error, meaning false positives. Type II errors underestimate the amount of on-time loads. Type I errors are a bias that is not in the interest of consignors because it reduces the perceived risk they face. In this scenario, the carrier being falsely on time is worse than being falsely late. Therefore, for-hire carriers would prefer models that optimize for reducing type I errors.

[c] False positives and false negatives are akin to type I and type II statistical errors, respectively. The null hypothesis is the claim that a load will be late, but 21 loads were predicted to be on time and yet were late. The type I error, accepting false positives, means that the model incorrectly rejected a true null hypothesis and overestimated the amount of on-time loads. Also, 43 loads were predicted to be late and yet were on time. The type II error, accepting false negatives, means that the model incorrectly accepted a false null hypothesis and underestimated the amount of on-time loads. These errors are not systematic mistakes but are due to random chance. Data containing anomalies might lead the model to make a type I or II error but that is a limitation in the data and not in the model's logic. Also, if there is a large difference between the events (e.g., 99% of the loads arrive on time) it must be remembered that only part of that is due to careful route planning. Another factor is random negative events that were avoided by chance. The solution to overcome anomalies and biases is to have more data. Predictions are not foolproof in an environment subject to random events because uncertainty is always present.

		Predicted Event		
		On Time	**Late**	**Total**
Actual Event	**On Time**	True Positive **387** correctly classified	False Negative **43** incorrectly classified	**430**
	Late	False Positive **21** incorrectly classified	True Negative **49** correctly classified	**70**
	Total	**408**	**92**	**Grand Total 500**

Fig. 6.1 Confusion matrix for model evaluation.

Of course, the model could be expanded to include more than two classifications. Such multiclassification models could expand beyond timeliness of deliveries to include incidence of damage (i.e., claims covered by the carrier's insurance or *force majeure* which would not be), the accuracy of the documentation (e.g., for customs clearance of international freight), etc. The confusion matrix would have multiple columns and rows but the downward diagonal would still represent the set of correct classifications. Regarding optical character recognition, a 10×10 matrix could indicate digits zero through nine. Each cell could be evaluated for the software's prediction regarding the numbers written on paper relative to what they actually were. Depending on the person's handwriting the number two could look like a four; a four could look like a nine, etc. Of course, a 26×26 matrix could be used to evaluate handwritten letters of the alphabet.

A good question would be how to evaluate the correct vs incorrect classifications. Indeed, the ratio of true positives and negatives to total loads is called the accuracy rate. Fig. 6.1 shows this to be $(387 + 49)/500$ or 87%. Conversely, the misclassification or error rate is $(21 + 43)/500$ or 13%. Other statistical tests include the F1 score and the Matthews correlation coefficient.[d] Another distinction is between the in-sample data which was used to "train" the model and out-of-sample data which is used to test the model's predictive power. This prevents the model from being "overfitted" to the in-sample time period and thus less relevant to out-of-sample and/or subsequent data. Of course, the choice does require some thought. For example, if the in-sample period includes the downturn in freight demand

[d] For a review, see Chicco and Jurman (2020) and Powers (2011).

due to, say, COVID-19 but the out-of-sample period does not, it is not too hard to imagine that the model will not work very well if this structural change is not present in both data sets.

Artificial intelligence

Would decision-making in for-hire transportation, supported by artificial intelligence (AI), be a VRIN input? Since the quality of AI is tied to company-specific algorithms using secured data from particular players it certainly has the potential. In other words, AI needs to be considered by any for-hire carrier wishing to keep up with the competition.

The challenge not long ago was how to turn data into information, and information into knowledge. A veritable avalanche of data is being gathered from customers and vendors, and from items in storage and in transit. The challenge was how humans could sift through this unending flow in order to make meaningful decisions. AI offers the promise of matching massive and rapid data flows with massive computations and rapid automated decision-making.

Acquiring technology is one thing; capturing a sustainable return on investment (ROI) from it is another. As already discussed, digitization is about turning information into digital bytes thereby making it computer-readable. Once readable it is now actionable, especially when used in an AI setting. Decision-making through AI is dependent on the structure of the algorithms (i.e., rules) into which these big data sets are fed. This is called deep learning—trying to imitate how people learn. These various algorithms, when used in tandem, form a neural network or artificial brain that "learns" tasks based on the "experiences" it gathers through identifying patterns in the data. Of course, the larger the data set the larger is the set of computer-based experiences. The more sophisticated the neural network, the more the computer learns.

After a while, the computer can take these accumulated "experiences" and aggregate them into statistics. Of course, statistics are always representations of reality and not reality itself. For example, if a motor carrier's average (technically, mean) travel time between points A and B is 38 h it is just a representation of the "typical" travel time. It is possible that none of the actual trips in that calculation were 38 h. In fact, in statistician-speak, if the sample of trips skewed heavily in terms of either quick or slow trips, or it had a high degree of variance, it is possible that most of the trips were nowhere near 38 h. What to do? The solution is for the computer to calculate many other statistics and compare them, apply rules of logic, and map out different types of travel scenarios. If after doing all that a solution to a problem comes into focus—say, the chosen route from A to B is reliably the fastest—that is part of the power of AI. Its solutions and forecasts are likely better informed through subtleties that a human cannot discern out of a mountain of data. In other words, AI provides a richer if-then analysis.

The ROI from AI is achieved when this mimicking of human decision-making power can be done with increasing speed while remaining scalable. In fact, once the data-gathering platform is in place it is highly scalable because website clicks from the customer base, signals from freight tracking devices, etc. have a marginal cost of uploading that is near-zero. This benefit is similar to how early industrialization relied on free-flowing water to spin watermills in order to work the machines used in flour milling, wood grinding, ore crushing, etc. Today a lot of customer data is free. Yet there is an ongoing public policy debate regarding the ownership and privacy of these cyber-streams of customer data.

Basically, AI is an attempt to simulate human intelligence. Machine learning is a subset of AI in that it refers to how the computer learns ways to simulate based on looking for patterns and making predictions. While predictive analytics is about developing a model from data, AI uses machine learning to adjust the model based on the continuous flow of incoming data. While predictive analytics sets up a well-defined model, the AI-induced model is more of a "black box" as far as the human observer is concerned. Nonetheless, it is important for the human trainer to look for systematic errors that the AI system might make. Good examples include handwritten documents being digitized using optical character recognition. For example, a human can readily discern when an error is due to confusing a zero with the letter O.

AI learns tasks based on the virtual "experiences" it gathers through identifying patterns in the data. In a less lofty sense, the AI system is being trained to follow rules (like chess) in order to achieve the desired outcome (like checkmate). The larger the data set the larger the set of "experiences." The more sophisticated the neural network, the more the computer learns.

A solid return on investment from AI will be achieved when it can mimic human decision-making with increasing speed. Self-driving vehicles and data-informed decisions on routes and delivery times that increase speed and reliability are good applications of AI. Another is preventative maintenance of machinery. Notice that AI is used to solve specific problems.

It should not be used to try to solve *everything* and to try to automate strategic decision-making. Even with AI, there is still plenty of room for supply chain managers to bring imaginative ideas and their personal skills to the table. In fact, AI should be seen as a tool to assist, not replace, human decision-making. Certainly, routine decisions that are not critical for production and revenue flows could be left to AI to plan out (acting as an autopilot, so to speak).

AI might optimize the purchase of office supplies, for example. But when decisions are strategic, AI's forecasts should be ruminated upon, not blindly followed. Remember, AI is only useful to the extent that the data is accurate, and the data set is rich enough. The danger of letting AI algorithms alone make important decisions is that all interconnected organizations may be triggered by their own AI programs to do the same thing. This is part of the reason behind modern day stock market crashes—and the need for circuit breakers. Also, AI develops deep learning "experiences" only within the current constraints the company faces. There is no reason to accept AI forecasts if these constraints can be, or ought to be, overcome.

Changing such things as vendors, countries of origin or destination, modes of transportation, ports of entry, and the ratio of capital to labor, etc. could nullify those AI forecasts. However, AI's forecasts might lead a manager to change certain constraints to try to improve subsequent AI forecasts. This is valuable human decision-making. Related to changeable constraints are unforeseen changes to the external environment. The COVID-19 pandemic is a case in point. This "black swan" event shut down markets around the world. Countries poured in different levels of fiscal stimulus. Business regulations were adjusted to different degrees in different industries. Consumer behavior switched markedly to online purchases, many of which were household cleaning supplies with hoarding of some of these items. Activities at border ports of entry fell sharply due to government-mandated travel bans. Passenger airlines took on more air cargo to try to maintain revenue flows. An AI system would not understand the context of all these sudden falls in sales, travel, etc. Facial recognition programs may be stumped by covered faces in crowds and along store aisles. Behavior monitoring programs might likewise be confused by shoppers moving erratically in order to maintain social distancing. Of course, any manager aware of current events would understand immediately what was going on. AI's human trainers would have to adjust the underlying algorithms accordingly so the systems could operate under a "new normal."

The three AI-based keys to a sustained value-add in supply chain management are richer data sets; faster computers; and algorithms demonstrating something akin to intelligence and human cognitive abilities. When the procedure is rules-based (i.e., chess) or requires encyclopedic trivia (i.e., the game show *Jeopardy!*), AI appears to have an edge. But when rules change, AI's power is limited by having to learn all over again—a slave to the old rules, biases, etc. built into the "experiences" without a broader context to possible changes.

Ultimately data is gathered by humans and used for the benefit of humans. The computers used along the way have the edge regarding speed and logic. But their value falls when decisions and/or outcomes are not binary. Not all decisions and/or outcomes are a simple either-or or a win-lose. There may be gray areas because the interaction does not follow a strict set of rules like chess. Subtleties, nuances, and idioms crop up in human interactions. The combination may be unique to a particular customer, vendor, negotiator, etc. In that regard, a person is likelier to derive more fulfillment from playing chess against an AI system than trying to register a complaint to an AI system about a recent purchase. Though self-driving cars are an emerging technology it is worth pondering the extent to which drivers would be willing to cede control to the onboard system.

Will cars in the future have steering wheels and foot pedals for acceleration and braking? Or will driver-assistance be the limit of car owners' AI acceptance? Passenger airplanes use autopilot while in-flight. But if AI could handle take-offs and landings as well, would passengers be willing to fly with no pilots on the flight deck at all?

What will be the future of work? It is a real debate. If AI decision-making combined with robots is better for a given company, it will switch out labor productivity for AI-robotic productivity. But if AI complements a worker's task, it makes sense to use a combination of both. Economists call this an increase in total factor productivity. In other words, the two inputs complement each other with a certain something that releases innovation and creativity. Nevertheless, the substitution vs complimentary effects of technology and labor are in battle within many industries.

Will the necessary stream of data be slowed by congestion? Data transmission and its processing using AI requires an infrastructure—a virtual highway. 5G (i.e., fifth-generation broadband technology) is the latest version to promise speed and the ability to handle the exponential increase in data set to come from autonomous vehicles. Therefore, information infrastructure needs to be considered alongside traditional infrastructure.

Blockchain

The support infrastructure for AI is made up of abundant data and fast computing. Regarding the latter, blockchain technology leverages speed and distribution in order to offer traceability, compliance, and security in accounting, finance, and operations among the multitude of the blockchain's users or peers. This peer-to-peer network eliminates the need for a central authority. It is a paperless method to share information and handle transactions. It also has the potential to assist to some degree with negotiations and contracting.

Blockchain technology was introduced in 2008 to support the development of bitcoin, a cryptocurrency. A blockchain is a digital ledger made up of connected blocks of information. The information is stored in a decentralized database, but everything is interconnected through cryptography. This is how a blockchain provides distribution of information along with security. A string of numbers, called a hash, is assigned to the block. Any update to the block is given a new hash. Importantly, all the hashes assigned to earlier states of the information are also connected to the current hash as a sort of record of all the updates. Anything encrypted is shared with peers who confirm the information. This widespread verification process, called a consensus mechanism, is intended to make the blockchain tamperproof. "Secured by math" is the term cryptologists use meaning that the huge string of hashes upon hashes to duplicate in order to copy or tamper with a current one makes it nearly impossible to reverse engineer. In effect, the longer the chain the stronger it is.

A public blockchain is open to anyone and all users remain anonymous. A private blockchain, on the other hand, requires that members be identified and possess the required credentials in order to validate blocks. For example, Maersk, the world's largest container carrier, teamed up with tech giant IBM in 2018 to launch a private blockchain platform called TradeLens. Their service is an electronically distributed ledger of immutable, time-stamped transactions along supply chains that are visible to their partners. While Maersk is a part owner of the platform's intellectual property it has made it available for other for-hire carriers to use. Apart from Maersk's subsidiaries (e.g., APM Terminals), the addition of other large container carriers,

CMA-CGM, Hapag-Lloyd, MSC, and ONE means that the status of more than half of the world's ocean container capacity is encoded within TradeLens. What will that mean for freight forwarders the bulk of which have been slow to adopt digitalization? The twin pressures coming from Flexport, as discussed above, and Maersk look similar to the twin pressures Sears felt from Amazon and Walmart. This is another example of the potential of technology to shake up staid businesses.

The difference between blockchains like TradeLens and those offering cryptocurrencies like bitcoin is that the latter is open to anyone who wishes to buy into it. Naturally, it makes sense that only those involved in the movement of freight (i.e., consignors, carriers, and intermediaries) be parties to what is happening with the freight and conveyances. The technical staff at Flexport and IBM (for their TradeLens platform) provide only the support infrastructure for the partners to perform their blockchain roles as certifiers of transactions. This will maintain a degree of trust and security. The blockchain could be used to facilitate a spot market among the partners if it uses an algorithm to sift through attributes of shipments to be tendered with capacity that is available. Any arrangement agreed to by a consignor and carrier would have a set of details involving the operation and payment recorded in the blockchain's ledger. These details would comport with the protocols the community of partners agreed to before their spot market became operational. In a less-than-truckload (LTL) environment, where loads are consolidated, a carrier can be expected to be dealing with two or more consignors simultaneously and devising individual bills of lading. Carrier-to-carrier contracts might also be arranged to facilitate interlining operations. Finally, various consignors might work together to self-consolidate their shipments in search of a bulk discount from a for-hire carrier with the necessary capacity.

The logical extension of blockchain technology is to automate the contracting process as well. Of course, what may be logical may not necessarily be right or even workable. Just like trust is a necessary ingredient in any contract the possibility of blockchain-generated contracts, based on a predetermined design, assumes that all partners trust the vetting process used to admit members into the blockchain. This is necessary since the players can be, for all intents and purposes, strangers to one other because the element of transactional speed is what the blockchain is offering. The administrators, no doubt, will vet for-hire carriers for insurance coverage, attributes of their conveyances, and perhaps company history and financial situation.

Naturally, any rating system cannot be 100% objective and nor can the process for when a partner is to be removed from the blockchain.

A smart contract is the term used for an algorithmic, computer-generated contract. The computer program draws up the contract using terms and conditions that are triggered by what each party is looking for based on the blocks of information they are uploading. Again, with speed being the issue in blockchain transactions it is assumed that both parties are not looking for legal nuance.[e] However, there are two problems with this. First, once the contract is set by the system and enacted it cannot be updated based on changing real-world conditions or mutual agreement by both parties. At best, the algorithm has to be able to turn terms and conditions desired by consignors and carriers into legalese. Of course, even typed-up and uploaded information by one or more parties are prone to idiomatic issues that might obscure intent when looked at later on by the other party. Second, a contract is not so much a codification of what the parties wish to do, it also codifies what happens if/when things go wrong. Will the two parties have enough time and experience to set these terms? If not, and there is no agreement if/when something unforeseen happens, the only recourse is litigation.[f]

Electronic bills of lading

Though less automated than smart contracts there is value in avoiding paper and using electronic documents. Transaction costs are lower when it comes to preparation, transfers, and regulatory compliance. This is especially true when multiple jurisdictions are involved. Consider ocean vessel carriers. The Digital Container Shipping Association (DCSA), a nonprofit formed in 2019, has been at the forefront of helping the ocean vessel sector pivot from paper to digital documents and improve the scheduling of containerized shipments. Of course, 2020 saw a lot of pivoting due to the COVID-19 pandemic and the surge in e-commerce related imports. The DCSA has suggested standards for carriers, ports, and terminal operators to adopt. But will they; and if so, when?

Data must be generated and shared among all the stakeholders. There is also the issue of acceptance. This is especially important when it comes to

[e] Lawyers refer to this as the intent of the parties. In other words, what were they thinking at the time relative to what economic and social conditions existed at the time the contract was enacted.

[f] For a highly critical overview of blockchains and the services connected with them see Gerard (2017). A more supportive overview is found in Ferreira (2021).

legal contracts. A common format for an electronic bill of lading (eBL)—i.e., the contract of carriage—needs to be accepted by regulators since, for example, customs officials will need to examine them during prearrival container screenings and during physical inspections at ports of entry.[g] Banks need to be involved since bills of lading form part of the process by which importers and exporters transact using letters of credit and documentary collection. Insurance companies will also need access should damage claims arise. An eBL must, therefore, be in a format that ensures interoperability across multiple user interfaces.

Given that the container liners are global businesses covering many jurisdictions, the DCSA is smart to leverage an eBL format suggested by United Nations Centre for Trade Facilitation and Electronic Business (UN/CEFACT). Still, a uniform eBL should not be the goal but rather a first step. After all, contracts are established between two unique parties; and each is entitled to negotiate over language and content whether it is in paper or electronic format.

Underlying the move to paperless transactions is the tension between establishing more formal service contracts and the vagaries of the spot market. Typically, trans-Pacific service contracts run from May 1 through April 30 and contain minimum quantity commitments in order to assist both parties in establishing the freight rate. This tension between fixed and variable rates serves to highlight differences among modes of transport. For instance, the International Air Transport Association (IATA) established an electronic air waybill (eAWB) in 2010 and it has become the default format for the contract of carriage used by its membership. The IATA's multilateral agreement formalized the eAWB on January 1, 2019. The DCSA is trying to follow a similar path.

Are consignors and container liners any more likely to cooperate in a digital setting compared to a paper one? Will the liners share data among themselves and with motor carriers? Will port congestion, especially at the ports of Los Angeles and Long Beach, see any relief as a result? Since the DCSA's membership represents about 80% of the container shipping industry on a TEU basis, it certainly speaks with a loud voice. The nine members are CMA-CGM, Evergreen, Hapag-Lloyd, HMM, Maersk, MSC, ONE, Yang Ming, and ZIM.

[g] Cargo manifests, which do not carry the same legal weight as bills of lading, have been handled electronically and used in regulatory compliance under section 343 of the Trade Act of 2002. For an overview, see Prokop (2017; pp. 81–83).

If the DCSA's standards are put into widespread practice the hope is that there will be more visibility and certainty in container shipping. Vessels can optimize on speed (i.e., maintain a steadier pace) in order to lower fuel burn and its concomitant pollution. Steadier speeds lead to more reliable arrival times which further assist ports and terminals when allocating equipment and workers to handle the off-loading of containers, the drayage process, and intermodal transfer inland to final destinations.

Consignors may wish to negotiate for higher minimum quantity commitments in order to lock-in space while carriers, knowing that capacity is tight, may wish to keep more space available for the spot market. Digitization is certainly overdue in the ocean vessel sector; but contracting, pricing, and capacity utilization are also dependent on conveyances, support infrastructure and the psychology of profit-seeking.

Data sharing and customer service

To shine light into the metaphorical black box where transporting items from point A to B takes place, reliable data is necessary to understand what is happening over the network as time passes by. Being a physical activity subject to time, and taking place over a defined route, for-hire transportation services are quite measurable. When data is generated it makes sense that it is shared among decision-makers. This includes consignors, consignees, for-carriers, and other intermediaries. Of course, when it comes to assessing customer service in transportation, data is certainly necessary—but it is not sufficient. Customer relationships and the nature of the contracts that the parties enter into will make or break the perceptions of customer service.

Simply put, customer service is the process of achieving a win-win outcome between a buyer and a seller. A win-win helps build relationships beyond the merely one-off, transactional type. If successful, the buyer is receiving fulfillment while the seller is building loyalty which may enhance the predictability of customer demand and, therefore, sales revenue. Of course, sellers must take care not to overpromise the scope and quality of customer service. This helps keep relationships and expectations sustainable.

Customer service is part of perceived quality. Yet quality measures can be either objective or subjective. Fuel efficiency and carrying capacity are objective measures of service capability since they are governed by the laws of physics. The type of fuel to be used (e.g., diesel vs electric battery) and how the capacity is to be allocated [e.g., truckload (TL) or less-than-truckload (LTL)] are subjective choices. Different people may make different choices because they have different valuations of the alternatives.

All the data in the world, finely honed into actionable statistics and scenarios through predictive analytics and AI, mean little if the contracted parties do not trust each other and they try to get around their obligations. For-hire transportation is an intangible service as opposed to a tangible item. Consignors and for-hire carriers can, and ought to, come to an agreement as to what a win-win outcome looks like before signing the bill of lading. Part of that win-win will be defined in terms of price, meaning value for money. If the scope and quality of the customer service being sought makes the freight rate appear too high for the consignor the transaction may not take place.

With an avalanche of data being generated daily in transport markets, some companies are looking to leverage it in order to enhance their services. In 2020 the founders of Uber Freight launched a new company called ISO. According to the company website, their services reconcile "data discrepancies between business partners in real time" and contextualize "service failures and create actionable insights." Their single cloud-based platform is intended to give all parties broader access to what is happening inside the metaphorical black box. Of course, it is assumed that all parties will share their data and, equally importantly, their performance metrics. After all, apart from homogenous data, one ought to have insight into what another party thinks the data means by way of the key performance indicator it is generating. For example, when is a shipment on time? Is it when the truck pulls into the consignee's yard or when the truck is parked at the dock and is ready for off-loading? Without agreement the situation is like two people looking at a Rorschach inkblot—they are looking at the same thing but are seeing two different things. This is the challenge when taking digitization to the next level. It is also a challenge when the terms of a smart contract are open to different interpretations.

Data transparency and visibility across different departmental silos is a good thing. But mistakes can happen in transportation. A none too rare example involves delivery to the wrong destination. If the for-hire carrier's dispatching department transmitted the wrong consignee's information to the driver the delivery will not only be late but potentially lost or damaged if unwittingly received. The dock personnel receiving the delivery and, indeed, the driver have little incentive to wade through the bill of lading to determine if the delivery is, in fact, a normal one for them or something is in error. Of course, the terms of the bill of lading confer on the for-hire carrier the responsibility to make the consignor whole when the latter tries to smooth things over with his customer (i.e., the true consignee). Fixing the mistake is still customer service, but it is akin to a contractual warranty for damages and defects.

Data sharing to enhance customer service is relatively easy for freight moved under service contracts. Here there is an expectation of a stream of consignments over a period of time. Relationships tend to be stronger as well. Things do not work as smoothly in the spot market for single shipments especially when using digital freight matching platforms (e.g., Uber Freight, uShip, etc.). Since there are multiple proprietary providers of such platforms the data is siloed. Consignors and for-hire carriers are, therefore, incentivized to post their requests on multiple sites in order to increase the chances of a quick match (much like someone being on multiple online dating sites). Once a match is made on one platform the others may still show availability which, of course, is no longer accurate. To the extent that these "off-the-market" players are chased by others, it leads to inefficiencies in route planning, capacity utilization, etc. Until these independent platforms agree to establish a clearinghouse like those operated in banking and stock markets, this problem will continue. Clearinghouses would allow all platforms to "clean house" once a match has been made at one of them.

Data accumulation and its usage are transforming transportation markets. This is a good thing. However, there is still much to learn as the parties try to pull a win-win out of the metaphorical black box they find themselves in. Providing consistent and reliable customer service is one of the most nebulous exercises in transportation management because of the number of moving parts involved.

Adoption and diffusion

Similar to the discussion in Chapter 3 which showed how a supply chain can be weaker than its weakest link, if an interoperable technology and/or database is shared among supply chain partners, the effects can be magnified. This "network effect" is akin to economies of scale and the gains to be had when codependent parties speak the same language when trying to achieve a common goal.

In order to leverage the full potential of these technologies, all of the players need to coordinate. This means interoperability of systems, sharing of data and forecasts, and joint decision-making. This is relatively easy in a command-and-control operation like in the military, or along a supply chain

		For-Hire Carrier	
		adopt	not adopt
Partner	adopt	A, A	0, 0
	not adopt	0, 0	N, N

Payoff (For-Hire Carrier, Partner)

A, N > 0

Fig. 6.2 All or nothing coordination game.

made up of companies with a common parent. It is not so easy among firms that are under limited contractual relationships along a supply chain. Furthermore, the contracts are only pair-wise meaning the company has a direct relationship with its vendor and not with its vendor's vendor.

The standard coordination game is played between the for-hire carrier and a composite of many partners. These could be consignors, interline partners, owner-operators, intermodal partners, port authorities, and 3PLs. The network effect is magnified when there are more partners who agree to adopt an interoperable technology.

The coordination game in Fig. 6.2 has two Nash equilibria where all players either adopt the technology or all decide not to and maintain the status quo in their business relationships.[h] Only with $A > N$ is there a Pareto improvement in switching from the (N,N) Nash equilibrium to (A, A). All players gain nothing if there is no coordination; in fact, the values could be negative instead of zero.

Another possibility is to try to coordinate between two technologies that are not interoperable, A vs B, as shown in Fig. 6.3.

In this game suppose there are multiple times the for-hire carrier and the partners (n) make their choices. A fraction of them (p) will choose technology A while $(1-p)$ of them will choose B. The choice is pnA vs $(1-p)nB$. Under these circumstances, A is the more profitable choice when

[h] The dollar values of the letters in the matrix are not important since it is their relative sizes that matter. This also means that the dollar values for the for-hire carrier and the partners need not be equal either.

For-Hire Carrier

		adopt A	adopt B
Partner	adopt A	A, A	0, 0
	adopt B	0, 0	B, B

Payoff (For-Hire Carrier, Partner)

A, B > 0

Fig. 6.3 Coordination game between rival technologies.

$$pnA > (1-p)nB \tag{6.1}$$

Solving for p gives

$$pnA + pnB > nB \text{ or } p(nA + nB) > nB \text{ meaning,}$$
$$p > B/(A+B) \tag{6.2}$$

Another way to interpret Eq. (6.2) is to say that if A is large relative to B it makes $B/(A+B)$ small. Thus, if only a small fraction (p) of partners chooses A it will, by nature of the larger payoff, entice other partners to switch to it. Through repeated interaction, the partners would, over time, be expected to adopt the technology with a higher payoff. This means that coordination should eventually lead to higher value-add assuming, of course, there are no coordination problems like lethargy, bureaucratic red tape, etc.

Issues and problems going forward

If blockchain systems truly eliminate the need for trust among contracting parties, can they truly eliminate the metaphorical black box that transportation activities go through? Obviously not, because not all parties along a public road, waterway, or airspace are part of a given blockchain. Trust requires verification and trust in the blockchain is ceded to administrators by the parties in the smart contract. In any case, trust is still required but the level of verification necessary is something that needs more understanding if this technology is to become widespread in the multifaceted transportation industry.

Of course, digitization and electronic documentation have obvious benefits in terms of speed and accuracy in documentary compliance. Adoption and diffusion of these technologies are ongoing but will not be uniform across the industry. This is because adoption may be through private initiative or through government mandate. Differences are also due to the nature of various modes of transportation. Certainly, diffusion across a more consolidated mode such as ocean carriers is easier than across the decentralized motor carrier sector. On the other hand, shared public infrastructure was the reason behind the government mandate for electronic logging devices on for-hire motor carriers.

References

Barney, J., 1991. Firm resources and sustained competitive advantage. J. Manag. 17 (1), 99–120.

Chicco, D., Jurman, G., 2020. The advantages of the Matthews correlation coefficient (MCC) over F1 score and accuracy in binary classification evaluation. BMC Genomics 21 (6), 1–13.

Ferreira, A., 2021. Regulating smart contracts: legal revolution or simply evolution? Telecommun. Policy 45, 1–16.

Gerard, D., 2017. Attack of the 50 Foot Blockchain. David Gerard.

Johnson, E., 2020. Flexport dominated maritime startup investment in 2019. J. Commerce 21 (1), 44.

Powers, D.M.W., 2011. Evaluation: from precision, recall and F-measure to ROC, informedness, markedness and correlation. Int. J. Mach. Learn. Technol. 2 (1), 37–63.

Prokop, D., 2017. Global Supply Chain Security and Management: Appraising Programs. Preventing Crimes, Butterworth Heinemann, Cambridge, MA.

CHAPTER 7

Problems in transportation costing

Joint cost vs common cost

Transportation presents challenges to measuring its cost from both an economic and an accounting perspective. A straightforward procedure is to divide costs into those which are fixed and those which are variable. If a cost remains constant over all levels of output (including zero output and, therefore, no operating revenue) then it is fixed. If, however, a cost is functionally related to changes in the level of output then it is variable.

What is more challenging is separating bundled costs and allocating them to their proper source. This problem was touched on in Chapter 1 regarding the traceability or separability problem in joint costs and common costs. It was also touched on in Chapter 5 regarding front-haul vs back-haul cost allocation. These issues have puzzled economists and accountants since the earliest days of railroads.[a] Unlike the relative ease of demarcating fixed and variable costs, it is often harder to decide when a cost is joint or when it is common. Basically, if two or more costs exist in a functional relationship, they are joint. If there is no functional relationship, they are common. For example, for every front-haul a domiciled carrier undertakes there is a back-haul to its domicile (which may or may not contain freight). In other words, there is a joint supply (i.e., a roundtrip) over two independent consignors' demands for front-haul and back-haul services. But how many passengers can be carried on an airplane or a train relative to the amount of freight held in the belly or inside the attached railcars, respectively? The fact is that an airplane, which offers passenger service, can also offer air cargo service. The reverse is not always true. Of course, if the airplane is configured to carry passengers and cargo these services are in joint supply because there is a fixed number of seats and fixed capacity in the belly.

A nagging question is what is the *output* of a for-hire carrier? Generically, it is ton-miles for freight or it is passenger-miles. Bulk commodities like coal

[a] For a classic review of these problems, see Locklin (1933).

https://doi.org/10.1016/B978-0-12-815415-1.00007-0

and iron ore are different raw materials. Boxes of pharmaceuticals and cosmetics are different consumer goods. But, from a service perspective, is the haulage of various bulk commodities and various packaged consumer goods over the same origin and destination the same service? If so, then these similar items are not being jointly supplied; rather, the supply of transport services is homogeneous and offered to the same subset of consignors.

The joint vs common cost debate started in the following fashion. One view, first championed by economist F.W. Taussig, notes that railways are dominated by fixed costs (e.g., the cost of building the rail line and other support infrastructure). Of course, railways can offer a variety of haulage services. Passengers could be tourists or commuters; and consignors could be moving bulk commodities or higher-value containerized freight. Furthermore, the frequency of consignors' demands over a given time period can also be different. In other words, heavy bulk shipments (which suggest allocating to them a larger share of fixed cost) may or may not be frequent. The same argument goes for containerized freight, which is likely less weight per cubic foot than bulk freight. Thus, these heterogeneous haulage outputs with their differentiated frequencies must share in the homogenous cost the railroad faces. The question is how? Taussig suggested charging based on the consignors' willingness to pay. In other words, the higher the passenger and consignor demand curves are for rail transport the more they are charged. The railroad must, therefore, artfully assign these differential freight rates across all passengers and consignors in order to cover all operating costs (i.e., fixed and variable). Costs are allocated according to what passengers and consignors can bear.[b]

Fig. 7.1 shows separable demands for transportation with joint supply of seats for passengers and freight space for consignors. The joint supply of a conveyance used for two distinct purposes is shown by the supply curve (S_c). For a given quantity of conveyances, there is a willingness to pay on the part of passengers for their trips and on the part of consignors for their freight. These are shown by the two demand curves for passengers and for freight, D_p and D_f. In this example, passenger demand is higher than consignor demand. The for-hire carrier is interested in charging prices to the two groups that will cover its costs (as mapped out on the supply curve). By vertically adding up the two demand curves the total demand for the conveyance (D_c) maps out the total willingness to pay by all demanders. Note that D_c becomes D_p once D_f falls to a willingness to pay of zero. In

[b] See Taussig (1891, 1933).

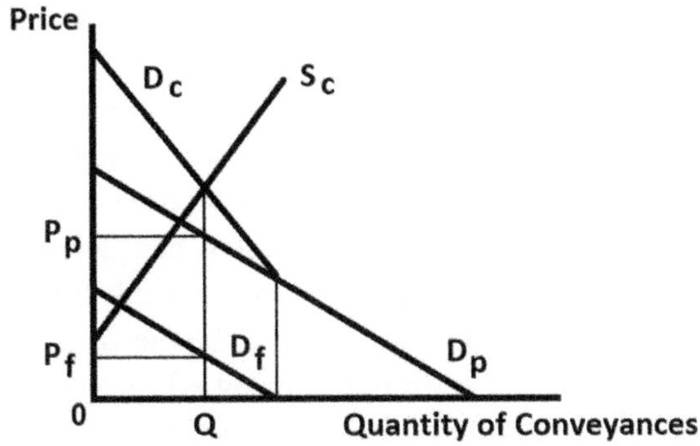

Fig. 7.1 Joint supply with separable demands.

effect, D_c is a kinked demand curve. By equating the supply curve with the summed demand curve, an equilibrium quantity (Q) of conveyances is determined. Charging a ticket price for passengers (P_p) and a freight rate for consignors (P_f), the sum of these two charges will cover the cost to supply those services.

Examining Fig. 7.1 can lead to valuable insights. For example, suppose the demand for freight transport increases. One would expect the freight rate to rise since more conveyances would have to be made available. But what would be the effect on passenger ticket prices? They would be expected to fall. The reason is that if the conveyance is designed for both passengers and cargo, it is a joint supply and the extra conveyances for freight mean an extra supply of seats. Ticket prices would have to fall in order to induce more passengers to purchase tickets. This can be verified in Fig. 7.1 by shifting D_f upward. This causes D_c to shift upward as well. The equilibrium quantity will rise; but since nothing has changed regarding the demand by passengers the new P_p simply slides down D_p.

Front-haul and back-haul demands are independent of each other, yet the supply used to fulfill them is joint. Of course, the same can be said for passenger and freight demands if it is on a common conveyance. Therefore, one would expect different freight rates or ticket prices for each independent demand under joint supply. All of these prices would have to add up to the marginal cost of providing the nth round trip or nth conveyance used to carry passengers and freight. These different prices under joint supply are not the same thing as price discrimination, which is about dividing up a demand for the *same* commodity according to different price elasticities of demand for subgroups. Technically, this signifies the sensitivity of quantity demanded with respect to price changes as opposed to the height of the demand curve (i.e., how intense the demand is).

Another view, contrary to Taussig, and first championed by economist A.C. Pigou, is that transportation service is basically the same across similar commodities and passengers over a given route.[c] There was no disagreement on the distinction between front-haul and back-haul services. These were still considered to be in joint supply. However, bulk freight rates over a given route by a given mode were expected to be the same. In other words, there is little material difference in transporting wheat vs corn, coal vs iron ore, etc. The same argument would apply to passengers (be they tourists or commuters) sharing a common origin and destination. Instead of transportation being jointly supplied, the carriers are dealing with a common cost, not a joint cost. If freight rates over a common class of freight were different over a given route this could only be due to the carrier practicing price discrimination.[d] In other words, different freight rates indicate prices set according to the carrier's understanding of different passenger and/or consignor classes. Exploiting these differences would be based on price elasticity of demand. This argument applies to differentiated services for the same transport. An example is first class vs economy seating on an airplane. Since an airline need not offer one or the other seating class there is no functional relationship between the two. The services are a common cost and different ticket prices are due to price discrimination.[e] LTL motor carriers offering a lower freight rate for the same commodity under a service contract vs the spot market is another example.

Of course, the counter to price discrimination is to argue that first-class travelers and consignors with service contracts have one thing in common—they both see themselves buying different services than economy passengers and spot market consignors. They see themselves buying higher quality, more flexibility, etc. If the for-hire carrier sees it that way as well, it would price according to marginal cost for each of these different services. In other

[c] See Pigou (1913, 1920).

[d] Technically, dividing demanders into distinct groups based on their price elasticity of demand is known as third degree price discrimination. For an overview, see Prentice and Prokop (2016; pp. 171–178).

[e] Charging a passenger or a consignor more than others for a shorter travel distance along a given route would also qualify as price discrimination. Of course, if the shorter distance were handled by a smaller conveyance and the longer route were handled by a larger one there would be a case for arguing that these are independent submarkets like a spoke-to-hub trip vs a hub-to-hub trip.

words, it is a common cost problem but without price discrimination. Simply use marginal cost pricing for the different services offered within the conveyance.[f] Like differential prices for wool and mutton supplied by the same sheep, meat and eggs from the same chicken, etc. they were the prices of heterogeneous services being jointly supplied by the same conveyance.

Context is very important. Pick-up, haulage, and drop-off for a consignor using a service contract or the spot market would be identical for the same class of freight. There is no functional relationship between service contract and spot market consignors and how carrying capacity is utilized. These are common costs. But for first-class- and economy passengers there is a functional relationship because each passenger sits in separate sections of the airplane differentiated by seat size, leg room, overhead space, etc. These are, therefore, joint costs.[g]

One reason why a for-hire carrier might resort to price discrimination is when costs are not separable but consignors' chosen services vary by degree. In this case, it becomes very hard to disentangle their effects on total operating costs. To illustrate, image a train proceeding from the origin with 10 boxcars attached. To keep it simple, let each boxcar contain a load tendered by a different consignor. The final destination sees the delivery of the 10th boxcar but there were nine other boxcar drop-offs along the way. Allocating the total operating cost of the train's journey suggests that an objective rule can be devised. But what would that be? Certainly, more costs are incurred the longer the boxcar travels, the higher the weight of the shipment, and any other special needs regarding loading/unloading and care in-transit. How would the railroad decide on a cost equation taking into account all of these variables in an objective way? It is not easy establishing the cost trade-off between adding a unit of distance but taking off a unit of weight. Price discrimination relieves any for-hire carrier from pondering

[f] In other words, the debate boils down to what transportation output is. Is it a series of different transportation services (i.e., Taussig's argument) or really the same service but facing different demand elasticities (i.e., Pigou's argument). For further discussion of these gray areas see Steiner (1957) and Phlips (1985).

[g] What is trickier is to account for price differences within each class. For example, the marginal cost of selling an empty seat a few hours before a flight departs is near zero. Yet, an airline is likely to charge a high price in order to deter passengers waiting for the last moment to secure a cheap flight. If the airline takes such last-minute behavior to mean price inelastic demand then it is an opportunity for price discrimination. Revenue management will be discussed further in Chapter 8.

over this so long as total operating revenue generated by the different freight rates covers total operating cost.

Another form of joint supply relates to time-use or peak-load. Railroads, pipelines, airports, and water ports need to build enough capacity to meet the peak level of service demanded over a given day, week, or season. Motor carriers, on the other hand, have more flexibility due to most of the infrastructure being publicly provided. They also have the ability to expand fleet operations using independent owner-operators. Infrastructure that is fixed has a cost of operation that needs to be divided among peak and off-peak users. Charging a congestion premium to peak users is not price discrimination but rather cost allocation of the joint supply of infrastructure to two different classes of user (i.e., those who cannot avoid peak usage and those who can).

Unlike providing labor-intensive services or those which are distributable over the internet, all modes of transportation involve some degree of fixed costs. There are also indivisibilities that can lead to excess capacity. For example, unless some minimum amount of freight is tendered or a certain number of passengers buy tickets a conveyance will not be dispatched. This argument can be extended in terms of expanding service by an extra container, extra rail car, etc. For-hire carriers have to decide the level of excess demand triggers investment in more infrastructure.

Total cost of ownership

The cost of transportation, or the cost of delivery as far as the consignee is concerned, is only one part of the total cost of ownership (TCO) of the item that was shipped.[h] If the seller of the item takes on the role of the consignor it is likely that most if not all of the billed cost of delivery will be passed on to the buyer as consignee. Other costs which make up the TCO for the consignee might include installation and maintenance of the item. Disposal of packaging and replacement or repairs should also be considered. Of course, disposal of the item itself after expiration or obsolescence might require further transportation if the item involves hazardous material, sale on a secondary market, etc.

From the for-hire carrier's perspective, TCO requires it to consider its conveyance or fleet of them as well as any support infrastructure it may own or lease. Components include acquisition cost, cost of depreciation,

[h] An overview of the TCO philosophy is covered in Ellram (1993).

maintenance costs, and subtracting any residual value of the asset. Labor costs (i.e., recruiting, wages, and retention), insurance, and energy costs are also major factors in order to fulfill operations. Naturally, the carrier will try to build as much of these costs as possible into the freight rates assessed to its consignors. The more market power it has the more likely it will be able to do this.

TCO, from the consignor's perspective, would start with the freight rate applied to the weight and/or volume of the shipment and append other costs that are, in effect, bundled with the act of transportation between a given origin and destination. Letting the for-hire carrier pick-up, take charge, and deliver the freight may be called the service acquired by the consignor to the ultimate benefit of the consignee. However, TCO would also include the consignor's cost of acquiring the service and any delivery-related problems that arise. These would be pre- and postservice costs.

Preservice would mostly involve search costs via a web portal if the consignor is using the spot market. Alternatively, it could involve more costs related to thorough negotiation if the consignor's intent is to establish a multiperiod service contract. The bill of lading could be signed as-is by the consignor or it could be negotiated in detail if the for-hire carrier is amenable to it.

Regarding postservice costs, it is important to note that while the consignor is legally required to be made whole if anything happens to the freight while under the for-hire carrier's charge, this does not include the cost of any loss of reputation in the eyes of the consignee. After all, if the seller of the item is the consignor, the consignee does not deal with the for-hire carrier except as a receiver at the time of delivery. The consignor takes on any loss of goodwill the consignee has if the carrier's services fall short of expectations. If this happens, the service contract may need to be renegotiated or possibly a new carrier will have to be selected.

Of course, the number of cost centers rises when intermediaries such as 3PLs and customs brokers are used. On the other hand, intermediaries assess specific charges to their clients. Things are murkier from a cost perspective if these duties were handled in-house by the seller or the buyer of the item. International transportation involves dealing with customs officials at ports of entry. Unlike other partners along the supply chain, customs officials look for a reason to detain and physically inspect shipments. This adds to time costs. Therefore, the cost of documentary compliance is a very important consideration on top of paying any applicable customs duties.

The transportation function is magnified if multiple carriers (and bills of lading) are needed. An import from overseas may require inland transport both before and after a trans-oceanic trip via an airplane or a water vessel. Intermediaries are certainly helpful in order to make sure the process is as smooth as possible. Of course, congestion at ports of entry and exits is another factor that must be considered when calculating the TCO.

The value of the TCO approach is derived from the data gathered and monitoring the flow of activities related to the set of services that comprise transportation. Consignors, for-hire carriers, and consignees should determine which of these costs are especially important to them. Tracking changes in TCO can inform choices related to planning shipment sizes, routes taken, and the timing of pick-ups and deliveries. Naturally, such planning is improved when there is collaboration among buyers and sellers as well as all the intermediaries involved in transportation.

The cost of demurrage and detention

Transportation processes can sometimes lead to stalls and back-ups in the process. It is inevitable because of the number of moving parts. A shipping container can make several moves across multiple countries especially when it is owned by an international ocean vessel carrier with global reach. There is no reason to expect each independent move, which was arranged by different consignors, to be well coordinated in terms of pick-up and arrival.

In 2021, there were about 5600 container ships operating internationally.[i] This global fleet had a carrying capacity of about 25 million TEUs. Ports saw a throughput of containers that reached about 775 million TEUs. Thus, a lot of containers need to be moved. Delays and congestion is inevitable over such a large system.

Demurrage and detention charges are used to compensate a port of entry/exit and a for-hire carrier, respectively. The compensation is paid for lost time and/or the container taking up valuable space for longer than expected. Carriers and ports calculate demurrage as the time in-between the import container's offloading from the vessel to it leaving the port's property. Of course, for exports the direction is reversed. Either way ports use demurrage charges to try to keep containers moving through their premises. These charges are assessed to the carrier. Of course, if the consignor is

[i] Data comes from Statistica (2021).

responsible for the container languishing at the port, the carrier would pass these charges to the consignor. One reason for this could be that the consignor did not arrange for the next leg of transport (e.g., motor carrier or rail) to pick up the container in a timely fashion.

Carriers calculate detention as the time the container is out of its charge. Typically, this means the time it is under the control of the consignee once the freight is delivered or under the control of the consignor when the freight is being loaded. If it is an ocean vessel carrier which owns the container, the time involved in transport to or from the port (technically, the ocean vessel's staging area) would also be part of the detention calculation.

While lack of coordination can cause demurrage and detention, other causes include congestion at ports of entry, delay in customs clearance, and shortages of drayage vehicles and/or drivers. Less frequent, though costly, sources include weather delays and labor strikes. It is incumbent on the consignor to verify that these charges are delineated in writing along with the freight rate. This is especially important when dealing with foreign countries. In 2021, average demurrage and detention costs across 20 of the world's largest container ports were $720 per container after a 2-week period. However, when congestion is pronounced, these costs can increase quickly. For example, the ports of Los Angeles and Long Beach were charging $2500 per container over the same period.[j]

Containers languishing in one place while needing to be elsewhere has concerned regulators for some time. In 2019, the US Federal Maritime Commission (FMC) took steps to promote "just and reasonable" (i.e., fair) demurrage and detention charges.[k] The FMC is the regulatory interpreter of the US Shipping Act (1984). The Act's two pillars are: (1) nondiscriminatory regulations and (2) providing an efficient transportation system. The first pillar is supposed to constrain the regulators and the second is supposed to mandate them to promote efficiency.

The complaints that triggered the FMC to set up new rules reached a peak in 2016 when the Coalition for Fair Port Practices (which represents thousands of US shippers) petitioned it for regulatory relief. Hearings gathered testimony of increases in charges that, according to the consignors, could not be validated. When disputes arose they found no clear dispute settlement mechanism to provide guidance when contacting the carriers.

[j] See Container xChange (2021).

[k] For more details on the notice of proposed rule-making, see Federal Maritime Commission (2019).

These are problems in the marketplace; but one can argue that they are contractual problems rather than regulatory ones.

Apart from which side of the freight market has a louder voice, or more political clout, is it possible to take an objective view in rule-making? Yes, if we consider the following question: Should we leave demurrage and detention charges to the market or would the market become more efficient if the FMC could establish a rule or rules for carriers and ports to follow? Notice the use of the word "efficient" rather than "fair." Efficiency is an objective term while fairness is always a subjective one (i.e., like beauty being in the eye of the beholder). Efficiency, being simply defined as more output for a given quantity or dollar value of inputs, can be standardized and more easily measured. Fairness, on the other hand, cannot because each beholder has his own personal measure.

The FMC seems to feel that demurrage and detention charges tend to create unfair costs or burdens on consignors and consignees. The issue is not that a consignor or consignee has caused financial harm to an ocean carrier and/or a port, it is how to assess an appropriate charge for it. Obviously, the carrier needs to be able to show that the consignor or consignee was negligent in respecting allotted times. A *force majeure* (e.g., severe weather) ought to relieve either of them from an accusation of negligence. Also, allotted times need to be agreed to and spelled out in the ocean bill of lading which is the legal contract of carriage signed by the consignor and the carrier. On the other hand, the consignor ought to insist on language in the bill that absolves him if, say, heavy traffic congestion prevents timely delivery or pick-up. The consignee (as the importer) may need to ask for similar representation from the consignor (who is, in effect, the seller/exporter of the freight). The tricky part is that the consignee is not a party to the bill of lading. Thus, carriers have an incentive to work with their consignors who, likewise, must work with their consignees to keep the market as efficient as possible.

The optimal charge is an amount to make the carrier and/or the port whole. Demurrage should cover the port's cost of dealing with a languishing container plus some punitive fee (agreed to, of course, and written into the bill of lading). Detention should cover the carrier's cost of not having its container when expected (which includes the opportunity cost of a revenue load foregone or the inconvenience of having to find another one when the container is finally returned).

In a related area, Incoterms, as a form of standardized commercial language, has served the transportation industry well. Of course, the parties ought to be able to use whatever language they wish in their bill of lading. But if the FMC uses "interpretive rules" to get into the business of suggesting appropriate allotted times, types of evidence constituting overcharging, and how to settle disputes, it will find itself in an extra-legal quagmire. It is better to have the parties figure it out on a contract-by-contract basis and let them take it to the courts if the dispute cannot be resolved.[l]

There is no denying that this process is complicated. Other actors playing roles in these disputes include the motor carriers and rail carriers, which move the containers into and out of the ports and any Non-Vessel-Operating Common Carriers (NVOCCs), which might be an intermediary between the ocean carrier and the US importer.[m] But if the focus is on efficiency (i.e., keeping the containers moving safely and securely as opposed to fairness) all parties may find it easier to work together. This might incentivize negotiating and writing better contracts as opposed to independently lobbying the FMC to choose sides.[n]

Cost of regulatory compliance

IMO 2020

In 2020, the United Nations' International Maritime Organization (IMO) implemented its low-sulfur fuel mandate. Referred to as IMO 2020, it updates Annex VI of the MARPOL (or Marine Pollution Treaty of 1973). Annex VI covers a variety of airborne pollutants from water vessels. Local jurisdictions, however, have the option to enforce even tighter standards. Thus, IMO 2020, as a minimum standard, applies to international waters.[o]

The scale of the pollution problem is highlighted in a 2018 study by Goldman Sachs.[p] The marine sector is responsible for 90% of the sulfur dioxide generated by all modes of transportation. Just 15 of the world's largest

[l] Blockchain technology and smart contracts, as discussed in Chapter 6, would likely exacerbate these problems.

[m] NVOCCs may be thought of as 3PLs, which specialize in water vessel transport.

[n] Recall the discussion in Chapter 3 of container no-shows and blank sailings. These gray area or off-contract activities are quite prevalent and are part of the challenge facing the ocean vessel sector as it strives to improve certainty in contracting and costing.

[o] International waters (also called the high seas) are beyond 200 nautical miles from a country's shoreline. This was set out in the United Nations Convention on the Law of the Sea (1982).

[p] See Goldman Sachs (2018).

ocean vessels generate more sulfur dioxide than all the automobiles in the world. Sulfur dioxide is a pollutant that is harmful to the respiratory system and adds acidity to the air, which can harm crops and vegetation.

The IMO oversees 174 signatory nations. The global fleet of merchant vessels is around 53,000 units with almost 18,000 being general cargo and 12,000 being bulk cargo. Containerized vessels, typically carrying the most valuable cargo per ton, are barely 5600 in number. Therefore, different types of water-based operations are affected by IMO 2020. Some of these carriers are better able to take on the extra cost of compliance.

Under IMO 2020, the maximum sulfur content of bunker fuel to be used on ocean vessels fell from 3.5% by weight, set in 2012, to 0.5% (i.e., an 86% reduction in sulfur content). This applies to all fuel used on board meaning in main engines, auxiliary engines, and boilers. This is certainly the largest one-time change in international sulfur emission standards and, though it has been on the industry's radar since the IMO announced it in 2016, many ocean carriers were scrambling in 2019–20 to comply. Of course, the IMO designated certain Emission Control Areas (ECAs) where the standard is even stricter at 0.1%. The ECAs cover: the Baltic Sea, the North Sea, and designated coastal areas of Canada, the Caribbean (specifically Puerto Rico and the US Virgin Islands), and the United States.

Ocean carriers faced three choices:

- convert to low-sulfur fuels;
- retain the heavier, and less expensive, bunker fuel but take on the cost of installing scrubbers (i.e., exhaust cleaning systems); or
- apply to the flag state[q] for a waiver on behalf of the IMO.

Of course, the ocean carrier would have to demonstrate that acceptable alternative fuels were not available for purchase. Flag states, for their part, are required under Regulation 18 of Annex VI to "take all reasonable steps to promote the availability of fuel oils which comply with this Annex and inform the [IMO] of the availability of compliant fuel oils in its ports and terminals." The IMO also noted that exceptions are possible for emergencies involving risk to life and damaged vessels. It is also up to each flag state to determine appropriate fines for noncompliance. Thus, while the rules are uniform the sanctions are not.

[q] Unlike other modes of transport, commercial water vessels must fly the flag of the state to which they are registered. In effect, the vessels become extensions of the state's territory, and subject to its laws. For a complete review see Prokop (2014).

Basic economics suggests that if demand for low-sulfur fuel rises faster than the available supply (via refinery output and inventory draw-down) prices will rise in the near term. Beyond basic economics are the logistical constraints of time, physical space, and location. This means that some ports may have enough compliant fuel to service their customers while others may not. If this is the case, one cannot expect supply chains and ocean transportation networks to adjust quickly enough to prevent such a price increase. Until adequate fuel supplies are available where needed, the adjustments likely to take place would involve what one would expect in any large neighborhood where there is only one gasoline station. Drivers would either: hoard their fuel early on (creating traffic congestion in the area); or drive more slowly and plan trips carefully all the while hoping that a fresh supply will be on hand before the gas tank runs dry. In like manner, ocean vessels would curtail their speeds in-between ports of call and hope to ride out any shortages.

Of course, IMO 2020 indirectly affects other modes of transport that use diesel fuel (i.e., trucks and railways). Very low sulfur fuel oil (VLSFO) also meets IMO 2020 standards and is available at the major ocean vessel ports (e.g., Rotterdam and Singapore). BIMCO, the world's largest association of ship owners, characterizes VLSFO prices as having been on a "rollercoaster" in the early part of 2020. Along the way the price spread between VLSFO and heavy bunker fuel reached a high of \$340 per metric ton before falling to \$284. Despite the narrowing price spread between the two fuels many carriers will likely invest in scrubbers. Installation cost per vessel starts at about \$2 million and can rise to several million more. This is the classic cost-benefit problem of taking on upfront costs vs estimating the present discounted cost of a more volatile commodity over time. Still, BIMCO estimates that using scrubbers will take anywhere from 0.5 to 1.5 years to have a lower cost impact than switching to VLSFO. This range is dependent, of course, on the installation cost, annual maintenance costs of the scrubbers, and the daily volume of fuel consumption.

Despite the eventual savings that come from scrubbers relative to VLSFO there is still a monetary risk from external sources. This is the classic *social* cost-benefit problem where a firm must consider larger environmental impacts beyond its own market. The IMO could eventually ban heavy bunker fuel and thereby invalidate the purpose of scrubbers. The scrubbers themselves could be banned due to the effluent that they generate, which must be disposed of after arrival at a port. As scrubbers become more prevalent under IMO 2020 will trading off sulfur particulate matter for effluent waste dumps, and the associated risk of ground contamination while awaiting treatment with caustic soda, be ignored by some future update to IMO regulations?

In any case ocean carriers are taking on more costs as they adjust to IMO 2020. They will certainly try to pass those costs along to their customers as a bunker adjustment factor (BAF) or surcharge. This will filter into annual negotiations. Typically, trans-Pacific contracts run from May 1 through April 30. Even before IMO 2020 was implemented big liners such as Maersk applied a BAF on December 1, 2019 to containers shipped under spot rates and under contracts of less than 3 months.

Who bears most of the regulatory burden is a problem that economists study at length. Again, carriers buying the same fuel type face roughly the same cost per ton but they may carry bulk or containerized cargo of much different values per ton. For consignors of bulk cargo vs those of containerized consumer goods, if each faced the same BAF in straight dollars, the latter would find it easier to absorb since the value of their shipments are higher on a per ton basis. On the other hand, any excess capacity in a shipping lane puts the consignor in a better position to hold off surcharges. Some consignors may feel pressure to accept the carrier's BAF formula while others may be able to negotiate its structure.

Liquefied natural gas (LNG), which generates only negligible sulfur emissions, is another option but the conversion from heavy bunker fuel is even more expensive. Since LNG density is lower than bunker fuel the LNG tanks need to be quite a bit larger. Of course, TOTE Maritime Alaska has been an early adopter of this technology. It was the first carrier in the United States to retrofit a vessel for LNG power. Its two diesel-powered Orca-class roll-on, roll-off (RO-RO) vessels (built in 2003) are to be retrofitted with two LNG cryogenic tanks placed on the weather deck behind the ship's bridge. Each tank has a 1100 m^3 capacity.

Retrofitting, the *North Star* and the *Midnight Sun* will be handled in stages over a 4 year period. Of course, as a Jones Act carrier,[r] TOTE would no longer be dependent, unlike other carriers, on oil refinery deliveries to

[r] As noted in Chapter 1, the Jones Act is a US regulation on domestic water vessel activity. A Jones Act carrier is one which flies the US flag and, as such, is authorized to pick-up and drop-off cargo between two or more US ports. Foreign flagged vessels can only drop-off US imports and/or pick-up US exports. Some see the Jones Act as a form of trade protection while others see it as necessary for national security. The idea is that in time of crisis only US-flagged vessels are plying US coastlines and waterways. US-flagged vessels are also US-owned and US-crewed.

US ports. TOTE is planning to buy its LNG at the Port of Tacoma from Puget LNG once the company begins operations in late 2021. Until then the two vessels will still be running on diesel. The *North Star* had one of its two engines converted to LNG in December 2019. Since these two vessels play a large role in the delivery of consumer goods to Alaska, it has been necessary to stagger the retrofitting process. While less than 5% of the global ocean vessel fleet runs on LNG, there is no doubt that IMO 2020 will boost its prospects when carriers consider new vessel orders over the coming decades.

The years of planning for IMO 2020 have paid off thus far. All key players were in it together so to speak—the ports, the carriers, and their flag states. Some flag states may be quick to fine carriers arriving at port with noncompliant bunker fuel and some may not. Some carriers may choose not to comply with IMO 2020 until caught. Such is the nature of a diverse global industry made up of developed and less-developed nations. In any case, such discretion adds slack when needed in the fuel markets. Green policies for blue skies will surely occupy business and government relations for decades to come.

Zero-emission vehicles

In 2020 California mandated that truck manufacturers must produce increasingly higher percentages of zero-emission vehicles. This mandate applies to any truck manufacturers of Class 2 (e.g., lights trucks like the Ford F-150) through to Class 8 (e.g., tractors suitable for 18-wheel semitrailers).

The California Air Resources Board (CARB) set the requirement to fulfill its mandate of getting more zero-emission vehicles on the road in order to relieve the air pollution in southern California. Of course, while the vehicles may be zero-emission the supply chains that facilitate their production are not. Still, CARB's website highlights rebates and other tax incentives available to buyers of such vehicles. However, that is not as intrusive as requiring private manufacturers to retool their assembly lines without any direct tax breaks of their own.

CARB's new rule is the first of its kind and it applies to vehicle production and sales as opposed to purchases. "Build it and they will buy it" must be the hope since this is a narrow supply-side regulation. Specifically, the requirement is that from 2024 to 2035 zero-emission trucks and/or chassis sales need to rise to 55% for Class 2b and 3 trucks and to 75% for Class 4 through 8 straight trucks. For large truck tractors the proportion is 40%. By 2045, every truck produced and sold in California must be zero-emission.

Given today's technology a zero-emission mandate strictly favors electric vehicles since natural gas power is not quite emission free. Negligible amounts of sulfur and nitrogen oxide are emitted. Yet even with electric vehicles there are two options. Battery electric vehicles (BEVs) take in electricity from a charger and store it in the vehicle's battery. This is the preferred technology used at Tesla, Inc. The other option is fuel cell electric vehicles (FCEVs), which use hydrogen and oxygen to generate the electricity on demand. The hydrogen must be pumped into the vehicle's fuel tank. Honda, Hyundai, and Toyota have various FCEVs on the market. Each technology, however, requires different infrastructure at fueling stations.

Mandating production and sales on the supply-side of the market while using tax incentives to promote purchases on the demand-side is a balancing act. Including economic uncertainty over recovery from the COVID-19 pandemic with concomitant adjustments in manufacturers' supply chains, this balancing act is on a razor thin tightrope if regulators expect sales to meet their targets in 2022 and beyond. Building something does not automatically lead to sales unless the seller lowers the price and eats into his own profit margins. What would this look like? Tesla, Inc. may have the brand recognition and economies of scale to handle promotional price cuts; but what about smaller companies that are not yet price competitive? What about other companies which still see profits in internal combustion engines? Basically, who ought to be responsible for pollution from vehicle emissions, the manufacturers or the users?

Of course, if Tesla is such a good innovator in this niche, does it need regulators to mandate it? Another question, apart from the fact that zero-emission vehicles are still an emerging technology that is untested in long-haul commercial trucking, what about the support infrastructure? Will original equipment manufacturers (OEMs) be able to ensure sufficient parts as production realigns over the 2024–45 timeframe? Will charging stations proliferate at rates necessary to support the new fleets and their delivery schedules? This is a problem. Regulations can, indeed, do things fast but they rarely do things effectively at the same time.

The only regulations that truly push markets are those that facilitate and stabilize them. Establishing the rule of law, property rights, contract enforcement, etc., form the foundation of the market economy. Beyond that, regulations begin to interfere with free enterprise because they distort incentives and price signals.

A regulation mandating purchases on top of CARB's rule mandating production would likelier achieve what the regulators want. It is true that more regulation forces a result; but it also stifles the free market. Regulations are always subjective and political. They are most effective when they fix market failures. Perhaps it would be better to let the zero-emission vehicle market blossom on its own. Mandating what private companies produce distorts markets from the dealers all the way back to raw material extractors. If pollution is costly to society, it ought to be taxed directly instead of a production mandate on how to avoid creating it.

Issues and problems going forward

The joint cost vs common cost debate gets to the nature of what transportation as a service is supposed to achieve. Since these costs are incurred by the for-hire carrier from across various consignors and passengers, it creates a cost allocation problem. Some costs are separable and allocatable while others are not. When they are not it becomes a matter of demand intensity or price discrimination. In other words, it is not just a matter of cost accounting on the supply side but also of preferences on the demand side. This means that costing in transportation operations may be quite variable even when a given conveyance is carrying similar items across a given route.

TCO is particularly challenging when it comes to emerging technology. The posttransaction is comprised of maintenance issues that are not fully understood. For-hire carriers looking to invest in electric and hybrid conveyances face this challenge. Indirectly, consignors and consignees are challenged with estimating the long-term impacts of these technologies on the freight rates that will be assessed to them. It will take more carriers taking on more of these vehicles in their fleets to better understand the life cycle.

Regulations, to the extent that they impact market transactions, will always be a mix of politics and economics. All modes of transportation are regulated to varying degrees. This means the cost of transportation can be quite different across modes. Intermodal activities add another layer to the complexity of regulatory compliance.

References

Container xChange, 2021. Demurrage and Detention Benchmark. 2021. https://container-xchange.com/.

Ellram, L., 1993. Total cost of ownership: elements and implementation. Int. J. Purch. Mater. Manage. 29 (4), 3–11.

Federal Maritime Commission, 2019. Interpretive Rule on Demurrage and Detention Under the Shipping Act. Washington, DC https://www2.fmc.gov/readingroom/docs/19-05/19-05_NPRM.pdf/.

Goldman Sachs, 2018. The IMO 2020: Global Shipping's Blue Sky Moment. The Goldman Sachs Group, Inc., New York. http://www.weltinnenpolitik.net/wp-content/uploads/2018/06/IMO-2020-Global-Shipping-Blue-Sky-Moment.pdf.

Locklin, D., 1933. The literature on railway rate theory. Q. J. Econ. 47 (2), 167–230.

Phlips, L., 1985. The Economics of Price Discrimination. Cambridge University Press, Cambridge.

Pigou, A.C., 1913. Railway rates and joint costs. Q. J. Econ. 27 (4), 687–692.

Pigou, A.C., 1920. The Economics of Welfare. Macmillan, London.

Prentice, B.E., Prokop, D., 2016. Concepts of Transportation Economics. World Scientific, Hackensack, NJ.

Prokop, D., 2014. International transportation management. In: Prokop, D. (Ed.), The Business of Transportation. Modes and Markets. vol. 2. Praeger, Santa Barbara, CA, pp. 70–89.

Statistica, 2021. Container Shipping: Statistics & Facts. https://www.statista.com/topics/1367/container-shipping/.

Steiner, P.O., 1957. Peak loads and efficient pricing. Q. J. Econ. 71 (4), 585–610.

Taussig, F.W., 1891. A contribution to the theory of railway rates. Q. J. Econ. 5 (4), 438–465.

Taussig, F.W., 1933. The theory of railway rates once more. Q. J. Econ. 47 (2), 337–342.

CHAPTER 8

Problems in transportation revenue management

Revenue and cost

Revenue earned from the sale of any good or service is defined as the quantity sold over a defined period of time multiplied by the price or prices charged per unit. This means that revenue is dependent on the magnitude of buyers' demand and their willingness to pay. In addition to buyer behavior, this also means that revenue flows are dependent on the level of competition the firm faces. The more alternative sources the buyers have, the more sensitive they are to price changes made by a particular seller. While cost is also a complex calculation, it is dependent more so on technology than buyer psychology.

Revenue and cost are not functionally related, but both are components of profit. Fig. 8.1 shows this relationship for a for-hire carrier that faces a high level of competition. As such, it takes the price it charges as given. It is much like the price of a commodity set on the world market. No one producer or even a group of them can influence the world price. The carrier is a price-taker. Raising the price would cede the market to its competition and lowering the price would reduce profits since all competitors would be maintaining a higher price.[a] Thus, total revenue is drawn as a ray from the origin with a slope equal to the market price. If the carrier sells a larger amount, it automatically increases the revenue earned because the price is constant. In this case, the price does not have to fall to induce more sales by the carrier.

The total cost function shown in Fig. 1.4 was linear for the sake of simplification. In contrast, the cost function shown in Fig. 8.1 is more realistic because it features increasing and diminishing returns as production increases. Initially, costs rise at a decreasing rate, but when congestion or

[a] The assumption is that the firm could not absorb all of the market demand if it attracted other buyers from its competition. Another assumption within the model of perfect competition is that a firm can sell all of its supply at the market price. In this way, it does not pay the firm to lower its price on its own.

Transportation Operations Management
https://doi.org/10.1016/B978-0-12-815415-1.00008-2

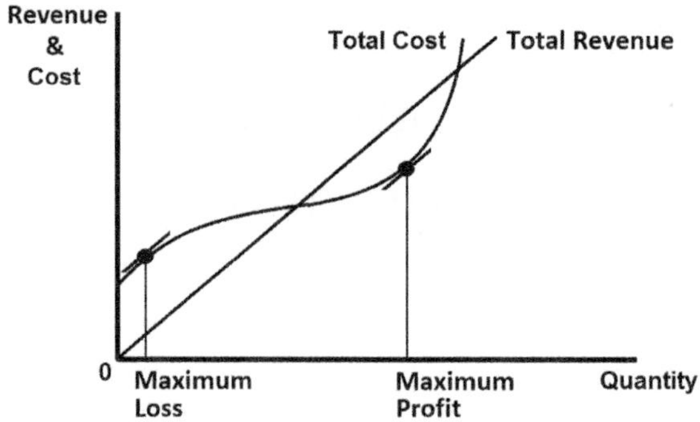

Fig. 8.1 Revenue and cost for a price-taker carrier.

crowding in the use of resources occurs, costs rise at an increasing rate. If the carrier wishes to maximize profit, it should sell a quantity where the marginal revenue earned on the last unit produced equals the marginal cost of production. The tangent line shown at the point of profit maximization in Fig. 8.1 is parallel to the slope of the total revenue function. The gap between the two functions is at its widest meaning that total revenue exceeds total cost by the largest margin. One can see on the total cost function that selling an extra unit would mean a steeper tangent line and therefore a narrowing of the gap. Selling one unit less means a flatter tangent line and a narrowing of the gap as well.[b]

Not all for-hire carriers are part of a perfectly competitive market. Only the motor carrier mode comes closest. For-hire carriers that have some degree of market power can set prices that differ from those of their competitors. Carriers may have products that are differentiated by their support services, quality of conveyances, etc. Even if the product and service were identical among carriers, prices may differ when delivery charges and other transaction costs are factored in. All carriers need not be in the same domicile; therefore, routes and distances of deliveries will differ. Certainly, the support infrastructure is not likely to be identical over various transportation networks. Fig. 8.2 shows a total revenue function that indicates a carrier with a degree of market power.

A for-hire carrier with market power has a total revenue function which is parabolic or semicircular in shape. Basically, total revenue rises and then falls based on the price elasticity of demand on the part of the consignors.

[b] Fig. 8.1 shows another quantity where marginal revenue equals marginal cost. However, that is the quantity where losses are maximized.

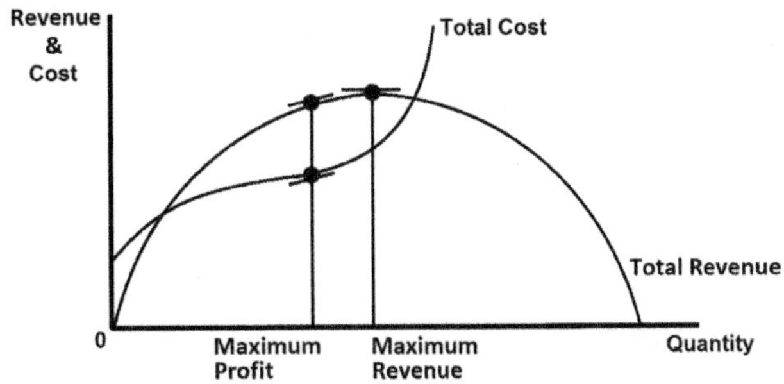

Fig. 8.2 Revenue and cost for a carrier with market power.

This is defined as the ratio of the percentage change in the quantity demanded to the percentage in the price that brought it about. Charging a very high price would lead the carrier to expect low quantities demanded. This means that total revenue would be zero or very low. By cutting a high price by some amount (say \$1), the demand response given its low starting point is likely to be a larger percentage increase. In this way, if the percentage fall in the price is less in magnitude than the percentage increase in the quantity demanded, total revenue rises. Of course, this effect does not go on indefinitely. As prices become lower and quantity demanded becomes higher, the percentage effects are switched. A cut of \$1 in an already low price combined with an increase in quantity demanded from an already large amount means that the percentage fall in the price is higher in magnitude than the percentage increase in the quantity demanded. In this situation, consignors therefore have a price-inelastic demand and total revenue falls as output increases.[c]

Fig. 8.2 shows that the point of profit maximization is not where total revenue is maximized. For-hire carriers therefore have to make a choice as to which is their preferred goal. Profit maximization may make sense from a purely financial perspective, but revenue maximization leads to more sales and potentially a higher market share. Indeed, some carriers may accept losses for a period of time if they feel that it is the price to pay in order to build brand recognition. In any case, revenue maximization always requires a level of production and supply beyond that for profit maximization. Fig. 8.2 shows

[c] Another way to trace out the shape of the total revenue function is to note that, given its market power, the carrier faces a downward sloping demand curve for its service. Examining the price elasticities of demand along the demand curve corresponds to the rise and fall of the total revenue function. For more information, see Prentice and Prokop (2016; pp. 33–40).

that marginal revenue becomes negative once total revenue is maximized. The only way to equate marginal revenue and marginal cost would be if the latter were negative as well. The only way this can occur would be if total costs fell as more production and supply were forthcoming. This, of course, is unrealistic.

Revenue management

Revenue management (RM), also called yield management, is a tool a for-hire carrier can use to manage consignor demand.[d] This in turn can assist in capacity management. For example, overbooking of passengers on certain air routes is not an accident; rather, it is an attempt by the airline to increase revenue. If a certain percentage of passengers are expected to cancel their reservations or be no-shows, then overbooking fills more seats and earns more revenue. The airline is attempting to manage the trade-off between the lost revenue from an empty seat due to a cancellation or no-show and the extra cost incurred by denying boarding due to overbooking and guaranteeing a filled seat. If a seat is double-booked, the opportunity cost of having an empty seat falls, but the expected cost of denial rises. The latter would be set in terms of the probability of a cancellation or a no-show. This, of course, requires past data to discern current passenger behavior.

Another example of capacity utilization takes the form of holding off on filling seats with discount passengers if a higher level of price-inelastic passengers is expected. Of course, the carrier has to be sure that competitors have limited capacity in order to keep the passengers from filling the seats on the rival plane. Passengers have price-inelastic demand when they feel compelled to travel at a certain time and do not have access to substitute airlines. Airlines need to be aware of major sporting events, conventions, etc. in particular cities since these raise the probability of a spike in demand along with a higher willingness to pay.

Dynamic pricing means that ticket prices are time-sensitive and employ other indicators of willingness to pay. This is not the same thing as charging more if the cost of provision is higher or the level of customer service (as assessed by the carrier) is higher. In fact, passengers know that this practice exists, though they may not know all the attributes that go into a carrier's RM system. Online booking adds convenience for the customer while at

[d] For a complete overview of RM modeling, see Talluri and Van Ryzin (2005) and Klein et al. (2020).

the same time giving the carrier more RM options than would be possible with static prices written in hard copy. Prices can be customized in ways that would not be tolerated by a group of customers browsing in one place at the same time. In fact, dynamic pricing can be automated on the carrier's website.

While RM has been a mainstay with passenger airlines for decades, it has applications in air cargo operations as well as other modes of transportation.[e] All-cargo air freighters present less of a challenge in capacity planning compared to passenger planes taking on air cargo. Since air cargo must share space with the passengers' luggage, a common cost problem is created. Also, the available capacity for air cargo is subject to the predictability of the RM system regarding seat utilization. Seat capacity is one-dimensional meaning the seat is either occupied by a passenger or it is not. Cargo, on the other hand, is multidimensional. It has weight, volume, and it may be constrained by the size of the air cargo container used to store it unless it is strapped down to the cargo deck floor with netting. On the other hand, as long as the cargo reaches its destination at the appointed time, it does not make much of a difference how many transfers take place. Passengers, to be sure, have less tolerance for multiple layovers at airports. One way a carrier can reduce uncertainty is through allotting capacity to consignors or freight forwarders which requires dedicated shipping. In this case, a stream of consignments is expected over some agreed to period of time.

When demand grows to the point where capacity becomes scarce, RM's value to the for-hire carrier grows. It is also not simply a matter of accepting or rejecting a consignor's request. A good RM system would also offer alternative routes between the origin and destination, some of which may cost more or less than the route desired.[f] However, a difference between RM for passengers and RM for freight is that the latter often relies on sales teams representing for-hire carriers. Since some consignors require multiple shipments over a specific period of time, these streams of transportation demand rely on negotiation. In this way, the sales team needs to be able to access and understand their carrier's RM process in order to explain to consignors why

[e] RM came into its own after the US airline industry was deregulated in 1978. Before then the airlines' operating licenses limited the routes they could choose and the ticket prices they could charge. For a complete review of the politics and economics which led to deregulation in multiple industries, see Kahn (1988).

[f] This process should be familiar to those who are used to booking airplane flights online. Routes could be direct or include one or more stops at transfer points with each showing departure and arrival times.

freight rates and shipping options appear the way they do. Seasonality may be the issue, or it may be something random which causes a variance in freight rates. Of course, for planning purposes, larger carriers, consignors, and freight forwarders can share data and forecasts directly using electronic data interchange (EDI) in order to examine, for example, surges in demand in particular areas, impacts due to infrastructure congestion, environmental issues, etc.

The intent of RM is to deploy the carrier's scarce resources in order to improve operating revenue flows. The goal may be to increase profit and/or market share through increasing network efficiency. Some routes may be more profitable than others, while some may be waxing or waning in that regard. Well-designed RM systems can be used to track these effects.

The five most important and interdependent components in RM systems are:

- inputs (i.e., the factors of production under the for-hire carrier's control);
- outputs (i.e., the tangible products and intangible services the carrier offers);
- customer base (i.e., the demands and willingness to pay by consignors/ passengers);
- competitors (i.e., the intra- and intermodal substitutes that consignors/ passengers have);
- government (i.e., the legal and regulatory constraints in which the for-hire carrier operates).

Consider these five points in turn. Availability of inputs and their cost at the times needed serves as a baseline for how much revenue needs to be earned in order to break even. Conveyances with sufficient capacity, labor for operations, and support infrastructure are the primary inputs. Beyond the cost of inputs are the extra costs necessary to turn these various inputs into outputs. These extra costs would include the use of technology and distribution channels to form and deliver the final product or service.[g] Determining the willingness to pay presupposes that the for-hire carrier has ways to ascertain customer behavior. Techniques include price discrimination and analysis of search behavior on the carrier's website. The former is an attempt to understand customers based on specific subgroups, while the latter separately

[g] Recall the concept of VRIN inputs covered in Chapter 6. Transportation services may be the source of a competitive advantage for the for-hire carrier. On the other hand, these costs may be difficult to allocate to specific consignors and/or passengers because they may be common costs as outlined in Chapter 7.

targets each individual. Predicting competitor behavior and how to match or surpass their prices is critical when there is high substitutability in the eyes of the customer base. While it may be difficult for a for-hire carrier to determine the range of products competitors have which are in direct competition, one technique is to examine spot markets to see if and when competitors try to match a carrier's change in freight rate or ticket prices. Slowness to react gives the carrier a chance to earn extra revenue.[h] Finally, the carrier must spend time and money complying with governmental constraints on operations. While most transport markets have been deregulated, there are still many regulations that impact operations. This is especially true for foreign carriers operating on domestic soil, along waterways, or in airspace.

Cargo RM when used in combination with passenger RM requires the airline to

- estimate the cargo capacity available (which will be the remainder after luggage is accounted for);
- allocate as much capacity as possible to dedicated consignors;
- allocate any remaining capacity to spot market cargo.

The cargo capacity estimate will have to factor in the expected weight, volume, and type (e.g., containerized or netted down). The cargo tendered through the spot market could be overbooked in order to increase revenue (given an estimated proportion of cancellations and no-shows).[i] Similar to "bumped" passengers, any cargo that cannot be accommodated would need to be routed on a different airplane operated by the carrier or a competitor.

While not as prevalent as in the airline industry, RM can also be used in container liner shipping. Unlike all-cargo air freighters and passenger airplanes, water vessels have much more flexibility regarding travel speed. Also, to some degree, cargo weight adds to the vessel's stability, whereas more weight in an aircraft means more fuel burn and more careful control of the route and elevation. If speed of delivery is not an issue, a water vessel can move slowly and idle in the ocean and offshore near a port of call. In contrast, an airplane burns fuel while in a holding pattern awaiting clearance for landing. However, fuel consumption is a major cost factor that liner companies' RM system must consider. Bunker fuel can account for as much

[h] This presumes that the for-hire carrier is raising prices due to the price inelasticity of demand and lowering them due to the price elasticity of demand.

[i] The capacity available and the proportion of cancellations and no-shows are best modeled as probability functions. For example, see Appendix A of Kasilingam (1996).

as 50% of the container vessel's operating cost.[j] There is a convenient relationship known as the admiralty coefficient (AC)[k]:

$$AC = \left(D^{2/3}\, V^3\right)/P \tag{8.1}$$

where D is the displacement (in tons), V is the velocity (in knots), and P is the propulsion or shaft power.

Displacement (D) is the weight of the water displaced by the vessel and is directly related to the weight of the cargo, fuel, equipment, and crew on board. Typically, AC is constant for similar vessels with values varying from 350 to 600. The higher the value, the more efficient the vessel is. As a source of cost, bunker fuel consumption on a given route therefore increases for vessels with lower AC. Also, D has a smaller effect on AC than does V. This means in order to keep AC constant, a percentage change in D requires a smaller percentage change in P (and therefore fuel consumption) than does the same percentage change in V. In other words, cargo on board is less of a burden on fuel burn than is maintaining velocity. RM optimization would therefore bias toward more loads on a given route as opposed to increased speed. This makes intuitive sense since the value-to-weight ratio for cargo tendered on water vessels is lower than that for air cargo.

A capacity constraint that a standard container vessel has is the limited number of places for refrigerated cargo containers, known as reefer containers or reefers. Typically, about 10% of the TEU capacity of the vessel may be devoted to reefer containers.[l] With extra care involved in order to deal with the refrigeration apparatus, the freight rate per TEU tends to be higher than for standard containers. While this process sounds similar to the extra care for first-class passengers on airplanes, the difference is that container slots not occupied by reefers can be used to hold standard containers. Airlines do not make a habit out of upgrading enough passengers to fill the first-class section of the airplane. Another difference is in the planning horizon. Container liners typically do not release slots for spot market

[j] See Notteboom (2006).

[k] For more detail on this relationship, see Harvald (1983).

[l] Of course, some vessels are equipped to carry refrigerated cargo exclusively in a break-bulk manner. Regarding container vessels, reefers may be carried above or below deck, but the cooling systems will work differently. Also, reefers carried below deck need to be plugged in, and the cargo hold needs to be equipped with blowers to deal with the external heat generated by the container's cooling system. For more details, see Maheshwar (2007).

purchases until 1–2 months before the vessel's departure. Also, booking usually closes about 1 week before departure in order to gather all necessary documents for government agencies. For international shipments, customs documents would be the most important.[m] Dedicated consignors typically have contracts for 1-year durations, and they still must book their slots on a vessel-by-vessel basis (though they will receive priority over spot market consignors). Industry practice allows for cancellation of bookings by consignors without penalty. This, of course, incentivizes overbooking. But unlike the airline industry, the containerized cargo is not as time sensitive and may be placed on a later vessel and/or a different route.

Price discrimination

If a for-hire carrier can separate out its consignors into various demand classes and charge different freight rates for the same service at the same time, it engages in price discrimination. Of course, the carrier needs market power in order to do this. To charge different prices for the identical product (size, quality, etc.), three conditions must exist for a price discrimination policy to be effective. First, the different market segments must exist; that is, they must have different demand characteristics. Second, an effective means of identifying the subgroups of consignors must be available and enforceable. Third, the subgroups must not be able to conduct arbitrage. This means the group paying a lower price cannot be allowed to transfer or sell its "privilege" to the group that is paying a higher price. There are three degrees of price discrimination. Each will be discussed in ascending order of market power.

Second-degree price discrimination is the weakest form. Different demands on the parts of consignors are known to exist, but the group members are impossible to identify directly. Consequently, for-hire carriers must rely on a method of self-identification. An example of second-degree price discrimination is freight rates that include bulk discounts. Lower prices induce those that would otherwise not enter the market to buy the carrier's services or, if already a consignor, tender even more freight. Dedicated consignors and those tendering enough freight to LTL motor carriers so that they in effect fill the entire truck would receive bulk discounts because of capacity utilization.

[m] For a list of all the US government agencies that play a role in international trade, see Prokop (2017), Table 4.1.

Third-degree price discrimination requires the market demand to be broken into identifiable subgroups by the seller. If the for-hire carrier faces the entire modal demand for transportation services along a route, or if a small group of carriers can cooperate effectively, the market demand may be broken into various classes of demanders. Bulk raw materials and manufactured goods certainly are easier to distinguish by their different haulage requirements. To the extent that these classes of demanders are different, their willingness to pay for services may be different, which is why their demands are distinct.

Freight rates charged are higher for the more price-inelastic class of consignors (net of any differences in special handling charges). A general result is that the freight rate set under third-degree price discrimination should be inversely related to the price elasticity of demand if the carrier wishes to increase revenue. Intuitively, if facing two classes of consignors, the higher price should be set where the premium in price is not offset by a greater percentage fall in the quantity demanded, thus leading to a fall in revenue. By definition, this is where demand is more price-inelastic.[n]

First-degree price discrimination requires monopoly power on the part of the for-hire carrier. It involves charging each consignor its maximum willingness to pay. First-degree price discrimination is also called Ramsey pricing. Ramsey's pricing rule assumes that the carrier, as a monopolist, is constrained by regulations to zero economic profits and prices are set according to the inverse of the individual consignor's price elasticity of demand. The more price-inelastic the consignor's demand is, the higher the markup charged. In this case, an efficient result occurs because the entire consumer surplus is appropriated by the monopoly. It can set production according to the long-run marginal cost and avoid welfare losses commonly associated with monopolies. The gains from price discrimination cross-subsidize the losses inherent in providing the optimal quantity. If the pricing yields a zero economic profit for the monopoly, then it is optimal.

Ocean carrier contracting and antitrust immunity

Transportation, like any other industry, is subject to laws against activity designed to achieve market dominance or monopoly. A notable exception is the limited antitrust immunity granted by the US government to international containership lines. This is an exemption to the Sherman Antitrust Act

[n] For a proof of this result, see Prentice and Prokop (2016), pp. 181–182.

(1890). The act states: "Every contract, combination in the form of trust or otherwise, or conspiracy, in restraint of trade or commerce among the several States, or with foreign nations, is declared to be illegal" (15 US Code § 1). Basically, monopolies and cartels were made illegal. Mergers and price policies designed to lead to monopolies were made illegal by the Clayton Antitrust Act (1914).

The United States offers limited antitrust immunity to international containership lines by allowing discussion agreements among the carriers. These are filed with the Federal Maritime Commission (FMC). It might be surprising to hear that it is US policy to grant such a degree of market protection to an industry that is mostly foreign-owned. Even as the industry moved away from US-flagged vessels to flags of convenience (e.g., those granted by Liberia, Panama, etc.) the protection remained. Such is the prominence and necessity of international container shipping to the US economy. Yet in 2017, a meeting of the industry's top CEOs in Sausalito, CA, was raided by antitrust officials wielding subpoenas for information. This nearly 2-year investigation was ultimately closed by the US Department of Justice (DOJ) in 2019 with no charges filed. There was nothing clandestine about the meeting. It was one of the biannual meetings of the International Council of Containership Operators (also known as the "Box Club"). US antitrust officials do indeed sit in on these meetings to make sure that the discussions do not veer into overt price-fixing. The group can discuss pricing guidelines (i.e., methods) but not actual prices. These guidelines are also taken by the membership to be voluntary when they set their individual freight rates. Anything more than that would be akin to cartel-like behavior. Nonetheless, the demand side of the market sometimes raises its suspicions. In other words, when do guidelines become price signals among the CEOs? It certainly is interesting that the DOJ felt it necessary to open a formal investigation into an organization it immunized. It was likely in response to recent consolidations among the world's largest container lines. Of course, the FMC approved all of these alliances in the first place and is aware of the inter-carrier discussion agreements. Thus, the regulators have a balancing act to perform.

This limited antitrust immunity was codified in the Ocean Shipping Reform Act of 1998 (OSRA) which prohibited carrier conferences[o] along

[o] Liner conferences is the industry term for cartel-like behavior; literally, having a conference to set freight rates among the carriers in order to control capacity and revenue flows in their shipping lanes.

US trade lanes. What did the carriers receive in return for this loss in market power? It was a lifting of the prohibition on negotiating confidential service contracts with preferred shippers. Naturally, big shippers like Walmart and Target were more than happy to leverage their ability to fill capacity on trans-Pacific routes from China as international supply chain activity accelerated. The power of liner conferences was greatly diminished anyway due to this hybrid of carrier cooperation and competition.

The FMC is the regulatory interpreter of OSRA. It is also important to note that this limited protection applies only to foreign-flagged carriers. Jones Act carriers (i.e., those transporting cargo from one US port to another) do not enjoy the protections codified in OSRA. In either case, price-fixing is illegal, and the DOJ has successfully prosecuted cases involving international and domestic trade lanes. A recent case involved Wallenius Wilhelmsen Logistics (WWL), "K" Line Japan, NYK Japan, and CSAV. Each paid fines in 2016 for price-fixing along trade lanes leading to the Port of Baltimore. In this case it involved roll-on, roll-off shipments of automobiles and trucks. WWL's fine after pleading guilty was $98.9 million. A case in a Jones Act trade lane involved Horizon Lines, Sea Star Line, and Crowley Maritime paying fines in 2012 related to price-fixing along the US-Puerto Rico trade lane. Horizon Lines pled guilty and agreed to pay a $45 million fine (though it was later reduced to $15 million). The complainants in this case were The Kellogg Company and Kraft Foods.

Ocean carriers and consignors have one thing in common—each wants certainty. Of course, each side differs on what ought to be certain. The container carriers will claim that they are only discussing availability among themselves and sharing capacity (i.e., discussing operational issues). One can argue that this leads to efficiencies through cost control which can be passed along to the consignors. However, consignors counter that covert price-fixing (rather than innocent sounding pricing guidelines) serves to keep freight rates higher and not lower. Also, as some claim, carrier operations can involve a liner alliance speaking for all members when negotiating contracts with tugboats, port operators, etc. A more mercantilist argument may also suggest that to the extent they do try to lower rates, do so only for the purpose of squeezing out nonmembers within a given trade lane. So, the argument would go, the liner alliances would be good for consignors only in the short run.

The FMC and the European Union's European Commission regulate an industry with a past legal practice of price-fixing. More of the carriers today are foreign and they are further consolidating. Just three alliances control

80% of the world's container vessel capacity. Their dominance is centered in Europe-Asia and Europe-US trade lanes. The 2M Alliance is made up of four liners of which Maersk and MSC are the world's two largest. The Ocean Alliance's six members include OOCL and CMA-CGM, the world's third and fourth largest. Finally, THE Alliance's six members include Hapag-Lloyd, the world's fifth largest. Despite this, the industry is characterized by overcapacity.[p] Also, an increase in Triple-E class vessels promises to exacerbate this problem in the years to come. These large vessels of more than 18,000 TEUs provide economies of scale and lower costs per TEU, but the supply chain effects are not always positive. Since liners need fewer vessels when switching over to the largest ones, this means that it takes longer to load and unload them at those large ports able to handle them. Thus, from the perspective of the demand side of the market, response time and flexibility are diminished. Only the mega-consignors would be able to easily adjust to mega-vessels.

Take an industry with huge capital costs, long lead times in acquiring vessel capacity and couple that with the uncertainty of global market conditions over that long time period. In this context, it probably never seems like a good time to invest in fleet size. But periodic investment must take place, and it is always a risk-taking exercise. Unless the United States and the European Union have the stomach for regulating international containership lines like public utilities, the current model of limited antitrust immunity may be the only way to stabilize an inherently unstable mode of international transportation. Basically, it is a regulatory balancing act.

Using auctions to find the price

In RM models, willingness to pay is not fully observable; that is, a for-hire carrier cannot know with certainty the entire demand curve for its customer base, their subgroups, or specific consignors. There is also uncertainty when prices are not well known due to newness of the product or service and if there is a high level of competition to purchase it. This is where auctions become useful. Instead of setting a price and hoping it earns enough

[p] The post-COVID-19 revival of international supply chains has shifted the problem from overcapacity to surges in demand leading to congestion at ports of entry and exit. In other words, it is easy to mandate shutdowns during a pandemic; however, resuming normal business leads to shortages and bottlenecks because activity does not resume in a uniform fashion.

revenue, an auction is used to, in effect, find the price. When an auction is well designed, willingness to pay is revealed.

For-hire carriers may desire to put their carrying capacity and available routes up for auction. Consignors would be demanders who bid for access to this limited but valuable resource. Recall, consignors view for-hire transportation as a purchasable input to facilitate their production and distribution processes. This is the basis of a standard auction. Of course, the situation could work in the reverse. A consignor who has a lot of freight to tender over a particular route or routes could hold an auction where the for-hire carriers as suppliers bid for access to this valuable stream of transportation demand. This is the basis of a reverse auction. While standard and reverse auctions have significant differences, what they have in common is that the host of the auction feels that the market is competitive enough to prefer receiving bids as opposed to negotiating individually or asking for submissions of business plans.[q] Contracts would still need to be drawn up after the winner of the auction is determined. This is necessary to make sure that each side fulfills the expectations of the other.

An auction applies a set of rules in order to foster competition for an item wanted by several bidders. The rules are important because their structure may either attract or repel potential bidders. The popular auction types noted below are stated in the context of the consignor holding a reverse auction. One should practice thinking about how these auction types would work in the standard setting. Doing this is much like learning to drive in both forward and reverse.

- *Reverse English auction:* Bids successively fall (sometimes in specific decrements), and each for-hire carrier is able to submit multiple bids.
- *Reverse Dutch auction:* The consignor sets a very low offering price, which rises in specific increments until a for-hire carrier says "stop" and accepts that price (i.e., freight rate). The increments could be called out by an auctioneer or by a special clock which ticks away from the low offering price until a for-hire carrier stops it.
- *Reverse Japanese auction:* The auctioneer continually lowers the offering price while for-hire carriers drop out of the auction. The remaining for-hire carrier is the winner and accepts the last (and lowest) offering

[q] In a standard auction, a single seller is looking for the highest willingness to pay from among the multiple potential buyers. In a reverse auction, a single buyer is looking for the lowest willingness to accept payment for inputs available from multiple potential sellers.

price from the consignor. Another way to do it is having a clock's hand tick away from the initial offering price over specific decrements until one for-hire carrier is left in the room or online.

- *Reverse first-price auction:* Sealed bids are submitted on paper in person, by mail, or online. The winning for-hire carrier is the one submitting the lowest bid.
- *Reverse second-price auction:* Sealed bids are submitted on paper in person, by mail, or online. The winning for-hire carrier is the one with the lowest bid, but the for-hire carrier is paid the second-to-lowest bid. Sometimes called a Reverse Vickrey Auction, this set of rules is thought to incentivize bidders to be more truthful (i.e., not inflating the valuation of their products and services).

Note that English and Dutch auctions could take place with all bidders physically present or online in real time. Reverse first-price and second-price auctions, on the other hand, are one-shot games, and submissions need not occur at the same time.

Firms wishing to hold standard or reverse auctions need to consider which set of rules is likelier to bring about an efficient result (i.e., buyers paying the highest possible price to a supplier or buyers accepting the lowest possible price from a supplier). Gregarious or aggressive bidders likely prefer the noise they can make in English auctions. Those who prefer a calmer atmosphere likely prefer Dutch and Japanese auctions. Finally, those who prefer not being in the presence of competing bidders, or even online in real time, likely prefer the sealed bid format of first-price and second-price auctions.

Auctions work best when there are many bidders because it fuels competition. A standard auction is said to be efficient if the winner is the buyer who is truly willing to pay the highest price—and actually pays that price. In the same manner, an efficient reverse auction has the supplier with the lowest willingness to accept win the auction and the demander actually pays the winner that amount. In addition to designing the auction's rules, the auction host needs to put thought into the preauction vetting process in order to screen out those bidders who may not have the ability to meet the expectations of the auction host. Whether it be a standard auction or a reverse auction, the for-hire carrier needs to know with some level of detail what the consignor is looking for. It is not just the nature of the freight and routes but also the timing and support services the for-hire carrier must provide to the consignor. The standard auction would have the for-hire carrier vet a pool of potential consignors. In the reverse auction, the roles are switched.

The vetting process is handled through a request for proposal (RFP) sent by the auction host to all potential bidders.[r]

The RFP requires a detailed exchange of information. The consignor's information provided to the potential for-hire carriers should as clearly as possible:

- define the transportation service being sought;
- provide detailed specifications of the freight being tendered;
- define any special needs regarding pickup, haulage, and drop-off;
- outline potential emergency situations and how they should be handled; and
- determine historical, current, and estimated future requirements

Similarly, the for-hire carrier's information provided to the potential consignor should as clearly as possible:

- provide specifications regarding cost;
- outline service capabilities; and
- describe how emergencies would be handled;

Basically, the preauction RFP is used to ensure that appropriate service value goes with the agreed to price.

When necessary, aftermarkets allow auction winners to sell their "winnings" among themselves in order to try to *improve* their collective results. How? Consider auctioning airport landing slots. These are the right for an airplane to land at the airport at a particular day and time and to receive service at a particular gate or spot on the tarmac. While such auctions may improve airport utilization, they are not the norm. Most airports allocate landing slots based on historical use. In this way, incumbent airlines may dominate hub airports, thereby making it difficult for new entrants to add competition. In 2008, the Federal Aviation Administration (FAA) attempted to auction off landing slots at two airports in New York (Kennedy and LaGuardia) and one in New Jersey (Newark). However, a court order issued at the behest of the

[r] Basically, a well-designed RFP guards against a highball bidder winning the auction, or a lowball bidder winning the reverse auction, but not following through on expectations. For example, the winning consignor agrees to pay the for-hire carrier a generous amount per ton-mile but tenders less freight tonnage than the for-hire carrier planned for. In a reverse auction, the winning for-hire carrier agrees to accept freight at a low rate per ton-mile but does not have the capacity on hand when it is needed by the consignor. The RFP must spell out all needs and how they are expected to be fulfilled. These details will form the basis of what needs to be included in the eventual contract between the for-hire carrier and consignor.

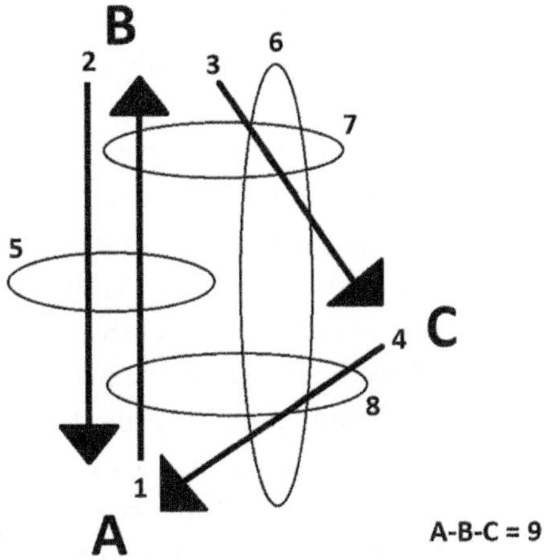

Fig. 8.3 Routes and segments in a three-node network.

Port Authority of New York and New Jersey stopped the effort. Subsequent administrations have not encouraged the FAA to pursue this option.

As an example, suppose a landing slot won at Chicago O'Hare were only valuable to the winning airline if a slot could be won at, say, London Heathrow. If it could not, the Chicago slot could be sold off to an airline which presumably has a London slot. Since the true value of a slot depends on the other slots the airline already has (or can obtain), an aftermarket allows airlines to bid for a slot more easily. The airline knows that it need not be stuck with a slot which it cannot effectively use later on when designing its flight network. Landing slot auctions cannot be looked at in isolation at each airport. In that regard, regulators should only restrict trading so that airlines do not monopolize hub markets.

Another example of matching winnings involves a motor carrier winning an A-B route and load from a consignor holding a reverse auction. Fig. 8.3 illustrates the situation. Unless the carrier also wins or has access to a B-A load, it would like to arrange a repositioning move to some other point (C). This would allow a B-C and/or C-A haul that would, presumably, lower the amount of empty backhaul miles. In effect, A-B-C-A is a triangular route. Such a three-node network, if it is in the consignor's purview, could have up to 9 different routes to bid on as shown in the figure.[s] For example, the fronthaul and backhaul for A-B is labeled route 5 while an empty repositioning move from the domicile at point A in order to haul

[s] This simple example is also discussed in Sheffi (2004).

along B-C and C-A is labeled route 6. Routes 7 and 8 involve some empty backhauls while route 9, which involves hauls along the entire triangle, does not.

The for-hire carriers, depending on their capabilities, may wish to bid for all the tendered freight in a particular route or just a fraction of it. The consignor in response needs to lay out the rules to establish the weighting used to find the winner of the auction. It should also lay out its objective. It could be to minimize the transportation expenditure over the network. Alternatively, it could be to minimize the delivery time over the network. It could also be a weighted average of expenditure and delivery time. In any case, the for-hire carriers need to know this so that they can make strategic decisions on their bids. In a weighted bid environment if a for-hire carrier has to bid high in order to incentivize providing the expected speed of service, it may not win the reverse auction. Of course, the for-hire carrier should not bid so high if speed is not one of its competitive advantages. Basically, the consignor's RFP will need to provide a complete set of rules, weighting formulas, etc.

There is an alternative to requiring for-hire carriers to try to balance their networks using aftermarkets for trades among themselves. The consignor could design a combinatorial reverse auction. As the name suggests, this auction allows for bids on a combination of routes that the for-hire carrier feels gives it the balance it needs regarding fronthauls and backhauls. Presumably, the packaged bid would be lower than the sum of bids of separate segments made independently. The reason for this is the package creates efficiencies through economies of distance, vehicle size, etc., while separate segments that may not be paired do not.[t] Naturally, a combinatorial auction has more moving parts, and therefore more care must be given to the rules and the RFP if the set of winners is to be able to use the transportation network efficiently.

Issues and problems going forward

Increasing revenue need not mean increasing profit. For-hire carriers, therefore, have a strategic decision to make when they consider how to price their products and services. Beyond airlines, RM is likely to become more prevalent over the coming years in the pricing decisions made by other for-hire carriers. Improvements in computer technology and data collection can

[t] Reviews of combinatorial auctions in transportation settings are covered in Gansterer and Hartl (2016) and Xu and Huang (2014).

assist in RM system design. Online auctions may also increase in usage. Beyond online spot markets, some consignors and for-hire carriers may find that customized auctions can lower their transaction costs and improve the contracting process. The motor carrier sector is a good candidate for these tools because it is a more fragmented mode and operates on lower profit margins.

In a well-designed auction, one side of the market is incentivized to act competitively. An RM system, when enhanced with price discrimination, is a way for a for-hire carrier to stand out from the competition. Of course, if the increase in RM and auction usage is slower than in other industries, the reasons are similar to those regarding the process of digitization and information sharing as outlined in previous chapters. This is a supply chain management problem more so than one of technology diffusion.

Revenue management, being related to the level of competition in the market, cannot be separated from how particular modes of transportation are regulated. The case of antitrust immunity and international containership lines highlights a unique example. Pricing and contracting are handled in unique ways as well. OSRA and the Jones Act play a large role in how business is conducted within that mode. Despite talks of reform that have occurred over the last decade, it does not appear likely that the US Congress would drastically change these regulations anytime soon. While each mode of transport is regulated differently, they are interconnected revenue-wise when intermodal transportation takes place. Of course, a source of revenue to one party is a source of cost to another.

References

Gansterer, M., Hartl, R., 2016. Request evaluation strategies for carriers in auction-based collaborations. OR Spectr. 38, 3–23.

Harvald, S., 1983. Resistance and Propulsion of Ships. Wiley Interscience, New York, NY.

Kahn, A., 1988. The Economics of Regulation: Principles and Institutions. The MIT Press, Cambridge, MA.

Kasilingam, R., 1996. Air cargo revenue management: characteristics and complexities. Eur. J. Oper. Res. 96, 36–44.

Klein, R., Koch, S., Steinhardt, C., Strauss, A., 2020. A review of revenue management: recent generalizations and advances in industry applications. Eur. J. Oper. Res. 284 (2), 397–412.

Maheshwar, C., 2007. Ships carrying reefer containers. Marine World 7, 31–32.

Notteboom, T., 2006. The time factor in liner shipping services. Marit. Econ. Logist. 8 (1), 19–39.

Prentice, B.E., Prokop, D., 2016. Concepts of Transportation Economics. World Scientific, Hackensack, NJ.

Prokop, D., 2017. Global Supply Chain Security and Management: Appraising Programs, Preventing Crimes. Butterworth Heinemann, Cambridge, MA.
Sheffi, Y., 2004. Combinatorial auctions in the procurement of transportation services. Interfaces 34 (4), 245–252.
Talluri, K., Van Ryzin, G., 2005. The Theory and Practice of Revenue Management. Springer Science + Business Media, New York, NY.
Xu, S., Huang, G., 2014. Efficient auctions for distributed transportation procurement. Transp. Res. B 65, 47–64.

CHAPTER 9

Risk management in transportation

Risk and uncertainty

When an item is secured in a warehouse there is still an element of risk and uncertainty in the form of damage or theft. When it is being transported the risk and uncertainty increase because there are more possibilities for bad things to happen. Of course, because supply chains are so interconnected, an item in a warehouse is likely dependent on some other item that is in motion. Very simply, most commercial items are reliant on the steady and reliable flow of electricity via a power grid. The power grid also empowers communication systems in order to share and update information related to the item. Just like supply chain management is a collaborative process among several players so is risk management.

Supply chains and the logistical flows within them are subject to a variety of threats. Beyond theft other threats can be economic, geopolitical, technological (e.g., cyberattacks), medical (e.g., chemical and biological), environmental, and terrorist related. Freight, conveyances, and support infrastructure are subject to risk and uncertainty from a variety of sources: human error, neglect, malfeasance, errors or damage attributable to machinery and technology, and emergencies due to the natural environment.

There is a distinction between risk and uncertainty. If the future cannot be known with 100% certainty the same can be said for the accuracy of any forecast for an event that has not yet happened. Knowing something with certainty is not, therefore, in need of forecasting. Considering the possible events or changes in states of nature that might occur is relatively easy. If, however, there is no way to assign probabilities to them then the observer is dealing with uncertainty and not risk. The US West Coast is subject to earthquakes. Global climate change is making weather more volatile in some parts of the world. The COVID-19 pandemic was financially beneficial for companies specializing in e-commerce and virtual meeting software while other companies were temporarily or permanently shut down. From a business perspective, it would be nice to home in on where and when a truly

Transportation Operations Management
https://doi.org/10.1016/B978-0-12-815415-1.00006-9

disruptive event might occur and how severe and prolonged it would be. Unfortunately, there is no way to know. Any assignment of probabilities would be guesswork. Probabilities are ratios of a particular event relative to the total number of possible events. This kind of reasoning does not apply to situations subject to uncertainty.

Unfortunately—for those who prefer only quantitative analysis—uncertainty cannot be ignored. To do so would be akin to a person looking for his lost car keys only under a lit streetlight because the other areas are dark. One may have to feel around in darkened corners in order to, with luck as opposed to skill, find those missing keys. In other words, dealing with uncertainty does offer opportunities. With multinational supply chains and transportation taking place over longer distances, there are more opportunities for things to happen—big and small; good and bad.

The matrix shown in Fig. 9.1 would be filled in with subjective valuations based on the best guess of the range of possible events and decisions which could be made. An example of a possible event concerns changes to consumer demand. Perhaps a large change, a small change, or the status quo is an acceptable range. Another example could be the impact of a natural disaster ranging from devasting, impactful, and no impact. Possible decisions, apart from doing nothing, involve changes to the business' financial, operational, and employee situations.

With the range of possible events being subjective so then is the appropriate decision to make. Should the preferred decision correspond to the one with the highest payoff cell? Should it be the one whose payoff row appears to have an acceptable range of payoffs (knowing, of course, that it is not

		Possible Events			
		1	2	...	Status Quo
Possible Decisions	1	payoff	payoff	...	payoff
	2	payoff	payoff	...	payoff
	...	...	...	...	...
	Do Nothing	payoff	payoff	...	payoff

Fig. 9.1 Uncertainty payoff matrix.

possible to take a weighted average since probabilities are not known)? Should the preferred decision take into account the opportunity cost of decisions not taken? One way to incorporate opportunity cost is calculating the maximum regret from all decisions not taken and then taking the decision that minimizes the regret. This is called the minimax regret decision.

Different decision-makers, and indeed the same person at different times, may differ in the psychological spectrum that runs between optimism and pessimism. The decision-maker may feel risk-averse if the negative impact of an event is high and/or it seems highly likely. Low impact events and/or seemingly unlikely ones may lead to risk-taking activity. These attitudes are subject to change based on new information and experiences. The point is that a decision should be made and validated. Doing nothing may be a valid decision as long as it can be justified against doing something. Standing idly by or making decisions at random are not good ways to deal with uncertainty.

Risk and uncertainty along the supply chain

Risk and uncertainty can impact any and all nodes along a supply chain either simultaneously or sporadically. In other words, prevention of all unwanted events is desirable but impossible. Yet it makes sense for for-hire carriers and consignors to understand their role within a marketplace and within society.[a]

Most of the time sellers and buyers take markets for granted. They appear to open and close based on economics. But there is more to well-functioning markets than economics. Markets require a foundation in which transportation plays a critical role. It all comes together like a pyramid. When a societal threat is large enough in magnitude this pyramid informs the emergency management process. Any emergency having commercial impacts reveals the nature of this pyramid and how fragile markets for goods and services can be.

Supply chains have become more complex and multinational without consumers much noticing. The ability to trade at a distance has fueled globalization with its concomitant drive to open new markets, increase competition, and lower the costs of production. The curse of not noticing this

[a] The effect of transportation disruption along the supply chain made up of various tiers of vendors is modeled in Wilson (2007). A model with random disruptions is presented in Azad et al. (2014).

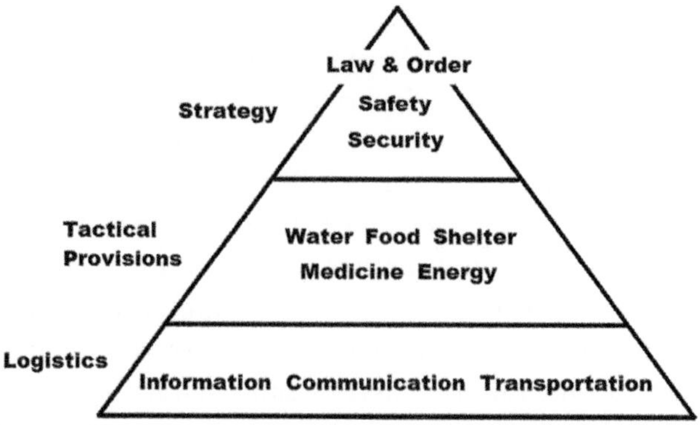

Fig. 9.2 Transportation in the logistics support structure. *(From Prokop, D., 2017. Global Supply Chain Security and Management. Elsevier. Fig. 4.1.)*

seemingly invisible logistics support structure is that one may not know when supply chain linkages start to strain or fray. The logistics support structure is the foundation of the pyramid as shown in Fig. 9.2.

The pyramid shows all components which need to be in place for markets to function efficiently. Since markets promote transactions between people it is their health, safety, and security that is paramount. Working from the top of the pyramid downward, people are willing to trade with each other only if law and order is assured within the vast areas between individual buyers and sellers. Not only does law and order provide the basis for entering into contracts, but it also provides the basis on which property can be owned and secured.

With law and order in place can firms open for business? Will transactions take place? Not unless the managers and workers feel safe at their places of business. It is also important to note that these people have families and other loved ones. Managers and workers will not come to work unless they feel safe in their homes. They need to know that their elderly relatives are secure in their own homes or care facilities, and their children are able to attend school.

For the strategic elements in the pyramid to function, certain tactical provisions are necessary. If reliable access to water, food, shelter, medicine, and energy is not assured people will not go to work. Reliable access to these necessities of life can make or break civil societies. Since these tactical elements are not located in one place, and all of their users are not located in one place either, reliable access is a matter of logistics. In this context, modern markets are really luxuries supported by reliable access to information, communication, and transportation.

The bottom of the pyramid shows the elements of logistical support. People require access to information in order to mitigate risks or deal with emergencies. They need to communicate with each other in order to share information and make decisions for themselves and for their loved ones. They need access to transportation networks in order to plan for emergencies or to overcome them. Moving all of the tactical provisions shown in the pyramid requires consignors and for-hire carriers to work well together. In emergency situations, the consignor would be the government or other relief organizations. Whether it be normal business conditions or actual emergencies, logistics simply cannot be ignored.

At any time, a critical piece of infrastructure can be impacted by traffic congestion or damaged by an accident, environmental disaster, or terrorism. If such an event impacts any of the elements shown in the pyramid, supply chain linkages will be strained and markets will slow down or shut down. In this context, one can appreciate the role of the government in having solid plans in place to provide emergency relief when called upon. In fact, emergency response procedures and the staging of the tactical provisions shown in the pyramid are exercises in supply chain management.

Compared to emergencies like 9/11 and Hurricane Katrina in 2005, the US government took the unprecedented step to shut down markets before the COVID-19 pandemic did it for them. Government officials were working on the assumption that their pro-active measures would "flatten the curve" of hospitalizations and death and reduce the pandemic's socioeconomic strain. Of course, a government can shut down commercial activity more easily than it can revive it.

Risk assessment

Though subjective features are involved, there is a systematic approach to handling risk. It requires defining the risk space and assessing what might occur within it. Naturally, each of the five modes of transportation is susceptible to different types of risk.[b] There are six cumulative steps in risk assessment:

[b] Since the term risk assessment is a popular one and does not always imply risk in the probabilistic sense it will be used here. However, it is more accurate to refer to it as an assessment of risk and uncertainty. Risk assessments across several modes of transportation are covered in Ke and Verma (2021), Khan et al. (2021), and Kontovas and Psaraftis (2009).

- Define the risk space (i.e., the jurisdiction of responsibility including the users or partners within it).
- Identify what could go wrong and where within the risk space.
- Assess the most impactful risks by investigating and estimating their possible magnitudes. Try to quantify the risk through monetary and probability measures whenever possible.
- Determine the cost of risk mitigation. Consider a proactive vs a reactive approach.
- Develop a risk management plan based on the results of the previous steps.

The risk space encompasses what is within the organization's area of control or influence. Areas beyond that are subject to uncertainty as opposed to risk. Regarding identification, as noted earlier, risk can occur due to human, technological, mechanical, and environmental sources. Any or all of these which make up the risk space need to be broken down further. This includes how labor and capital are deployed, how they interact within the risk space, and where are the potential sources of error, neglect, damage, or malfeasance. Managerial oversight must also be included in terms of identifying how information is gathered and acted upon in order to keep the system running smoothly.

Assessing impactful risks could be illustrated as a variation in Fig. 9.1. The rows could list the range of impacts of the event rightward from, say, minor to devastating. The columns could list the frequency of occurrences over some time period. These could range downward from frequent to rare. The cells could be filled with the number of actual events that occurred over the time period being assessed. This captures the history of the organization's risk. Another option is to place numbers on a Likert scale in order to make forecasts. These two options could be applied separately to each type of risk (i.e., human, machinery, technology, and the natural environment). In this way, different managerial segments of the organization (e.g., human resources, information technology, engineering, etc.) could devote their time and energy to a matrix targeted to their core competencies. Cells with numbers considered too high are the ones that deserve the most attention.

Targeting the most impactful and frequent events will set out what needs to be in the mitigation plan. The procedures need to be monetized and compared to the revenue flow and/or cash on hand to deal with it. This is very much a cost-benefit analysis. The organization will have to decide if it can afford the mitigation or simply live with the risk. These are tough but necessary decisions.

Force majeure

For-hire carriers are responsible by law for loss, damage, or delay in any freight under their control. This is a form of risk mitigation that benefits consignors and consignees. Of course, there are exceptions such as an "act of public enemy" (i.e., enemy acts in time of war), an "act of public authority" (i.e., the conveyance is commandeered by the government), inherent vice (i.e., unknown or hidden defects in the freight itself), and force majeure (i.e., an act of God). Service contracts between consignors and consignees may also have clauses that specify the conditions for force majeure.

Global supply chains have been challenged by the uncertainty that has burdened the transportation sector since COVID-19 surfaced in Wuhan China in December 2019. But a testimony to how mutual trust simultaneously strengthens supply chains and makes them more flexible comes in the discussion around adjusting the terms of existing contracts. If a sincere attitude is necessary in order to enter into a contract it is certainly necessary if and when it needs to be adjusted.

An example of some of the pitfalls that can occur when cross-border transportation occurs was seen with the China Council for the Promotion of International Trade (CCPIT), a government organization. In March 2020, it issued over 4800 force majeure certificates to China-based companies holding supply contracts ranging from thousands of yuan to billions of yuan. The total contracted value translated to about $50 billion. The CCPIT claimed to be helping "enterprises safeguard their legitimate rights and interests and reduce the losses caused by the [COVID-19] epidemic."[c] Referring to the legal weight this carries, the CCPIT noted that "one party of the contract may claim partial or complete exemption from the liability of nonperformance, incomplete performance or delay in performance of the contract by virtue of the certificate."[c] This means that any nonperformance penalties noted in contracts are not enforceable in Chinese courts—and the duration of these certificates were for an indefinite period of time. This development adds risk to international companies with supply chain linkages through China.

[c] China Council for the Promotion of International Trade (2020).

Narrowly considered, a contract of service is designed to protect each party's interests. But beyond "the four corners of the contract" which lawyers focus on are the unwritten relationships that can flow from it. Ideally, both parties need to share a mission and develop a strategy which ultimately serves the final customer at the end of the supply chain. Without the final customer buying the good or service a lot of upstream activity would not take place. Basically, transparency is not achieved when one contracted party can appeal unilaterally to the government for protection on otherwise shaky legal foundations.

Assuming the contracts between the China-based and international business partners even have force majeure clauses within them, it is hard to see COVID-19 as an act of God in a strictly legal sense, especially since it was government action (or, more likely, inaction) that led to its spread within Wuhan and then around the world. Human actions could be a source of force majeure but under common law and international law, these are typically spelled out in the contract as opposed to just inserting the force majeure term as a catch-all.

Those international companies which have no choice but to deal with their China-based vendors may decide that it is simply better to maintain the relationship, hoping for an eventual and steady resumption of supply, than to take their chances in Chinese courts willing to give legal weight to the CCPIT's force majeure certificates. A good practice in supply chain management is to let the partner who is better able to assume cost and risk do so. This is in the spirit of shared burden. The ugly twin of that practice is to pass along the burden to the partner least able to avoid it.

There is a problem in thinking of transportation as a transactional function rather than a relational one. If the discussion is only about the freight rate it is merely a zero-sum game between the consignor and the for-hire carrier. But if it is a discussion about services then the result could be a positive-sum game. Quality of service from the carrier combined with a commitment from the consignor to purchase capacity is a win-win if it can grow out of a well-honed contract.

China's rapid economic growth since the 1990s and the international trade relationships which grew out of it seemed to fixate both sides of the container liner market on price and not service. This is ironic since within the terms of the US Ocean Shipping Reform Act (OSRA) of 1998 was the opportunity for confidential service contracts rather than the container liners sticking to freight rates formerly set by carrier conferences (i.e., cartels).

Yet the container liners continued to merge into mega-alliances to try to ensure their own profitability or, in bad years, mitigate losses. Here, too, relational options may exist in the form of sharing and integrating digital platforms. Many players—the for-hire carriers, the consignors, the intermodal partners, and the ports—are investing in digital solutions and artificial intelligence (AI). Will they share their data in the spirit of relationship-building or hoard it out of mistrust? As supply markets readjust in China, or as buyers shift to other Far East Asia locales, new opportunities to collaborate may present themselves.

An example of the government working to assist with contract compliance regards providing relief to domestic and foreign airlines' use of their landing slots on routes in areas susceptible to spikes in COVID-19. The Federal Aviation Administration (FAA) took the lead in March 2020 by suspending the so-called 80/20 rule through the end of May of that year. The International Air Transport Association (IATA), whose membership of 300 passenger and cargo airlines account for about 80% of the world's air traffic, asked other jurisdictions to follow the FAA's example. In this case, they asked the airports (most of which are government owned) to consider relaxing contract enforcement. Of course, this is not the same thing as the CCPIT's extra-judicial interference in the business activities between two private parties.

The 80/20 rule is a "use it or lose it" requirement. Air carriers must make use of the time-and-day specific landing slots they purchased at airports at least 80% of the time. Failure to do so leads to forfeiture. Naturally, when the US imposed travel bans on non-US residents from China and Europe (excluding the United Kingdom), many air carriers needed to adjust their routes, times, and frequencies. Relaxing the 80/20 rule gave them the flexibility they needed to make efficient decisions as they adjusted capacity in the face of lower demand for air travel.

The role of government is exemplified in creating incentives for private agents to enter into contracts backed by a judicial system which will enforce them. It is best when governments do not go down the road of interfering extra-judicially in contracts by, in effect, picking winners and losers.

General average

The spirit of shared burden within service contracts takes on a unique form in the water vessel mode. Cargo insurance which for-hire carriers rely on to make their consignors whole is a mainstay in motor carrier, rail, and air transport.

Water vessel transport is quite different. Being the oldest of the five modes of transport it has a lot of history and precedence to draw from.

The world's news media watched as the MV Ever Given got stuck in the Suez Canal between March 23 and 29, 2021. This ultralarge 20,000 TEU vessel was in the middle of its voyage from the Port of Tanjung Pelepas in Malaysia to the Port of Rotterdam when, according to the vessel operators, strong winds made it run aground. Its 430-yard long hull nestled obliquely along both edges of the narrow canal.

Once the MV Ever Given was dislodged from the canal, the news media moved on much like passers-by at a road accident. The vessel was towed out of the narrow canal and into the adjacent Great Bitter Lake in Egypt. World trade resumed once more through this critical international choke point. On average, about 50 vessels per day pass through the Suez Canal.

The legal aftermath began soon after the vessel was dislodged. The first move was the vessel owner's declaration of so-called general average. This implies, for insurance purposes, that a danger to the vessel existed while it was trapped. Though leased by Taiwan-based Evergreen and operated by Germany-based Bernhard Schulte Shipmanagement (BSM), the Panama-flagged vessel was actually owned by Japan-based Shoei Kisen Kaisha. The subsequent investigation showed no damage to the vessel or the containers on board.

When a claim of general average is upheld, all consignors have to pay a bond to have their cargo released from the vessel once it reaches an appropriate port. How much would this be? Typically, it is a salvage value set at some percentage of the cargo's value. The exact amount is up to the maritime insurance adjustor once the investigation is completed. These can take months or even years. Until then all consignors have to wait. Of course, consignors who maintain their own maritime cargo insurance can file their own claims while waiting for the process to work itself out, assuming their policies cover losses due to a declaration of general average. Those consignors who do not have such insurance may lose their cargo if they cannot or will not pay the salvage value assessed.

General average is a part of maritime law codified in the York Antwerp Rules (1890). In fact, the concept goes back to ancient Greece. In those days throwing cargo overboard in order to save the vessel was deemed a loss to be shared by the for-hire carrier and all the consignors. Today, as in the past, general average is used by the for-hire carrier to force all parties to share proportionally in the costs associated with rescuing the vessel from a dangerous predicament.

In the case of the MV Ever Given, other directly affected parties included the Suez Canal Port Authority, which had to marshal the necessary dredgers and 11 tugboats to free the vessel, and the approximately 400 other container vessels that were waiting in the queue. Vessels on Asia-Europe routes wishing to avoid the blockage had to steam around the Cape of Good Hope which added an extra week to their trips.

The International Federation of Freight Forwarders Associations noted for its shipper customers that a claim of general average need not require any physical damage or other loss of property.[d] In fact, any expenditure of funds used to rescue the vessel is interpreted as a loss of property that must be shared proportionately. BSM noted that the vessel passed independent inspection by the American Bureau of Shipping and was deemed seaworthy. Unfortunately for the consignors who had to await access to their property, the Suez Canal Port Authority sought a court order to detain the vessel, with crew on board, pending the vessel owners paying a compensation claim of $916 million. Though not part of the general average process itself, the two parties undertook their own negotiations for the release of the vessel.

There is never a good time for supply chain disruptions to occur, let alone as international trade flows try to stabilize amid the blockage of a critical choke point. The effect of congestion on transport predictability, the cost of demurrage and detention, the need to build supply chain resiliency, etc., will preoccupy logistics professionals indefinitely.

Insurance and reinsurance

Transportation facilitates trade. But if it is too expensive for the consignor then trade does not take place. Likewise, trade does not take place if importers at the manufacturer or wholesaler level feel that their retail customers downstream along the supply chain will not pay them. Importers take on the risk of holding excess inventory. They also take on risks when selling items on credit (typically, with 1–3-month terms). This, in effect, offers interest-free loans. Their customers can earn revenue and pay down the cost of goods sold retroactively. Doing more with other people's money always looks attractive. Of course, importers can mitigate the risk of holding past-due accounts receivable by also holding trade credit insurance. About $600 billion of annual US sales are protected in this way.

[d] International Federation of Freight Forwarders Associations (2021).

Just like transportation facilitates trade—due, in part, to for-hire carriers holding cargo insurance—trade credit insurance takes some of the worries out of the import process. Of course, even those not trained in actuarial science can see that the insurers themselves were facing increased risk due to the COVID-19 pandemic and the global recession it precipitated in 2020. The likelihood of defaults and bankruptcies was higher than they were pre-pandemic. This would lead to more trade credit insurance claims. Thus, insurers became leery about issuing more coverage. If there is less insurance on offer there will be less liquidity along supply chains and, therefore, less trade and transportation.

Atradius, Coface, and Euler Hermes, three of the largest trade credit insurers, called for the US government to assist the industry in the face of a higher likelihood of claims. Their jointly commissioned report proposed variants of risk-sharing models (known as reinsurance) between the private insurers and the US government. The intent was to implement one of these models on a temporary basis to ride out the pandemic. The report, released in 2020 by Econ One, a consultancy, noted that about 60% of trade credit insurance is issued to small and medium-sized enterprises (SMEs).[e] The report also found that coverage over 2019–20 had already been cut back by 14%. Fear of a second wave of COVID-19 in 2021 prompted insurers to cut back even further. In any case, less insurance coverage raises importer risk which permeates the supply chain. The alternative is to require downstream partners to pay in advance or upon delivery. Given the economic stakes involved the National Retail Association stated its support for a government-backed reinsurance program.

Uncertainty in the insurance market is shared by all parties. On the supply side, how liquid are the insurance companies and the banks? Likely more so now than just after the 2008 financial crisis. But the problem during the COVID-19 pandemic was not a credit crunch, it was a government-mandated spending crunch. On the demand side, what are the importers doing to raise their insurability? Hopefully, they are improving their supply chain management skills. Building better relationships with their foreign sources, for-hire carriers, and downstream customers are a must. Basically, it is about trying to make things steady and predictable, which insurers prefer, as opposed to erratic and uncertain. Time and money must be invested in good relationship-building.

[e] Litan and Xu (2020).

Another worthy investment is in digitization. Often talked about in the context of transparency and logistical efficiency, getting the paper out of transactions between exporters and importers (including the intermediaries they rely on) speeds trade flows, avoids errors, and offers a degree of standardization, which is not the norm in paper-based international trade. It would likely also speed up the processing of insurance claims. It is certainly a good signal to send to any insurer during uncertain times.

A single window

Seamless trading in data and documents, that is, transparency, has merits. Supply chain partners want to collaborate. However, there are limits based on legacy systems, different partners wanting to use different enterprise resource planning (ERP) systems, for example.[f] Lack of transparency adds to the risk of suboptimal performance or even loss. Of course, overlaying a system-wide program adds risks as well. Apart from buy-in across the supply chain the information flow has to be bi-directional, a two-way street of sharing and accountability. Thus, any system-wide overhaul must be phased in over different parts of the supply chain. This has risk in the form of interoperability during the phase in. Finally, no matter what system is in place each requires data accuracy.

The Port of Los Angeles, as a municipal organization, was discussed in Chapter 6 in the context of offering a cloud-based electronic portal for its customers. At the federal level, the United States-Mexico-Canada Agreement (USMCA) came into force in 2020. It includes innovations that were not available when its predecessor, the North American Free Trade Agreement (NAFTA), came into force in 1994. Consider the single-window entry point for electronic document submissions as outlined in USMCA Article 7.10.[g] Using the World Customs Organization Data Model as a basis for gathering data elements, the idea is for importers to have a more streamlined system for tracking the status of an item moving within the North American trade bloc. The intent is to increase transparency and speed the release time from the respective customs agency. If this works according

[f] US Customs and Border Protection manages international trade flows using a single-window called the Automated Commercial Environment (ACE). Data on conveyance, freight, and containers are shared among 12 federal departments and eight independent government agencies. For an overview see Prokop (2017), pp. 68–73.

[g] The full text of the agreement may be found at the United States-Mexico-Canada Trade Agreement (2021).

to the plan it should lower compliance costs and increase trade flows. Of course, this is only harmonization regarding an electronic portal. It is not harmonization of customs regulations and procedures themselves as noted in USMCA Article 7.11. Such a thing would move the agreement along the lines of a customs union which neither trade partner negotiated for. Each USMCA country maintains the right to run its customs agencies as it sees fit.

Issues and problems going forward

Unless and until all activities involving transport from point A to B are measured and open to probabilistic calculations there will always be uncertainty in transportation. In effect, to eliminate uncertainty the black box of transportation would have to be eliminated and planners would also need perfect foresight. Every conveyance would have to be made autonomous of human drivers and controlled in a mass by a central authority. Supply chain partners, within domestic and cross-border activities, would have to share information in real-time in order to achieve complete transparency. Of course, even if all this were to happen, emergences due to human error, the criminal element, and the natural environment cannot be mitigated completely.

Risk and uncertainty remain in various degrees across different modes of transportation, along particular routes, and within different jurisdictions. Risk assessments, and therefore mitigation plans, can differ because of the subjective nature of the process; and risk attitudes can differ across supply chain partners. Flexibility in business choices is the hallmark of innovation and competition and so, therefore, is the need for risk management. This must be a part of the contracting process between for-hire carriers and consignors. Risk-sharing could be strictly defined like the general average concept, or it could be more flexible like force majeure. In any case, thought should be given to how strong the logistical support structure is which facilitates the market for goods and services.

References

Azad, N., Davoudpour, H., Saharidis, G., Shiripour, M., 2014. A new model to mitigating random disruption risks of facility and transportation in supply chain network design. Int. J. Adv. Manuf. Technol. 70, 1757–1774.

China Council for the Promotion of International Trade, 2020. CCPIT Issues the Force Majeure Certificates of Novel Coronavirus Disease (COVID-19) for Enterprises. https://en.ccpit.org/infoById/40288117668b3d9b017080e1f9b5072f/2.

International Federation of Freight Forwarders Associations, 2021. MV Ever Given Owner Declares General Average. http://fiata.com/index.php?id=990.

Ke, G., Verma, M., 2021. A framework to managing disruption risk in rail-truck intermodal transportation networks. Transp. Res. E Logist. Transp. Rev. 153, 1–18.
Khan, F., Yarveisy, R., Abbassi, R., 2021. Risk-based pipeline integrity management: a road map for the resilient pipelines. J. Pipeline Sci. Eng. 1, 74–97.
Kontovas, C., Psaraftis, H., 2009. Formal safety assessment: a critical review. Marine Technol. 46 (1), 45–59.
Litan, R., Xu, Y., 2020. A Strong Recovery Requires a Healthy Trade Credit Insurance Industry. Econ One, Washington, DC. https://www.econone.com/wp-content/uploads/2020/07/A-Strong-Recovery-Requires-a-Healthy-Trade-Credit-Insurance-Industry.pdf.
Prokop, D., 2017. Global Supply Chain Security and Management: Appraising Programs, Preventing Crimes. Butterworth Heinemann, Cambridge, MA.
United States-Mexico-Canada Trade Agreement. (2021). Washington, DC. Office of the United States Trade Representative. https://ustr.gov/trade-agreements/free-trade-agreements/united-states-mexico-canada-agreement.
Wilson, M., 2007. The impact of transportation disruptions on supply chain performance. Transp. Res. E Logist. Transp. Rev. 43 (4), 295–320.

CHAPTER 10

The future of transportation operations

Coordinating physics and psychology

The supply of for-hire transportation services, taking the form of carrying capacity and infrastructure, will always be hard to synchronize with consignor demand. Carrying capacity and infrastructure will waiver between being underutilized and in short supply relative to consignor demand. Even the interface between carrying capacity and infrastructure will have problems with coordination. Consider this in the context of the five modes of transport. Water ports either have the dockage space and appropriately gauged gantry cranes to handle large container vessels or they do not. Airport runways and terminals must be sized appropriately to handle the largest air freighters that need to use them. In other words, capacity decisions must be envisioned during water port and airport design and construction. Pipelines are designed with a circumference necessary to handle the anticipated flow of liquid or gas. Of course, if these capacity needs should decline over time (e.g., an oil field's production passes its peak) the pipeline's operation and maintenance activities will have to change. Of course, railways and highway lanes have standard widths that conveyances conform to. Still, depending on capacity needs, railways must consider parallel runoff and staging trackage in order to manage flow along the network. Motor carrier regulations covering weight, axles, and trailer configuration are an attempt to manage traffic flow and minimize undue stress on the road's surface.

Indivisibilities cannot be overcome completely due to different peak and off-peak consignor demands. Downstream demand is ultimately in response to the consumption preferences of the final customer at the end of the supply chain. For-hire transportation will, therefore, always be a means to an end and not an end unto itself. Dealing with the physics that governs supply and the psychology that governs customer demand at the retail level, whether directly or indirectly, will always be a challenge in for-hire transportation. The balancing act involved in managing economies of scale, as covered in Chapter 2, is everchanging and cannot be overcome by technology alone.

Transportation Operations Management
https://doi.org/10.1016/B978-0-12-815415-1.00004-5

Economies of scale is a cost concept, but for-hire carriers cannot lose sight of the revenue side of the profit equation.

It is difficult politically for democratic governments to systematically take on large-scale infrastructure projects. Typically, the timeline for benefits to be felt by the users is long after the electoral cycle and its usual rancor over taxation or borrowing to finance the project. It is true, of course, that the United States has built the massive interstate highway system from the late 1950s over multiple decades; but the impetus for the Federal-Aid Highway Act (1956) took place when the country was flush with post-WWII economic confidence. Furthermore, the system was also intended for national defense and not just commercial and leisure transportation activity. In other words, many powerful constituents supported the project.

Human activity has been trending toward urbanization since the early days of the Industrial Revolution. People have moved farther away from the primary supply sources that fuel the supply chains that lead to consumer goods and services. Still, with great distances separating most cities, coupled with a demand for final goods sourced from around the world, geography will remain a business constraint. Short of developing a Star Trek transporter machine to reduce items and people to a fanciful energy state, beaming them from place to place, serving different locations beget the problem of distance. Physical transport from point A to B over a diverse physical space will always cost time and money.

Additive manufacturing (i.e., 3D printing) may be considered a disruptive technology as far as the logistics of procurement, production, and distribution are concerned. But additive manufacturing cannot overcome the fact that all vendors, producers, and customers cannot be in the same place at the same time. Transportation of at least the printing resins and alloys will still be necessary once the 3D printer technology is shipped in and set up. It is true that transporting bulk printing material and printed subassemblies will be easier than finished goods. But transportation will nonetheless still be a necessary part of the additive manufacturer's supply chain.

The politics of infrastructure provision combined with the desire for mobility will, as noted in Chapter 4, keep policymakers thinking about network congestion. For-hire carriers will likewise remain concerned with how to manage their fleet over their networks. As noted in Chapter 5, the back-haul problem will remain so long as a conveyance has a domicile to return to and consignor demand is not guaranteed in both directions. In other words, these constraints weigh into cost and revenue management.

Since for-hire transportation is a means to an end, and private fleets are not within the core competency of most businesses, the market structure of for-hire transportation is not likely to change very much in the years ahead. Costing and revenue issues discussed in Chapters 7 and 8, respectively, will be a regular part of any for-hire carrier's business. Buyers and sellers of goods will still have to decide on who takes on the role of the consignor, or who will hire a 3PL as an intermediary. The frequency of shipping and the importance of the freight to the buyer and seller will determine if relationships with for-hire carriers need to be transactional or relational. As discussed in Chapter 3, spots markets and service contracts are choices which must be considered carefully. Finally, as discussed in Chapter 9, risk and uncertainty cannot be eliminated completely when it comes to transportation decision-making. Leaving aside the role of geography and the natural environment, of which humans have little control, there are simply too many moving parts, both physically and in terms of supply chain partners, to avoid problems with coordination. Supply chain management, and considering for-hire carriers as critical partners, is a good way to account for risk and uncertainty.

Automation and labor

Chapter 6 discussed how information technology (IT) could improve the transportation function. Indeed, the movement of information electronically along a communicative supply chain is similar to the movement of physical goods. Each can enhance the value-add of the other. IT is more controversial, however, when it applies to automating jobs; or more specifically automating workers out of their jobs.

Time, physical space, and location will always be logistical constraints. As long as time is scarce, physical space has obstacles, and suppliers and demanders are not situated in the same place transportation will be necessary and will add to the cost of market-based activities. The COVID-19 pandemic of 2020–22 disrupted a lot of jobs. However, like health-care workers, transportation workers were also essential. Workers at the office, factory, or working from home still relied on deliveries for production and/or personal consumption purposes.

Related to the quality and extent of available infrastructure is the way it is used. This means labor productivity and hours of operation. Labor is a necessary component for airports, water ports, etc. to function. With respect to water ports, the gantry cranes could be automated but this necessarily reduces the labor pool. This is challenging for ports which rely on unionized labor. Large ports in Asia operate every hour of every day while US ports operate an average of about 16 h/day.[a]

Robotic gantry cranes may replace some operators; however, the remaining ones would be more productive if they can operate more than one via a remote monitor. Automation tends to make some people nervous. Ever since the invention of the steam engine (which displaced the Pony Express), for-hire carriers have since been expected to become ever faster, more reliable, and offer larger carrying capacity. Couple this with cheaper and faster access to information. This also makes some people nervous—from the original printers (which displaced medieval scribes) through to the one-click-away Uber/Lyft drivers (who are now displacing traditional taxicab companies). In all these cases, markets became more efficient (i.e., using fewer inputs to generate higher-value outputs). As a result, jobs were lost and those remaining were re-tasked to utilize the latest technologies. These structural changes are rarely smooth but, at the same time, they are hard to stop.

Automation is now being widely discussed for application at container ports. Actually, it is more accurate to say that the latest form of automation is under brisk discussion because the process of automation is never-ending. The modern shipping container itself changed the nature of dock work by making it less labor intensive and more efficient. Locked and sealed ISO containers move from origin to destination by way of various transfer points. Avoiding the unloading and re-loading of the cargo at all those points save time, money, and lowers the risk of theft, damage, and terrorist tampering. Today, the tide of automation is leading to driverless container carriers and remote-controlled gantry cranes.

A 2019 study by Toronto-based Prism Economics and Analysis noted job loss as part of the economic impact of partial to full automation of port activities in British Columbia.[b] The report was sponsored by the Canada chapter of the International Longshore and Warehouse Union (ILWU). Naturally, the ILWU is concerned with the activity that might lead to job loss among its membership. It had taken a strong stand against increased automation at the Port of Los Angeles, though that effort did not succeed and APM Terminals deployed its first set of automated straddle carriers in 2019. However, the

[a] Tirschwell (2021a). p. 54.

[b] See Prism Economics and Analysis (2019).

ILWU and APM Terminals did reach an agreement on worker retraining. This is the sort of push-back to be expected from trade unions in the coming years because the number of unionized jobs will surely decrease. Unfortunately, because of protected wages and benefits, labor is the highest variable cost in port operations.

While the Prism report suggests that productivity may decline and the return on capital invested may be lower than otherwise, it also notes that the number of fully/partially automated ports in the world are likely to increase beyond the 60 identified. If this is the case the risk versus return on capital does not seem to be a strong deterrent to at least some investors and governments. Still, of concern was the upfront capital expenditures necessary to move to more automation. Of course, some in the 1950s made that same argument when they contemplated the upfront expenditures on gantry cranes. In due time it became widely understood that such cranes were a necessary price to pay before ports could realize the full benefit of lift-on, lift-off (LO-LO) containerized shipping. A further benefit from containerization was the spurring of intermodal transport. Using gantry cranes to speed loading and unloading of containers incentivized investment in more trucks and trains to handle the extra demand for inland container transport. In like manner, one can expect the largest ports to invest in the newest technologies because of their economies of scale.

Remote-controlled gantry cranes mean the operator does not deal with the physical movements and equipment noise and vibrations that come with operating the crane atop in a sealed compartment. The remote operator, sitting in a more comfortable workspace, could be "moved" from one crane to any other across the terminal by the push of a button to call it up on his monitor. The future could see an operator handling more than one crane simultaneously. The Port of Rotterdam, an early flashpoint in this effort, suffered a wildcat strike on this very issue in 2013 with further strikes occurring in 2015 and 2016. Thus, it will take some time to implement the latest automations because some degree of union buy-in, or at least their reluctant resolve, will be necessary. Jobs will be fewer; but they will be more comfortable and dependent on computer technology. At the same time, trade unions at the ports will be under increasing pressure as new labor-saving technologies become available. Caught in the middle will be the state and local governments which own and oversee the major US ports. If the aphorism "all politics is local" still holds true one can expect a lot of lobbying and counter lobbying on the future-of-work in the years ahead.

In addition to gantry cranes, remote-controlled vehicles moving containers on and off the docks allow for coordinated activity beyond what independent human drivers in separate vehicles can do. In other words, faster and more coordinated activity allows for a denser concentration of activity. This is attractive to ports with limited terminal space. Naturally, unions are reluctant to give managers a free hand to automate jobs, and this is expected to be a point of contention when collective bargaining occurs.[c]

Can conveyances be driverless or can more than one be operated simultaneously in a caterpillar-like fashion with a driver in the lead vehicle? Yes, they can. Of course, the practice is still in the experimental stage for commercial activity. The National Highway Traffic Safety Administration (NHTSA) lists six levels of vehicle automation.

- Level 0: A human driver operates the vehicle at all times.
- Level 1: An advanced driver assistance system (ADAS) is available on the vehicle to assist the human driver with either steering or braking/accelerating, but not both simultaneously.
- Level 2: ADAS can control both steering and braking/accelerating simultaneously under some circumstances. The human driver must continue to pay full attention (i.e., to the driving environment) at all times.
- Level 3: An automated driving system (ADS) on the vehicle can perform all aspects of the driving task under some circumstances. In those circumstances, the human driver must be ready to take back control at any time when the ADS requests the human driver to do so.
- Level 4: ADS on the vehicle can perform all driving tasks and monitor the driving environment (i.e., handle all the driving) in certain circumstances. The human need not pay attention in those circumstances.
- Level 5: ADS on the vehicle can handle all the driving in all circumstances. The human occupants are just passengers and need never be involved in driving the vehicle.

Vehicles with levels 4 and 5 capabilities are not commercially available as yet, though NHTSA is preparing for the day when they might be.

A challenge for fully automated vehicles is the method of control and ensuring protection against cyberattacks in order to wrest control. Another challenge, as noted in Chapter 6, is training ADS to mimic basic human decision-making over a wide range of scenarios. Simply put, an object not sensed by ADS does not, so to speak, exist. This includes a stop sign

[c] For a review of the emerging issues for labor on the US West Coast and East Coast, see Tirschwell (2021b). p. 62.

covered in snow, a pedestrian near but not within ADS' visual sensors, etc. Humans, on the other hand, do not have to sense objects to know that they still exist. If the stop sign was there the day before the snowfall it is probably there today; and, even if the sign is totally covered there is still the tell-tale evidence of the sign's support pole sticking out of the ground, the pile of snow on top of what appears to be the sign, etc. There may also be lag effects in machine learning. For example, ADS will know that it should stop the vehicle at a red light. However, further training must teach it to cross the red light when it detects an on-coming emergency vehicle. How fast it detects the vehicle compared to a human driver and how it navigates into opposing traffic will indicate a lot about ADS' efficacy. Mass control of the traffic would improve the aggregate result, but it would cost more and raise issues of independence. This debate will unfold in the years ahead.

The challenge facing automation is the setting of the goal. Will it lead to the replacement of human operators or will it offer a symbiosis? Tasks that are repetitive and well-defined are suitable for automation. The challenge is in designing the robots and other automatic devices so that their processing functions mimic humans. This is why, in comparison to assembly lines, automation has been slow regarding driving and the loading and unloading of conveyances. In each, there are numerous out-of-the-ordinary situations. Traffic is subject to random events that can be dangerous for many people if not handled properly. Loading and unloading are most predictable when the shipments are homogenous in shape and packed in a uniform way. Any deviations and stray objects can stump robotic loading devices. Of course, if a robot is used successfully to load an empty trailer, container, etc. it should be able to unload it as well. It would be the same set of actions in reverse.

Energy usage

Global climate change has been politicized for the last few decades and there is no reason for this to change in the future. Emerging technologies to deal with climate change are set within a tangle of market forces and political incentives. As discussed in Chapter 7, regulations, taxes, and subsidies may spur on these technologies or they may interfere with normal market incentives.

Are we approaching the end of mass-produced vehicles with internal combustion engines? Are hydrocarbon energy sources (i.e., crude oil, natural gas, and coal) soon to be supplanted by cleaner alternatives? Not for decades, it would seem. On the other hand, electrification and alternative fuels are steadily progressing. The problem is that wind, solar, and battery power still have an efficiency gap to surmount relative to hydrocarbons. "The annual output of Tesla's Gigafactory, the world's largest battery factory, could store three minutes' worth of annual US electricity demand. It would require 1000 years of production [given today's technology] to make enough batteries for two days' worth of US electricity demand. Meanwhile, 50–100 pounds of materials are mined, moved, and processed for every pound of battery produced."[d] Thus, a small carbon footprint generated via battery power comes at the expense of the larger carbon footprint in the supply chain that manufactured it. The same argument can be made for manufacturing wind turbines and solar panels. From a supply chain perspective, the production process for solar panels, wind turbines, and batteries will generate pollution to the extent that raw materials (e.g., cobalt, lithium, nickel, and rare earth minerals) are not located in one place. After mining and extraction, these materials must be transported often along multicountry supply chains. At any rate, hydrocarbons have accounted for about 80% of fuel needs over the last few decades. The transition to alternative fuels will be neither easy nor fast.

The impetus for alternative energy sources is government pressure and the incentives to reduce greenhouse gas emissions—specifically, carbon dioxide. The biggest challenge in this hoped-for transition to a clean energy economy is requiring speed to replace hydrocarbons as opposed to carefully diversifying the energy grid. Water, steam, and oil power followed overlapping paths of usage without overarching regard for environmental sustainability. There was no sense of urgency let alone a feeling of crisis as there is today at the political level. This complicates the flow of capital and business planning in the manufacturing and transportation sectors. It is also important not to conflate the information revolution with the hoped-for energy revolution. Both technologies overlap in that the information sector uses energy while the energy sector must concern itself with the physical challenges of exploration, mining, and storage. In short, information is much more scalable than energy, engines, and conveyances because information has the public good attributes of nonrivalry and nonexcludability as noted in Chapter 6. Of course, computer technology has increased the efficiency of exploration, mining, and storage of energy. More information on hand, faster calculations, and forecasting have improved preventative maintenance to be sure. But without nonrivalry in usage, transportation's efficiency gains will always lag behind those of the information sector.

[d] See Mills (2019). p. 4.

Electrification itself is not emission free because power needs to be generated and many plants still use coal. Hydropower is attractive so long as the water resources are available. An alternative source is natural gas. This is an intermediate solution between fossil fuels like coal and crude oil on the one hand and zero-emission sources like wind and solar on the other. High-emitting coal and crude oil sources would require the development and extra expense of carbon-capture technology to be compliant with current and emerging emissions regulations. Wind and solar are emission-free but are not as reliable a power source as coal and crude oil. This explains why natural gas is a so-called bridge fuel. Indeed, natural gas-fired power plants generate about half the emissions of coal-fired ones on a BTU basis. An argument against natural gas, however, is that it is a by-product of crude oil exploration and, in that sense, could be a brake on the transition away from crude oil. Also, natural gas emissions include methane, another greenhouse gas that is even more potent in the atmosphere than carbon. What would the trade-off of less carbon dioxide but more methane be in terms of climate change? Of course, apart from the combustion process itself, natural gas extraction, liquefaction and/or compression, and transportation via pipeline or other conveyances generate further emissions

Shifting out of fossil fuels combined with the desire for mobility and publicly provided infrastructure will mean new taxes to fill the void left by lower revenue streams from gasoline and diesel taxes. The US federal gas tax finances publicly provided infrastructure that will be needed by gas and alternative fuel-powered vehicles alike. Yet the tax was never used to mitigate externalities from driving; that is, air pollution. Of course, that is less of a problem with vehicles using alternative fuels. Taxes on distance, direction, duration, and conveyance type are superior to taxes on the fuel usage itself. The mirror image would be like the government subsidizing book purchases but having no way to know if the books are actually being read, let alone being put to "good use."

The wild cards in the decades ahead, apart from changing technology, is the political resolve to create net-zero emissions economies and how the demand for energy grows across the world. All of these forces are interconnected with their own feedback loops. The tangle of business and political interests, each using science for their own purposes, will intensify in the years ahead. Recall that, on the basis of cost to the consignor, for-hire transportation either facilitates or hinders production and trade. Energy costs will surely be passed along from carrier to consignor.

References

Mills, M., 2019. The "New Energy Economy": An Exercise in Magical Thinking. The Manhattan Institute, New York, NY.
Prism Economics and Analysis, 2019. Economic Impact Study of Digitization and Automation of Marine Port Terminal Operations in British Columbia. Prism Economics and Analysis, Toronto, ON. https://ilwu.ca/wp-content/uploads/prism-ilwu_report-a3-aug14.pdf.
Tirschwell, P., 2021a. Freight policy's 'third rail'. J. Commer. 22 (9), 54.
Tirschwell, P., 2021b. Watching the West Coast. J. Commer. 22 (18), 62.

Index

Note: Page numbers followed by *f* indicate figures and *t* indicate tables.

D

E

F

G

H

I

J

L

M

N

O

P

R

S

T

U

V

W

Y

CPI Antony Rowe
Eastbourne, UK
July 04, 2022